CHURCH CONFLICTS

CHURCH CONFLICTS

The Cross, Apocalyptic,
and Political Resistance

ERNST KÄSEMANN

Edited by Ry O. Siggelkow
Translated by Roy A. Harrisville
Foreword by James H. Cone

Baker Academic
a division of Baker Publishing Group
Grand Rapids, Michigan

English edition published as *Church Conflicts: The Cross, Apocalyptic, and Political Resistance*
© 2021 by Baker Publishing Group

Originally published as Ernst Käsemann, *Kirchliche Konflikte*, Band 1
© 1982 by Vandenhoeck & Ruprecht GmbH & Co. KG, Göttingen

Published by Baker Academic
a division of Baker Publishing Group
PO Box 6287, Grand Rapids, MI 49516-6287
www.bakeracademic.com

Printed in the United States of America

Library of Congress Cataloging-in-Publication Data
Names: Käsemann, Ernst, author. | Siggelkow, Ry. O., editor. | Harrisville, Roy A., translator.
Title: Church conflicts. The cross, apocalyptic, and political resistance / Ernst Käsemann ; edited
  by Ry O. Siggelkow ; translated by Roy A. Harrisville ; foreword by James H. Cone.
Other titles: Cross, apocalyptic, and political resistance
Description: Grand Rapids, Michigan : Baker Academic, a division of Baker Publishing
  Group, [2021] | Translation of: Kirchliche Konflikte. Band 1 / Ernst Käsemann. Göttingen :
  Vandenhoeck & Ruprecht, 1982. | Includes bibliographical references and indexes.
Identifiers: LCCN 2020030438 | ISBN 9781540960108 (cloth)
Subjects: LCSH: Theology—Miscellanea.
Classification: LCC BR118 .K34513 2021 | DDC 230/.044—dc23
LC record available at https://lccn.loc.gov/2020030438

21   22   23   24   25   26   27   7   6   5   4   3   2   1

Contents

Foreword

James H. Cone (1938–2018)

I am very thankful for the invitation to write a reflection on my relationship with Ernst Käsemann. I really wish someone had asked me to write about him about twenty years ago when I had more time and energy to reflect on Käsemann in a manner that he deserves. Even though I would love to do it, please accept my deepest regrets for not being able to write a serious reflection at this time for a man I admired very much.

Käsemann was a very distinguished scholar. I have read extensively in his work and appreciate him very much. His book *Jesus Means Freedom* was one of the first books that excited me about him, even though I knew and had read his work about the "new quest for the historical Jesus," challenging some of the assumptions of his teacher Rudolf Bultmann. As I look back, I can see how his challenge to Bultmann led directly to his affirmation of liberation theology and my work.

We first met in 1973 when I lectured at the University of Tübingen and had dinner with him and his wife during my stay there. We had extended conversations about his daughter, who at that time was in Argentina. I never will forget the dinner we had together in his house with his wife as they told me about their daughter among the rebels in Argentina. Käsemann told me that he wrote about the meaning of liberation theology, but his daughter

---

This foreword consists of a compilation of personal email exchanges between James Cone and the volume editor, Ry Siggelkow. It is printed posthumously with Cone's expressed permission communicated before his death on April 28, 2018. (Email correspondences dated October 11, 2017, and March 19, 2018.)

lived it. Both he and his wife expressed grave concern for their daughter's life. Unfortunately, a few years later she was killed, becoming a martyr for the cause of justice. We also talked a lot about black liberation theology, and I appreciated deeply his words of encouragement to me. Among all the German theologians, or Europeans for that matter, whom I came to know when I began writing, Käsemann was the only one who understood me. He was a man of my own mind and heart and wrote concretely about what I was trying to express in my own situation.

Editor's Introduction

Ry O. Siggelkow

What you hold in your hands is a translation of the first volume of Ernst Käsemann's *Kirchliche Konflikte*, a collection of essays, lectures, Bible studies, meditations, and sermons spanning the late 60s to the early 80s, compiled and published in 1982.[1] The projected second volume of *Kirchliche Konflikte* has already been translated and included in the book *On Being a Disciple of the Crucified Nazarene*.[2] The meticulous labor of Käsemann's friend and colleague Roy A. Harrisville is behind the translations of both volumes. As the editor of this translation, I include here an introduction to the life and theology of Käsemann, which I hope will provide the reader with something of a guide to the material that one will encounter in this volume. Käsemann often reflected on how his experiences shaped his theology, sometimes even writing in vivid detail about his childhood years, the specific sequence of events that led to his arrest and imprisonment by the Gestapo, the turmoil of World War II and the postwar period in West Germany, his engagement with the ecumenical movement, his shifts in perspective, and his often quite intense conflicts and disagreements with teachers and colleagues, for which he was well-known. Here I foreground some significant, and more proximate, historical context for understanding Käsemann's theological development evident in the material found in this

1. Ernst Käsemann, *Kirchliche Konflikte*, vol. 1 (Göttingen: Vandenhoeck & Ruprecht, 1982).
2. Ernst Käsemann, *On Being a Disciple of the Crucified Nazarene: Unpublished Lectures and Sermons*, ed. Rudolf Landau and Wolfgang Kraus, trans. Roy A. Harrisville (Grand Rapids: Eerdmans, 2010).

volume. In particular, I highlight the abiding significance of the 1967–68 West German student movement, the life and death of his daughter Elisabeth, and Käsemann's encounter with the freedom struggles of the Third World through his participation in the global ecumenical movement. This context is critical to grasping the changing shape and movement of Käsemann's thought, which both extend the insights drawn from the German dialectical theology movement into the postwar period and substantially depart from certain dimensions of dialectical theology that failed to sufficiently challenge the ideological status quo. What begins to emerge from the material of this volume is what might be called an *apocalyptic theology of liberation*.[3]

The Early Years and Theological Studies

Ernst Käsemann's life spanned nearly the entire twentieth century.[4] Born in 1906, Käsemann grew up in the working-class city of Essen in northwest Germany, an industrial center of German coal mining.[5] When Käsemann was only nine years old, his father, who had been enlisted into World War I, was killed in battle on the Eastern Front. Left alone to raise two young children, Käsemann's mother was forced, in his words, to "tough it out" in the aftermath of postwar Germany. At the age of nineteen, Käsemann enrolled as a student at the University of Bonn. At Bonn, he found himself captivated by the lectures of Erik Peterson, a professor of church history, who would later, famously, convert to Roman Catholicism. Peterson's lectures on the church as the worldwide body of Christ drove Käsemann to call into question the liberal Protestant tradition as well as the evangelical pietism he had been exposed to in his youth. Out of fear that he, too, was already well on his way to Rome, Käsemann left Bonn to study under Rudolf Bultmann in Marburg, where he would, in his words, swallow the pill of Bultmann's historical criticism as an "antidote."[6] While studying at Marburg, Käsemann learned more about the dialectical theology movement, working his way through the writings of Kierkegaard, Barth, and Heidegger. In his fifth semester he left for Tübingen for further study under Adolf Schlatter.

---

3. See also Ry O. Siggelkow, "Ernst Käsemann and the Specter of Apocalyptic," *Theology Today* 75, no. 1 (April 2018): 37–50.

4. For an extended narration of Käsemann's life on which this account heavily relies, see Roy A. Harrisville, "The Life and Work of Ernst Käsemann (1906–1998)," *Lutheran Quarterly* 21 (2007): 294–319.

5. The city still features a number of monuments in memory of Käsemann as well as in memory of his daughter Elisabeth, who is discussed below. For example, in Essen there is a square the size of half a city block called Ernst-Käsemann-Platz.

6. Käsemann, *On Being a Disciple*, xv.

The Pastoral Years and the Resistance against Nazism

After completing his initial theological studies, Käsemann took up a position as a teaching vicar in Zieverich, about a hundred kilometers south of his hometown of Essen. While there he completed his first theological examinations at nearby Koblenz, and by 1931, under the direction of Bultmann, he submitted his doctoral dissertation on "the theme of the worldwide body of Christ."[7] Then, after briefly serving as vicar of the synod of Barmen, Käsemann was called to serve as pastor of a congregation in Gelsenkirchen-Rotthausen, where he would remain for the next several years.[8] In the midst of firsthand experiences of a mounting civil war in Germany, and having little time for involvement in politics while writing his dissertation and completing his exams, the young Käsemann describes himself as one who "eagerly longed for order." He recounts his experience of that time: "In family and school we continually heard that the Treaty of Versailles shamefully humiliated us Germans. Finally, the war left behind six million unemployed in our country. So my friends and I agreed that only a strong government could help us."[9] Along with many others, Käsemann would cast his vote for Adolf Hitler and join the right-wing Hitlerite movement of German Protestantism, the Deutsche Christen (German Christians). Before long, however, Käsemann grew mistrustful of the regime after Hitler intervened on behalf of a criminal storm trooper in Silesia. But Käsemann admits that he still naïvely thought that Germany could wait until the next election, four years later, to vote Hitler out of office.

Käsemann changed his mind when, in the summer of 1933, his congregation witnessed a dramatic increase in membership of the Deutsche Christen (from four to forty-five members).[10] When the Reichsbishop sought to recruit the evangelical youth group into the Hitler Youth in September 1933, Käsemann decided to join the Pastor's Emergency Union (*Pfarrernotbund*), founded by Pastor Martin Niemöller, publicly declaring that the Reichsbishop had become a "traitor to the evangelical church."[11] In response to his public stance against

---

7. Ernst Käsemann, *Leib und Leib Christi: Eine Untersuchung zur paulinischen Begrifflichkeit* (Tübingen: Mohr Siebeck, 1933).

8. Richard Walter, "Ernst Käsemanns Wirken als Gemeindepfarrer im Kirchenkampf in Westfalen 1933–1946," *Kirchliche Zeitgeschichte* 12 (1999): 201–4.

9. Käsemann, *On Being a Disciple*, xvii.

10. Harrisville, "Life and Work of Ernst Käsemann," 295. See also Hammann's discussion of Bultmann's exchange with Käsemann. Konrad Hammann, *Rudolf Bultmann: A Biography*, trans. Philip E. Devenish (Salem, OR: Polebridge Press, 2013), 278–83.

11. Käsemann, *On Being a Disciple*, xviii. See also Hammann, *Rudolf Bultmann*, 282–83; Walter, "Käsemanns Wirken als Gemeindepfarrer," 204–5.

the Reichsbishop, the district leader in Gelsenkirchen denounced Käsemann as a traitor to Germany and recommended him for assignment to a concentration camp. In the fall of 1934, Käsemann heard news that the Confessing Church had been contemplating an official separation from the German Christians, at which point he, along with two colleagues and twelve members of the Confessing Church, "resolved immediately to go on the offensive."[12] On the Day of Repentance and Prayer on November 15, 1934, Käsemann, along with his colleagues and friends from the Confessing Church, publicly dismissed before the altar the forty-five members of the Deutsche Christen from membership in his congregation and presented forty-five members of the Confessing Church to replace them.

In response to the planned action, a group of Nazis from Gelsenkirchen had prepared a plan of their own. As the service was about to commence, a group of Nazis formed in front of the church, determined to stop the service from happening by having the pastors "flogged" out of the church. A group of women in the congregation—"the backbone of the congregation," in Käsemann's words—formed the key opposition against the Nazi group. While the Nazis did not threaten the group of women violently, they promised to "participate aggressively" if the situation demanded it. By this point, many curious onlookers from all ages and walks of life began to gather in front of the church to see what was going on. In Käsemann's words, the front of the church had been transformed into a "battle arena." In response to what appeared to be an impending riot, a man named Graf Stosch, a Nazi advocate for church affairs in the district of Westphalia-North, appeared with fifty policemen and ordered everyone to clear the area "in the name of the state." Stosch had earlier informed Käsemann and others preparing for the service that he had received a commission from Berlin to arrest the pastors and prevent the service from taking place. In response to his query as to whether they would still continue the service, the Confessing Church pastors answered, "Yes." Stosch said that he would ensure that the pastors would be protected, and he informed Berlin that he would secure law and order. Although he was not sure what had motivated Stosch to allow the service to continue, Käsemann found this action very moving, going so far as to say, "The climax of our struggle is bound up with him."[13]

The service proceeded as planned. Stosch even joined the congregation in worship. On that day, Käsemann delivered a sermon on Jeremiah 7:1–15 ("Thus says the LORD of hosts, the God of Israel: Amend your ways and your

---

12. Käsemann, *On Being a Disciple*, xviii.
13. Käsemann, *On Being a Disciple*, xix.

doings, and let me dwell with you in this place. . . . Has this house, which is called by my name, become a den of robbers in your sight?"). Then Käsemann, along with the other pastors and leaders, introduced and presented before the congregation the forty-five members of the Confessing Church who were to function as substitutes for the forty-five discharged German Christians. Käsemann read the name of each outgoing member and each incoming member. "We could see the older people weeping there," he recalled.[14] Such a public excommunication was an unprecedented action among German Protestant churches at the time.

Käsemann's actions on that day isolated the congregation from the rest of the synod in Westphalia, but not from the working-class community of Gelsenkirchen. Much of the labor force of Gelsenkirchen consisted of immigrant workers originally from Masuria, Poland, many of whom were miners and communists who would later be given sanctuary in Käsemann's congregation in the midst of the struggle against Nazism. The congregation at Gelsenkirchen quickly became a fellowship of proletarians. Together with the Masurian communists and the members of the Confessing Church, the congregation became determined partisans against the Deutsche Christen, resisting any talk of "reconciliation" or compromise with the national church. In 1935, Käsemann preached on Joshua 7:13b ("You will be unable to stand before your enemies until you take away the devoted things from among you") and spoke of the German church's penchant for self-preservation and its refusal to move "out of the encampments of this world into No-Man's-Land."[15] In response to the sermon, Käsemann received another warning, and the German authorities eventually levied a charge against him.[16]

Incarceration by the Gestapo and Involuntary Military Service

When seven hundred evangelical pastors were imprisoned by the Nazis in 1937—including Martin Niemöller, who was forced into a concentration camp—Käsemann again preached a provocative sermon at a service of intercession, this time on the text of Isaiah 26:13 ("O LORD our God, other lords besides you have ruled over us, but we acknowledge your name alone"). In the sermon, Käsemann spoke out against the many voices pressuring the Protestant church to throw out the Old Testament, the apostle Paul, and the Bible as a whole in the name of the supremacy of Germany and an Aryan

14. Harrisville, "Life and Work of Ernst Käsemann," 296.
15. Quoted in Harrisville, "Life and Work of Ernst Käsemann," 296.
16. Harrisville, "Life and Work of Ernst Käsemann," 296.

Jesus.[17] He was immediately reported for treachery. "On the following day," Käsemann writes, "the Gestapo came and got me."[18] Käsemann spent the next month in a Gestapo prison completing a commentary on Hebrews, subsequently published as *The Wandering People of God* (*Das Wandernde Gottesvolk*), which he would later describe as a commentary on the struggle of the Confessing Church (12). To this day, if one is willing to climb the rickety steps up to the very top of the Gelsenkirchen church tower, one can see engraved on the bell the passage from Isaiah 26:13, a text with which Käsemann was buried upon his death.[19]

In 1940, Käsemann was drafted into the German military (*Wehrmacht*). He was sent first to Charleroi, a mining region in Belgium, where he contracted a serious infection that required the extraction of his fingernails. He was then sent to Paris, where he served in the telephone exchange. While his congregation was able to reclaim him as their pastor in 1941, only two years later, in 1943, he was drafted into the Wehrmacht again and sent to work in Greece in a light artillery unit. Viewed by his commanders as not particularly fit for armed combat, Käsemann was sent to work in the mailroom. In 1944 Käsemann's unit was forced to retreat from Greece to Yugoslavia (what is now Bosnia-Herzegovina and Croatia) because of the Soviet occupation of Bulgaria and Romania. During his travels, Käsemann was shot in the hand by a rebel outfit and spent several months recovering in a military hospital in Sarajevo.[20]

The Field of Misery: The Death of Dietrich Käsemann and Life in a US Concentration Camp

After his recovery, Käsemann received news from his wife, Margrit, that their eldest son, Dietrich, had died of diphtheria. In March 1945 Käsemann was granted a temporary release from the military to return to his family. On his way back to Germany from Yugoslavia, much of which he traveled by foot, and within only twelve kilometers from his home, he was captured by the Americans and became a prisoner of war at Bad Kreuznach.[21] The prison at

17. Käsemann, "Predigt im Bittgottesdienst am 15.8.1937 in Gelsenkirchen-Rotthausen," in *Dienst in Freiheit: Ernst Käsemann zum 100. Geburtstag*, ed. Jens Adam, Hans-Joachim Eckstein, and Hermann Lichtenberger (Neukirchen-Vluyn: Neukirchener Verlag, 2008), 87.
18. Käsemann, *On Being a Disciple*, xix.
19. In the summer of 2015, I had the opportunity to visit the church in Gelsenkirchen-Rotthausen to see the bell in the tower. Special thanks to Pastor Rolf Neuhaus for opening up the church to give me a personal tour.
20. Harrisville, "Life and Work of Ernst Käsemann," 296.
21. It was in a personal conversation with Eva (Käsemann) Teufel that I learned he had made this journey mostly by foot.

Bad Kreuznach was one of twenty US-led camps in which an estimated four hundred thousand German citizens were held indefinitely in what amounted to an open-air concentration camp, lacking severely in food, water, medicine, and space.[22] As a prisoner of war, Käsemann was assigned the job of throwing prisoners who had died of starvation or disease "over the wire."[23] As Harrisville describes it, "Sick with malaria, huddled in an underground cave dug with a pocket-knife, a spoon and a can, Käsemann was finally released, returned to his congregation."[24]

Upon his return home, with little time to recover from the war and to mourn the death of his son, Käsemann learned he had been appointed as professor of New Testament at the University of Münster in Westphalia. In that same year, Käsemann delivered a paper at the Evangelische Akademie in Gelsenkirchen in which he maintained that the tyranny of Nazi Germany did not happen overnight but was the culmination of modern Western history itself.[25] At a time when Nazism was understood by liberal observers as the opposite of humanism, Käsemann maintained that it was, in fact, its bitter fruit. It is here that Käsemann begins to turn to apocalyptic imagery to describe theologically the contemporary reality of evil:

> Life is a clash between cosmic powers, as one might, perhaps, formulate it today. The Bible says more simply and perhaps also more adequately: a confrontation between God and Satan. The spheres of power overlap in the struggle, they shift and divide anew in each new generation. The earth is the battlefield, the human being the true object of the fight, in which, however, the whole of the earth is also swept. And, in any case, the cross of Christ is

22. Among all the US camps along the Rhine River, Bad Kreuznach had the highest mortality rate. Officially, the prisoners were deemed "Disarmed Enemy Forces," which was a convenient way for the Supreme Allied Commander, General Dwight D. Eisenhower, to avoid granting the legal rights due to prisoners of war under the Geneva Convention. See the article by Richard Wiggers, "The United States and the Refusal to Feed German Civilians after World War II," in *Ethnic Cleansing in Twentieth-Century Europe*, ed. Steven Béla Várdy, T. Hunt Tooley, and Agnes Huszar Vardy (New York: Columbia University Press, 2003), 281.

23. A large monument has been erected—a massive wooden cross wrapped in barbed wire—in memory of those who died at the concentration camp. The location, now an empty field bordered by vineyards, has come to be known as the "Field of Misery" (*Feld des Jammers*). The camp was one of an estimated twenty US POW camps along the Rhine. See Christiane Wienand, *Returning Memories: Former Prisoners of War in Divided and Reunited Germany* (Rochester: Camden House, 2015).

24. Harrisville, "Life and Work of Ernst Käsemann," 298. Because the prisoners had no shelter, they slept in holes dug in the ground. Wienand, *Returning Memories*, 183.

25. Ernst Käsemann, "Die evangelische Kirche im deutschen Zusammenbruch: Vortrag vor evangelischen Akademikern Gelsenkirchens am 4.12.1945," in *Theologie und Wirklichkeit: Diskussionen der Bultmann-Schule*, ed. Martin Bauspieß, Christof Landmesser, and Friedrike Portenhauser (Neukirchen-Vluyn: Neukirchener Verlag, 2011).

the place at which the division of the spirits and powers constantly comes into view.[26]

Käsemann never made it to Münster. Someone had intervened and denounced his appointment on account of his association with the Masurian communists in his former congregation in Gelsenkirchen. Instead, Käsemann went to teach at the University of Mainz, then to Göttingen, and finally to Tübingen, where he would spend the last thirty-seven years of his teaching career as professor of New Testament.

Professor of New Testament Studies

In the years after the war, Käsemann taught thousands of students and published widely. Many of his essays were compiled and published in the two-volume *Exegetische Versuche und Besinnungen*,[27] later translated into English as *Essays on New Testament Themes* and *New Testament Questions of Today*.[28] In these essays, written in the 1950s and early 1960s, Käsemann established himself as a prominent voice in the field of New Testament studies and was perceived by many to be the most significant representative of the Bultmann school of New Testament interpretation. And yet, Käsemann entered into fierce conflict and debate with his former teacher on virtually every topic in the field—from Bultmann's interpretation of Johannine theology,[29] Pauline theology, and the theology of the Synoptic Gospels to Bultmann's hermeneutical program of demythologizing and his categorical rejection of historical Jesus research. Even when his criticisms of Bultmann were most severely enunciated (and, as I will highlight in more detail below, their differences were profound and highly significant to Käsemann's later theological development), Käsemann always acknowledged his great debt to his teacher. In the late 1960s and into the 1970s, Käsemann published *Der Ruf der Freiheit*, translated into English as *Jesus Means Freedom*,[30] and another collection of a series of lectures on Paul, most of which were initially delivered before US

26. Käsemann, "Kirche im deutschen Zusammenbruch," 232. My translation.
27. Ernst Käsemann, *Exegetische Versuche und Besinnungen*, 2 vols. (Göttingen: Vandenhoeck & Ruprecht, 1965).
28. Ernst Käsemann, *Essays on New Testament Themes*, trans. W. J. Montague (London: SCM, 1968); Käsemann, *New Testament Questions of Today*, trans. W. J. Montague (London: SCM, 1969).
29. Ernst Käsemann, *The Testament of Jesus: A Study of the Gospel of John in the Light of Chapter 17*, trans. Gerhard Krodel (Philadelphia: Fortress, 1968).
30. Ernst Käsemann, *Jesus Means Freedom*, trans. Frank Clarke (Philadelphia: Fortress, 1969).

audiences.[31] In 1973, Käsemann published *An die Römer*, and after several revised editions in German, it was finally translated into English in 1980. To this day, Käsemann's *Commentary on Romans* is regarded as an important contribution to New Testament studies.[32]

With the exception of *Der Ruf der Freiheit*, most of Käsemann's published work is often technical, focused on historical and exegetical issues in New Testament research. While he never hid his theological motivations, Käsemann's distinctiveness as a constructive theologian in his own right has often been underappreciated. In common with his teacher Bultmann, he always viewed himself as at once a theologian and a historian in the field of New Testament. The theological import of his work, however, has become much clearer, at least to the English-speaking world, since the publication in 2010 of *On Being a Disciple of the Crucified Nazarene*—a translation of a wide variety of Käsemann's theological reflections on biblical themes, reflections previously unpublished or available only in German.[33] Now with the appearance of *Church Conflicts*, the breadth and depth of Käsemann's theological engagement with social and political issues has become clearer still. What is perhaps most striking about these two volumes is Käsemann's trenchant criticism of the German evangelical church's complicity in white supremacy, capitalism, and militarism, as well as his attention to the theological significance of the freedom struggles of the Third World.[34] Käsemann had always regarded himself as a political nonconformist, but after 1967–68 his work

31. Ernst Käsemann, *Perspectives on Paul*, trans. Margaret Kohl (Philadelphia: Fortress, 1978).

32. Ernst Käsemann, *Commentary on Romans*, trans. and ed. Geoffrey W. Bromiley (Grand Rapids: Eerdmans, 1980).

33. *On Being a Disciple of the Crucified Nazarene* is an English translation of the posthumously published *In der Nachfolge des gekreuzigten Nazareners: Aufsätze und Vorträge aus dem Nachlass*, ed. Rudolf Landau and Wolfgang Kraus (Tübingen: Mohr Siebeck, 2005). Käsemann had actually intended to publish many of the essays in that volume in what would have been a second volume of *Kirchliche Konflikte* (Church Conflicts).

34. I use the term *freedom struggles* to refer to the anticolonial movements that emerged in the 1950s—especially in Latin America, Africa, and Asia—that sought to articulate a self-consciously internationalist political project. See Vijay Prashad, *The Darker Nations: A People's History of the Third World* (New York: The New Press, 2007). As Prashad puts it in the opening lines of *The Darker Nations*, "The Third World was not a place. It was a project." However, Prashad overlooks the theological work that, in fact, formed a critical dimension of the Third World project. From the mid-1970s through the 1980s, at the center of this were the gatherings of the Ecumenical Association of Third World Theologians (EATWOT), which took place on a regular basis and produced some of the most under-read and undervalued theological literature of the twentieth century. The gatherings of the World Conference of Churches also became an important site for Third World theologians to contest the legitimacy of the imperial and colonial framework of European theology. For a historical introduction to EATWOT, see Virginia Fabella, *Beyond Bonding: A Third World Women's Theological Journey* (Manila: Ecumenical Association of Third World Studies and the Institute of Women's Studies, 1993)

displays a definite political radicalization—we might even say a *conscientiza-tion*, to use Paulo Freire's term—about the concrete ways in which the demonic powers enslave the earth.[35] This is important to highlight, in part, because the "apocalyptic theology" currently in vogue in much academic theology and biblical scholarship, which owes much to Käsemann, has often missed the concrete political dimension of Käsemann's theology.[36]

The Postwar Years in Germany

The year 1945 has been described as "the most profound of the caesurae marking the history of modern Germany."[37] The year marked the defeat of National Socialism in Germany, along with the devastation of German cit-ies and the loss of territory, and precipitated a national moral crisis as the depth and breadth of the crimes of Nazism came into clearer focus among the general public. Only a few years later, two new German states had been established, each with its own set of constructed moral and political narratives and traditions. As the two German states sought to rebuild and reconstruct not only cities but new senses of national identity that would decisively break from the horrors of the preceding years, it was as if the clock of German history had been reset. For these reasons, these years have been described as

---

and M. P. Joseph, *Theologies of the Non-Person: The Formative Years of EATWOT* (New York: Palgrave Macmillan, 2015).

35. Paulo Freire, *Pedagogy of the Oppressed: Thirtieth Anniversary Edition*, trans. Myra Bergman Ramos (New York: Bloomsbury Academic, 2017), 67.

36. Even where the political dimension of Käsemann's work on apocalyptic is acknowledged, it is often abstracted from the concrete revolutionary struggles that he supported, effectively reducing his understanding of apocalyptic to a formal point about the sociopolitical or "cosmic" dimensions of a Pauline description of sin and salvation against Bultmannian existentialism. For a representative example, see Martinus C. de Boer, "Paul's Mythologizing Program in Ro-mans 5–8," in *Apocalyptic Paul: Cosmos and Anthropos in Romans 5–8*, ed. Beverly Gaventa (Waco: Baylor University Press, 2013), 1–20. While it is no doubt true that the New Testament scholarship that relies on Käsemann is usually more concerned with the particularities of his biblical exegesis and interpretation than with the particularities of his politics, the effect is that the concrete political commitments of Käsemann's work become obscured or lost altogether. This is no less true in the field of theology. For an influential and representative example, see Philip G. Ziegler, *Militant Grace: The Apocalyptic Turn and the Future of Christian Theology* (Grand Rapids: Baker Academic, 2018). Ziegler relies heavily on Käsemann in his constructive articulation of a soteriology that prioritizes what he calls an "apocalyptic account" of the lordship of Christ and the sovereignty of God. Yet his use of Käsemann remains mostly formal. Again, the claim is not so much that Ziegler is wrong to discover in Käsemann's interpretation of apocalyptic resources for a revision of Christian doctrine, it is that in the process Käsemann's politics become merely ancillary.

37. Timothy Scott Brown, *West Germany and the Global Sixties: The Antiauthoritarian Revolt, 1962–1978* (Cambridge: Cambridge University Press, 2013), 84.

a *Stunde Null*, a Zero Hour, in the history of modern Germany.[38] And yet, recent scholarship has problematized this narrative, emphasizing the extent to which no matter how much German leadership desired to break with the past and begin anew, continuities remained, and the crimes of the past could not so easily be forgotten.[39]

In the late 1940s and into the 1950s West Germany experienced a period of tremendous economic growth, due in no small part to foreign aid from the United States. Demands for justice for the perpetrators of the crimes of National Socialism were often stultified as a result of Cold War geopolitical interests that perceived West Germany to be a central ally in the fight against the communism of the Eastern Bloc. Public outcry in the 1950s tended to be shaped more by a concern to grant leniency to the perpetrators of National Socialist violence than by a commitment to justice and reparations for the victims of violence. Indeed, the persistence of authoritarian and racist social and political attitudes in West Germany after the war along with explicit right-wing nationalist and anti-Semitic sentiment were symptomatic of the ways in which the politics of the past continued to determine the present.[40]

The West German Student Movement of 1967–68 and the Anticolonial Struggles of the Third World

In several essays included in this volume, Käsemann reflects on the impact that the 1967–68 student movement in West Germany had on his own theological development. In order to grasp the significance of Käsemann's development and the distinctive shape that his theology takes in these essays, it is important to provide some historical context.

The German student movement of 1967–68 emerged, in part, as a response to the perceived failure of a generation of West Germans to adequately come to terms with Nazi crimes. Moreover, the student movement claimed that the fascism of National Socialism, far from receding out of public life, persisted in the form of global capitalist exploitation, support for colonial and neocolonial regimes in the Third World, and the German alliance with US imperial interests worldwide.[41] The student movement of West Germany, while responding to local issues in Germany, was also part of a larger global

---

38. Peter Alter, "Nationalism and German Politics after 1945," in *The State of Germany: The National Idea in the Making, Unmaking, and Remaking of a Modern Nation-State*, ed. John Breuilly (London: Longman, 1992), 154.
39. Brown, *West Germany*, 85–86.
40. Brown, *West Germany*, 91–92.
41. Brown, *West Germany*, 98.

resistance movement that occurred throughout the 1960s, which included uprisings in Berkeley, Paris, Prague, Mexico City, Dhaka, Tokyo, and many other cities across the globe. The networks of these movements were at times quite closely connected. The student movement in West Germany, in particular, was significantly shaped by a dramatic increase in the number of Third World students from Africa, Asia, and the Middle East who organized and mobilized West German students and deepened and broadened the student movement's political critique and demands to include critical issues raised by anticolonial liberationist struggles of the Third World.[42]

While the extent to which Käsemann himself had direct connection with Third World students is unclear, one can nonetheless discern an important resonance between Käsemann's evolving political perspective evident in this volume and the voices emerging from the West German student movement, particularly those shaped by Third World anticolonial struggles and the Black Power movement in the US. His engagement with the German student movement and his encounter with global liberationist struggles, moreover, provides the historical context for Käsemann's warm reception of James Cone in Germany, their friendship, and his deep appreciation of Cone's Black theology of liberation.[43]

In the opening essay of this volume, for example, which is intended to function as an introduction to the central theological outlook of the book, Käsemann refers to the impact of the German student movement on his theological development. Käsemann observes that the German student movement began as an inquiry into the role of the older generation in the crimes of the Third Reich but quickly turned into a wild "brush fire" of open revolt and rebellion against "all institutions and more or less everything older" (29). The polarization that had been latent, yet in certain respects limited, in German society now expanded and became all-encompassing, to the extent that "hate ate its way as far as into families" (30). Käsemann witnessed many of his colleagues in the academy and in the church respond by succumbing to a reactionary politics in which state repression and the "club of the police" (131) were repeatedly defended over openness to compromise and "presence of mind" (*Geistesgegenwart*) (chap. 10). For his own part, Käsemann interpreted

42. See especially Quinn Slobodian, *Foreign Front: Third World Politics in Sixties West Germany* (Durham, NC: Duke University Press, 2012).

43. The appreciation was mutual. See the foreword to this volume, as well as Cone's references to Käsemann in many of his published works. For an important reading of Cone's theology within the context of anticolonial struggles and Third World theology, see Matthew M. Harris and Tyler B. Davis, "'In the Hope That They Can Make Their Own Future': James H. Cone and the Third World," *Journal of Africana Religions* 7, no. 2 (2019): 189–212.

the student movement, despite its flaws, as a time of reckoning with the "bitter truth" of German history—namely, that the reconstruction of postwar Germany had culminated in a "dance around the golden calf" (30).

Käsemann describes this time of reckoning in the late 1960s as a conversion, a critical turning point in his theological career that furnished his work with "an unmistakable and most concrete goal" (30). Käsemann's theology had long emphasized that the Christian life is never a private affair, that the Spirit leads one into the world and into everyday life, and that the central theme of preaching must take as its basis the freedom *from* principalities and powers, which is to be demonstrated in the work of resistance against idols among the disciples who follow their Lord, the Crucified One, into the "no-man's-land" of the earth (77, 155, 202). But what became "unmistakable" and "concrete" in Käsemann's theological work in the wake of the student movement was the particular idol that must be resisted in the contemporary world—namely, the global reality of white supremacy, which, Käsemann maintains, demonically possesses and systematically exploits the Third World, defending itself with science, technology, weapons, and the exploitation of the earth's resources. "It is not enough," Käsemann writes, "to demythologize texts with Bultmann."[44] Recalling his earlier critiques of Bultmann's theology, Käsemann asserts that while demythologizing is critical to the theological task, before demythologizing the demonic powers of the New Testament one must be willing to demythologize human beings, and especially the powers of the modern world. It is not only religious superstition, Käsemann maintains, but the modern Western ideology of "self-mastery" that needs to be demythologized. Such demythologizing only occurs "in the power of the gospel."[45]

The Death of Elisabeth Käsemann

In the late 1970s Käsemann would experience yet another trial when he received news that his youngest daughter, Elisabeth, had been detained, tortured for weeks, and executed by the US-backed junta in an Argentine detention center whose walls were "coated in polystyrene and decorated with swastikas."[46] In 1968, at the height of the West German student movement, Elisabeth had left Germany to serve in Bolivia on a five-month internship. After her internship was over, Elisabeth took a six-week tour of South America. Witnessing the misery of the slums of Bolivia and Buenos Aires, Elisabeth decided to

---

44. Käsemann, *On Being a Disciple*, xii.
45. Käsemann, *On Being a Disciple*, xii.
46. Harrisville, "Life and Work of Ernst Käsemann," 298.

extend her stay in Argentina to join the fight alongside local union organizers against economic neocolonialism and the military dictatorship. As the political situation in Argentina worsened and became increasingly dangerous, the family encouraged Elisabeth to leave the country and return to Germany. In response, Elisabeth explained that she could not leave the struggle because so many of her friends had already gone missing or been killed.[47] She wrote to her parents about her decision to stay in Argentina, explaining that she had begun to identify with the fate of the Argentine people.[48]

The last time Ernst and Margrit Käsemann saw their daughter was when they visited her in Argentina in April 1976. In August of that same year, she wrote to her parents saying, "The conditions are very bad. . . . Thousands of people are missing of whom no one knows anything. . . . There are concentration camps everywhere, a human life is worth very little, and you get used to the fact that everywhere people disappear and you hear nothing more of them."[49] In the spring of 1977, Elisabeth went missing. Her friend Diana Austen, a student at Union Theological Seminary whom she had met in Argentina, was also detained and interrogated in the same building. Diana never saw Elisabeth, but she reports hearing her scream in the next room.[50]

Käsemann worked tirelessly to learn the details of what had happened to his daughter, to retrieve her body from Argentina, and to ensure that the military and the executioners did not have the last word. The autopsy report concluded that Elisabeth had been shot in the back by an automatic weapon, and three times in the neck and heart; her body showed signs of having been tortured. Käsemann responded to the news saying, "This is the way executions are done."[51] He invited his friend and colleague Jürgen Moltmann to deliver the eulogy at Elisabeth's memorial service.[52] Moltmann wrote, "Your Elisabeth dedicated her love and her hope to the liberation of a humiliated people, in order that space would be made for the poor and their affliction would find an end! On this road to the freedom of others, she has fallen

47. See Diana Austen, "Fear and Remembrance: Back to Argentina," *Christianity and Crisis*, August 19, 1991, 246–48.

48. When I asked Eva (Käsemann) Teufel about her younger sister Elisabeth's decision to stay in Argentina despite the dangerous conditions, she said, "Elisabeth was her father's daughter."

49. Elisabeth Käsemann, a letter to her parents, August 1976, as quoted in Koalition gegen Straflosigkeit, "Ein Leben in Solidarität mit Lateinamerka," available from Deutsche National Bibliothek, May 2007, https://d-nb.info/991004361/34 (translation mine).

50. Austen, "Fear and Remembrance," 247.

51. Arthur Dobrin, "Disappearing in Argentina," *Christianity and Crisis*, November 26, 1979, 301.

52. Moltmann later recalled that Käsemann had demanded, "The sermon: not more than 10 sentences!" Jürgen Moltmann, *A Broad Place: An Autobiography* (Minneapolis: Fortress, 2007), 149.

victim to the oppressors of the people. She has entered the community of the countless, nameless victims of acts of violence."[53]

Käsemann was deeply affected by Elisabeth's murder.[54] He wanted justice for his daughter, but he did not seek revenge, nor did he want her remembered as a martyr.[55] Instead he expressed hope that her death might "open people's eyes so that the reality of [Argentina], so beautiful and yet harboring an inferno, can be seen."[56] Käsemann was not afraid to speak out against the political situation in Argentina. He wrote, "As grotesque as it appears to the observer, those presently in power in Argentina lay claim to . . . the primacy of a cultural nation, and downright blasphemously, to a pronounced liberal tradition. . . . With the aid of the army and the police great wealth protects itself against the protest of the proletariat."[57]

After the death of Elisabeth, Käsemann's theology takes on a new tone.[58] When Käsemann speaks of the cross, the life and death of Elisabeth are not far from view. When he speaks of resistance, liberation, freedom, and the call of discipleship, the life and death of Elisabeth are present in his mind. This is not to say that Käsemann idolizes his daughter. But the struggle for which she died in Argentina forms a crucial part of the context in which to read the essays written in the years after 1977. Profoundly shaped by the relationships she made while organizing in Argentina, Elisabeth had discerned the connection between the struggle of the Argentine people against a military dictatorship and the internationalist socialist commitments of Third World

53. Quoted in Koalition gegen Straflosigkeit, "Ein Leben in Solidarität" (translation mine).

54. As, of course, was her mother, Margrit, who kept a calendar marking every week that passed since the day of Elisabeth's murder. According to personal conversations with Eva (Käsemann) Teufel, her mother and father never fully recovered.

55. Ernst Käsemann, quoted in Elaine Magalis, "Murder in Argentina," *Christian Century*, November 9, 1977, 1033. In July 2011, a Buenos Aires court convicted retired General Hector Gamen and Colonel Hugo Pascarelli for committing crimes against humanity at the El Vesubio prison, where Elisabeth was tortured (along with at least 2,500 other "subversives" between 1976 and 1978). Tony Paterson, "Argentina Jails 'Dirty War' Officers Accused over Killing of German Girl," *Independent*, July 16, 2011, http://www.independent.co.uk/news/world/americas /argentina-jails-dirty-war-officers-accused-over-killing-of-german-girl-2314585.html.

A verdict was never made against the man convicted for the murder of Elisabeth Käsemann, because the defendant, Jorge Videla, died before the end of the trial in May 2013. For more details on Elisabeth Käsemann's case, see "The Käsemann Case," Elisabeth Käsemann Foundation, http://www.elisabeth-kaesemann-stiftung.com/kaesemann-case.html.

56. Magalis, "Murder in Argentina," 1033.

57. Ernst Käsemann, "Tod im argentinischen Dschungel," *Evangelische Kommentare* 8, no. 10 (August 1977): 469–71, quoted in Harrisville, "Life and Work of Ernst Käsemann," 299.

58. Dorothee Sölle, a former student and friend of Käsemann, dedicated many of the essays in *The Strength of the Weak* to the memory of Elisabeth. Dorothee Sölle, *The Strength of the Weak: Toward a Christian Feminist Identity*, trans. Robert and Rita Kimber (Philadelphia: Westminster, 1984), 7.

anticolonial movements.[59] Indeed, it is precisely this insight that her father was so drawn to in his essays from the late 1970s until his death in the late 90s, an insight that, in significant ways, broke away from the standard Cold War political conflicts of postwar Germany—between the West and the East, the so-called First and Second Worlds—and pushed him toward a socialism informed by and attentive to voices emerging out of the Third World project. What Käsemann heard in these voices was nothing other than the Crucified Nazarene.[60]

The Ecumenical Movement

Three years after Elisabeth's death, in 1980, Käsemann was invited to speak at the World Council of Churches Conference for Mission and Evangelization in Melbourne. Käsemann had previously participated in the global ecumenical movement, having attended and delivered papers at the World Council of Churches "Faith and Order" conference in Montreal in 1963 and in Nairobi at the Fifth Ecumenical General Assembly in 1975. But his experience in Melbourne left a lasting impression, deepening his awareness of the changing landscape of global Christianity, anticolonial Third World resistance to racial capitalism,[61] and the importance of reimagining the work of theological reflection in light of contemporary political realities. The ecumenical movement, particularly the theologies of liberation articulated by Latin American theologians, caused him to rethink the "marks" of the visible church in the world and the "heart of the gospel." No longer could he view the marks of the visible church in the terms of the Augsburg Confession—which identifies the proclamation of the Word and the administration of the sacraments as the criteria of the true church. Instead, Käsemann speaks of the "presence of the poor" as the critical third dimension of the visible church, which takes form as a resistance movement of the exalted Christ serving the freedom and liberation of the oppressed (225). "For us, the kingdom of God is not primarily a theory but a praxis"; it is that praxis whereby the first commandment—"no longer uttered from the clouds at Sinai"—is given concretion in the "crucified, risen, Son of the heavenly Father, and at the same time the new Adam"

59. See Koalition gegen Straflosigkeit, "Ein Leben in Solidarität."

60. One can see a deepening of these themes after 1980, especially a more explicit affirmation of liberation theology in the essays included in *On Being a Disciple of the Crucified Nazarene*.

61. The term *racial capitalism* comes from Cedric Robinson. It refers to the idea that "racialism . . . permeate[d] the social structures emergent from capitalism." See Robinson, *Black Marxism: The Making of the Black Radical Tradition* (1983; repr., Chapel Hill: University of North Carolina Press, 2000), 3.

(200). Käsemann here describes the church as a resistance movement of the exalted Christ, the "fellowship of the free," given by the power of the Spirit to live in bodily service and in solidarity with an earth that groans for redemption under the weight of demonic possession. "We have understood nothing about [Christ]," Käsemann writes, "when we seek him at the wrong place and proclaim him under false mottoes" (201). As the Crucified, he is to be found only among those who "[sit] in darkness and in gloom, prisoners in misery and in irons," as the psalmist writes (201). It is among those "who hunger and thirst after righteousness" that the Spirit of God is present and active, making dry bones live, and de-demonizing the earth of tyrants (203).

Deepening and Extending the Fronts of Resistance

In 1934, de-demonizing the earth as resistance to tyranny took concrete form in the struggle against National Socialism. Käsemann's experience in the struggle of the Confessing Church, informed by the dialectical theology of Barth and Bultmann, had profoundly shaped his theological perspective. But after 1967–68, Käsemann was pressed in genuinely new directions on account of what he had come to learn from his students in the West German student movement, the witness of his daughter in the freedom struggle in Argentina, and his encounters with Third World liberation theology in the ecumenical movement. "We once said at Barmen," Käsemann writes, "that no area of life is omitted by the gospel. Conversely, . . . [it] can no longer be ignored . . . [that] Christianity is no longer determined by the White Man. Today, the majority, according to its number and its passion for departure, is in the world of the people of color" (224). The anti-fascist character of Käsemann's theology was deepened and extended toward new fronts of resistance.

Käsemann saw his friends and colleagues in the Confessing Church wrongfully believing that the war had ended, too quickly settling into the comfort of bourgeois existence, failing to open their eyes to the scope of the tyrant's possession over the earth. The fascism of National Socialism was merely symptomatic of a modern tyranny of demonic proportions, manifesting itself in a class war in which the white propertied possessors exploited people of color in the majority of the world through colonialism and neocolonialism and converted God's good earth into a living inferno for most of its creatures. "What is harmlessly camouflaged as a free market economy and promises to benefit all," Käsemann writes, "is in reality the continuation of imperialism and colonialism by a capitalist system. It lives from the Third World's yielding its raw materials and accepting our finished products, to which, particularly heinously, all sorts of weapons belong. The result is that the slums, the reverse side of our affluence, continue to grow, and for three-fourths of humanity our earth becomes a hell in which hunger, murder, and prostitution rule, each person wrestling with the other for survival" (225).

Apocalyptic Theology and the Praxis of Discerning the Spirits

The recovery of Christian apocalyptic theology had long been a touchstone of Käsemann's contribution to New Testament research. Against the demythologizing of his acclaimed teacher Rudolf Bultmann, Käsemann insisted that "apocalyptic was the mother of all Christian theology," determined as it was from the beginning by the imminent expectation of the parousia, the return of Christ.[62] For Käsemann, the apocalyptic mythology of the New Testament retained an ongoing theological significance, especially in its perception of the cosmic dimension and scope of the power of sin and the power of grace. Apocalyptic theology offered the critical insight that the Risen One remains for us the Crucified, and the earth remains for us a battlefield in which, still awaiting the new creation, ongoing struggle and resistance are necessary.

After the experiences in which Käsemann was opened up to the reality of anticolonial struggles against white supremacy coming especially from the Third World, apocalyptic came to express the truth of Golgotha and its contemporary meaning—namely, that God is present with and among "the crucified peoples of the earth," in the memorable words of Ignacio Ellacuría,[63] an offense to the satiated, to the propertied, and especially to the bourgeois church that clamors for law and order in the face of revolution. "To reduce it to a common denominator," Käsemann writes, reflecting on the impact of the student movement on his theological development, "I unlearned the spiritualization of the Beatitudes of the Sermon on the Mount" (225). In the face of anticolonial freedom struggles, the German church had sided with the oppressors and the propertied class, refusing to remember the critical lessons learned in the struggle against Nazism. Because the Risen One, the Spirit of the Crucified on earth, apocalyptically conceived, is the Spirit that drives out demons and heals the possessed, the Risen One is also the Spirit of resistance and freedom from bodily enslavement, signaling an

---

62. Ernst Käsemann, "The Beginnings of Christian Theology," in *New Testament Questions of Today*, 102. See also his response to critics and further elaboration of the earlier essay, "On the Subject of Primitive Christian Apocalyptic," in *New Testament Questions of Today*, 108–37.

63. See Ignacio Ellacuría, "The Crucified People: An Essay in Historical Soteriology (1978)" in *Ignacio Ellacuría: Essays on History, Liberation, and Salvation*, ed. Michael E. Lee (Maryknoll, NY: Orbis Books, 2013), 195–224.

open heaven, the gospel of liberation for the children of God seeking healing, truth, and freedom.

The Spirit of the Crucified demands the work of concrete political judgment, discerning the spirits, which is the task of both theology and discipleship. Indeed, the task of theology, for Käsemann, is nothing else but "instruction in the praxis of discipleship" as it seeks to "[aid] toward discerning the spirits, and from out of love it weighs to what extent historical realities are and remain possibilities for moving into the present, or where and how they made dust of arable land, which needs plowing again in order to give bread to the world today" (224). Discernment always occurs, for Käsemann, in the praxis of discipleship: "There can be no mere prattle about it; we must live it" (226). Because it is oriented by and toward life in the world—that is to say, *praxis*—theology is a contextual task that must refuse the temptation of abstraction. To fail to concretely discern the spirits on the battlefield of the earth, to fail to act, or to seek after neutrality and balance in the face of anticolonial struggle against the exploitation of the earth by the White Man, not only marks the failure of discipleship of the Crucified, it is a decision to side with the antichrist, with the propertied tyrants of the earth. "Resistance to the Nazis in our youth is an illustration of this. It would be senseless if we wanted to hide the fact that today the burden of this decision has become heavier, its dimension wider, its necessity clearer. For it continues. . . . All creation cries and in yearning waits for the glorious freedom of the children of God" (226).

From an Apocalyptic Theology of Hope toward a Concrete Apocalyptic Theology of Liberation

In *God of the Oppressed*, James Cone commented on what he called the "white 'hope' theologians"—e.g., Moltmann, Pannenberg, and Metz—who had taken their "cue" from Käsemann's work on apocalyptic but ignored the struggles of the peoples of the Third World. Cone expressed his bafflement that Hope and the Future of Man, a 1971 conference in New York City, included no presenters from Africa, Asia, Latin America, or Black America. "How can Christian theology truly speak of the hope of Jesus Christ," Cone inquired, "unless that hope begins and ends with the liberation of the poor in the social existence in which theology takes shape? In America this means that there can be no talk about hope in the Christian sense unless it is talk about the freedom of black, red, and brown people."[64] Cone argued that the

64. James H. Cone, *God of the Oppressed* (Maryknoll, NY: Orbis Books, 1997), 117.

refusal of "white 'hope' theologians" to take seriously the voices of hope in the struggle of oppressed peoples renders their theology "abstract talk, geared to the ideological justification of the status quo."[65] While one could argue that certain aspects of Käsemann's theology might also be subjected to a similar critique, in risking the work of concrete discernment and political judgment, Käsemann, we might say, moves away from the "abstract talk" that Cone diagnosed as ideologically dangerous. Indeed, it is precisely in risking concrete discernment of the spirits, the work of *naming* the contemporary tyrant concretely as the "White Man" in possession of the earth's resources and *naming* the concrete presence of Christ among the crucified peoples that Käsemann's apocalyptic theology departs from a "white" theology of hope and moves in the direction of an apocalyptic theology of liberation. With Cone, Käsemann insists that theology must entail such concrete discernment of Christ's presence not only in words but in praxis.

It is precisely here that Käsemann's theology marks a significant departure not only from the so-called "white 'hope' theologians" but also from the German dialectical theology that shaped the Confessing Church, specifically the theology of his teacher Bultmann and the apocalyptic theology of the early Karl Barth. It is a difference that Cone himself recognized when he drew on Käsemann over and against Barth's theology of the Word and Bultmann's skepticism about historical Jesus research, and one that he acknowledges again in the Foreword to this volume.[66] With Käsemann, Cone worried that Bultmann's kerygmatic theology displaced the concrete history of Jesus Christ as the Crucified One, and in so doing removed God from God's concrete identification with oppressed peoples. "Taking seriously the New Testament Jesus," Cone writes against Bultmann: "Black theology believes that the historical kernel is the manifestation of Jesus as the Oppressed One whose earthly existence is bound up with the oppressed of the land."[67] Here, Cone rightly discerns the motivating concern of Käsemann's critique of his teacher Bultmann. Käsemann is not interested in reopening "the quest for the historical Jesus" but in articulating the sense in which Jesus is unreservedly given over to the damned of the earth. He is thereby motivated to revise the doctrine of the righteousness of God and the justification of the ungodly christologically—according to God's preferential option for the poor and oppressed.[68] The result is that the

65. Cone, *God of the Oppressed*, 117.
66. James H. Cone, *A Black Theology of Liberation: Fortieth Anniversary Edition* (Maryknoll, NY: Orbis Books, 2010), 118.
67. Cone, *Black Theology of Liberation*, 119.
68. John Barclay grasps this point in Käsemann well. John M. G. Barclay, *Paul and the Gift* (Grand Rapids: Eerdmans, 2015), 146.

fulcrum of Christology becomes a *theologia crucis* concretely discerned in the Crucified Nazarene's movement into the inferno of the earth. And so, Käsemann is able to insist that God's righteousness is always partisan, which means good news for the poor and judgment for the wealthy and satiated.[69]

For Käsemann, to maintain the material relation between the earthly historical Jesus and the risen *kerygmatic* Christ, the disciple must discern the activity of the Spirit in the everyday apocalyptic realities of the earth, affirming and proving in discipleship that the eschatological kingdom of God reaches out to those who bear the weight of the world on their shoulders. It is for these reasons that Käsemann insists that the cross of Jesus is not an "edifying picture" but the sign of one who "dies a death on the gallows because he did not erect principles, law, and order but unmasked the inhumanity of our earth by accepting its damned and oppressed."[70]

In important ways, Käsemann would remain a dialectical theologian within the tradition of Barth and Bultmann. Indeed, God's otherness from the world, for Käsemann, is located christologically as it is in Barth and Bultmann. The critical difference is that for Käsemann, as well as for his friend James Cone, in the discernment of the spirits, Christology takes on a concrete specification— indeed we might even say a location—because Christ is the one who is actively present with and among those who resist oppression.[71] God's apocalyptic otherness in relation to the world is articulated as God's solidarity with the oppressed in the Crucified Nazarene who is present precisely in historical struggles for liberation, which express the freedom of the children of God from the demonic structures that possess the earth.

---

69. Käsemann, *On Being a Disciple*, 18.

70. Käsemann, *On Being a Disciple*, 250. See also James H. Cone, *The Cross and the Lynching Tree* (Maryknoll, NY: Orbis Books, 2011), 26.

71. On the importance of "concreteness" and even "sociological concreteness" with reference to the theology of James Cone, see especially Paul L. Lehmann, "Black Theology and 'Christian' Theology," in *Black Theology: A Documentary History, 1966–1979*, ed. James H. Cone and Gayraud S. Wilmore (Maryknoll, NY: Orbis Books, 1979), 145–46. Christopher Morse does not find Lehmann's discussion of "concreteness" to be sufficient. He explains, "For whether in the case of metaphysical or sociological modes of thought, the issue of *concreteness* poses particular problems with respect to what are most often designated as 'apocalyptic' claims" ("Apocalyptic Concreteness: James Cone's *The Cross and the Lynching Tree*," *Theology Today* 70, no. 2 [Summer 2013]: 203). In the same essay, Morse takes up J. Louis Martyn's concept of "apocalyptic rectification" in Paul as a way of articulating not just "sociological" concreteness but what he calls the "apocalyptic concreteness" in Cone's *The Cross and the Lynching Tree* ("Apocalyptic Concreteness": 207).

Translator's Preface

ROY A. HARRISVILLE

If there is a single theme threading through these essays and sermons, it is that the discipleship of the Nazarene involves corporeality. That is, the disciple, like the Master, is enjoined to come to earth, where the dispossessed and disadvantaged suffer from tyranny and exploitation. With this move, like Israel's exodus from the fleshpots of Egypt, or Abraham's abandonment of his father's house and his friends, the disciple waves goodbye to self for the sake of the other. Such a concentration delivers from the narcissism of the pietist, everlastingly feeling his or her own pulse, and from the captivity of the orthodox to unaltered, fixed tradition. The move may, perhaps, be slow, taken step by step, in the face of the tyranny of the powers that hold the majority of those who live on the earth enslaved, or in the face of the indifference of an affluent middle class, throwing alms to the poor to satisfy its guilt. And the rations to be taken along on this trip will be "iron," as Käsemann puts it, reduced to a minimum, with only enough to keep body and soul together.

If this move, this "descent," is required of the individual disciple, it is no less a requirement for a religious community, for the church. Concern for the dispossessed, for those in the third and fourth worlds, should move the church to abandon what is confessionalist, fundamentalist, whatever separates one body of Christians from the other and restricts fellowship at the "table of the Lord." Käsemann's interest in the ecumenical movement was nothing if not a hailing of a period in which churches and denominations were at the point of transcending their differences for the sake of a world in need.

Whatever the objection, the move, the "exodus," after the pattern of Israel and Abraham, was bound to have political consequences. But Käsemann was dissatisfied with the liberation movements of the secular society of his time. The genuineness of the move on behalf of the earth and of those for whom it was a hell could only be guaranteed by the discipleship of Jesus. Before the liberal reader registers surprise at this exclusivist claim, it should be noted that it serves the conviction that the life for the other was total, unconditional, without exception, in the suffering and death of the Crucified, and so it must be for the disciple. For this reason also, Christology had to be the criterion by which whatever the church said or did was measured; it had to be the key to the interpretation of the biblical witness to the Crucified. This explains what for the conservative represents a radical criticism of the New Testament, relegation of a portion of the Jesus-tradition to the legendary, and impatience with the debate over the empty tomb. If the reader misses this concentration on Christology as criterion and key, the criticism will appear merely as an eagerness to destroy or dismantle.

Beneath it all lay Käsemann's commitment to eschatology, in contradiction of his teacher Rudolf Bultmann, for whom anthropology, existence, self-understanding, the individual, lay at the center of the New Testament message. For, through that embracing of corporeality, God was at work to win back the whole world he had made. The kingdom of God, the kingdom of the end time, had begun with the Crucified, and it was to be brought to its completion through those who were his. Corporeality, then, was the end of the ways of God.

The context in which Käsemann lived and worked has altered radically. Germany is no longer divided, and the ecumenical movement has lost much of its attraction. Whatever of the arcane may attach to that context now, and be of interest only to the historical researcher, theologically it still maintains its relevance, since without it Käsemann's passion for his theme would be an abstraction, left in the air.

The old classicists had a term for it: *Traductor traditor* (The translator is a traitor). Käsemann's style, in the words of one of his younger colleagues, is "dense." Aside from the syntax, that heaping up of dependent clauses, or that German habit of delaying the verb, and at times allowing it to do double or triple duty, the innumerable adverbs made reduction necessary. But however dire the betrayal, the intent was to be as faithful as possible to what my friend had to say. He deserves it; in fact, he deserves much more.

Author's Preface (1982)

Ernst Käsemann

The essays in this collection of lectures and meditations have been individually published in many different places over the course of fifteen years, and some have already been translated into other languages. The first essay indicates the theme of the volume and is intended as an introduction. Conversation partners, opponents, and constantly changing situations forced me to reconsider my own way out of ever-shifting perspectives, leading me to abandon earlier positions and to steer another course. The old Adam remained nonconformist. I am not sure if the miracle of the new Adam expressed itself in me in the fact that I was permitted, compelled, or enabled to remain in German provincial churches of conservative or reactionary stripe. In any case, a good theologian does not swim with the secular or ecclesiastical current, which is why, despite many temptations, I was never able to become Roman Catholic or Orthodox. At least on earth, Protestants are always indispensable.

It seemed useful to me to look far back into the past. In this way, the development becomes more obvious, which I did not anticipate, but now fully affirm. The exegetical reflections show that I have tried to listen, as a disciple should do, according to Isaiah 50:4.[1] I have become increasingly conscious of

---

1. "The Lord God has given me the tongue of a teacher, that I may know how to sustain the weary with a word. Morning by morning he wakens—wakens my ear to listen as those who are taught" (Isa. 50:4).

This preface was written by Käsemann during Easter 1982 to accompany the German edition, *Kirchliche Konflikte*, volume 1.

the fact that the Bible is a subversive book, at least in relation to the norms prevailing among us today. The Bible judges the church so severely that the criticism of those who do not simply and wholly submit themselves to it only seldom has any force. Authority is legitimized by service alone; tradition is legitimized by that rationality which, in every case, Paul has most intimately connected with love. No hierarchy and no bureaucracy may limit the freedom of those who still seek to radically follow the Nazarene. An old man would like to encourage young rebels, at their own peril, to risk with the One whom not even the church replaced, and who allowed his disciples to leap over ecclesiastical boundaries and barriers.

∴ 1 ∴

Aspects of the Church (1982)

Since my youth I have experienced church fellowship, have been most strongly determined by it, and for my part have sought to be informed by it in all phases of my life. For me, as for Zinzendorf, there is no Christianity without it. Conflicts are by no means excluded in such fellowship and its individual forms. Genuine and deep human bonds always lead to conflicts, even must prove themselves directly in them. They have been heaped up on my journey. The causes, arenas, opponents, problems, and results have changed. For this reason I have constantly ended up in different positions, was never dependent on a party for any length of time, had disputes with former friends, while onetime adversaries became partners. To live in church fellowship remains an adventure for me. At times, one does not become merely an outsider but a partisan between or behind all kinds of fronts. Sometimes offense has been taken at this assertion. Usually one forgets, if one ever knew at all, that church fellowship has never existed without loners. Criticism and opposition are indispensable to it, and in a certain respect not only the preacher in the pulpit, the theologian at the lectern, but every Christian must be a counterpart to the other members of a community if one is not to founder unfruitfully in it. Amos and Paul were undoubtedly almost unbearable companions for the churches of their time. Many have been excommunicated who wanted to serve, had an important task to fulfill, and later were sometimes actually canonized. Abraham had to leave his father's house and his friendships. Exodus is not just a part of every normal growth, but it pertains to discipleship as well. For we can hardly arrive at the kingdom of heaven on well-trodden paths and in columns. One's own thinking and independent steps are not made superfluous by faith. No one can dispense with midwives, as Socrates wanted to be for his students. Conversely, grace does not continually make babysitters available to us. Very often, teachers, like-minded persons, adherents prove to be a particular danger, whereas troublemakers, nonconformists, even heretics prove to be guides, even if only by putting uncomfortable questions to us, indicating alternatives, or bringing us out of familiar routine. The cloud of witnesses envisaged by Hebrews 11 is, in any case, not only made up of the representatives of particular confessions, schools, and groups, though most who watch over order wish it so, and in their field believe it necessary to shape everything according to their own image and the breadth or narrowness of their horizon. Our God differentiates according to 1 Corinthians 12:13ff. and sets tensions without which there is no solidarity. The only one who is carried is the one who is also able to carry.

Perhaps young people will benefit more if an old man narrates his life in and with the church as a story of conflicts, rather than harmonizing what on earth is never harmonious. It is not even settled that one should regard heaven primarily as a sphere of harmony. In any case, I would like to leave behind a testament, as it were, for friends and opponents, as to how I learned to see the church over the years and under what circumstances that changed in each case. Perhaps others will gain courage, patience, and comfort from it.

The Body of Christ

Faith cannot do without thinking. Otherwise it becomes sterile. When I took up my theological study in Bonn in 1925, out of curiosity I got into Erik Peterson's[1] lecture on the Epistle to the Romans, and I was so fascinated by it that his explanations, even to the point of their wording, stuck in my mind and for decades furnished me with the problems of my own academic work. Even the theme of my dissertation on the church as the body of Christ was conceived under his influence. Though I have often been urged to do so, I have not allowed the work (published in 1933) to be reissued, and I can no longer understand why my Marburg teachers, Bultmann and von Soden,[2] gave it high praise. I have never allowed my students the lack of restraint with which I sought to speculatively reconstruct not only the prehistory and the religious-historical sphere of the motif but also its relevance for the theology

1. Erik Peterson (1890–1950), professor of New Testament at the universities of Göttingen and Bonn in the 1920s, converted to Roman Catholicism in the 1930s.
2. Hans Freiherr von Soden (1881–1945), professor of church history at Breslau, finally of church history and New Testament at Marburg.

of Paul and his pupils. Since then I have learned that research decidedly rests on the capacity for limiting its horizon, and the boldest sketches must be open to radical self-criticism. Nonetheless, the investigation, undertaken in a hurry and monstrously rank in growth, betrays the fact that Peterson's understanding of the Pauline letters from the Hellenistic environment and the epochs following it, which I described as "early Catholicism," so captivated me as can only happen in a first semester.

Disillusion over what otherwise would soon have taken the route of romanticism, toward Rome, occurred in Marburg through the "dialectical theology" dominant there, as well as the sedulous readings of Luther that, under the aegis of the so-called Luther renaissance, were then almost obligatory. Already prepared for it by pietism, I became consciously and irrevocably "Protestant," while Schlier[3] at the same time, at the same place, and associated with me through Bultmann's seminars, wandered in the opposite direction. Later, one of my friends called it "contrast harmony." For me the primacy of Christology prior to and above ecclesiology could from now on no longer be infringed on in the least. The relation is irreversible. Only where Christ is, is there church. Factually it is acknowledged that church fellowship is normally shaped by Christ and oriented to him. But this should not be allowed to be explained apodictically and dogmatically. There are always churches of the antichrist that intend to expropriate the glory of the Nazarene, and that even in their worship services. And everywhere there are those churches that render their Lord unbelievable, see in him only the model of a religious affiliation, and no longer allow their criterion to be the Crucified One who unmasks all idolatry and problematizes the Christian worldview. But precisely this is involved in the concept of the body of Christ that marks the earthly sphere of the Exalted One's lordship, realized in his members. The church is mirror and tool, the "organon" of his glory. But it is legitimately such only in the shadow of his cross; and it is, even there, only a most deficient breaking in of the new creation.

Seen from this insight, only later gained and formulated precisely, my dissertation nevertheless encountered two important determinations. Without immediately calculating the extent of the decision that seemed obvious to me, I had most intimately connected Christology and anthropology when I first inquired what "body" meant before and in Paul. In doing so I assumed that the function of the body of Christ was analogous to that of the human body. The doctrine of the *Corpus mysticum* [mystical body] in the later history of

3. Heinrich Schlier (1900–1978), professor of New Testament at Halle, Saxony-Anhalt, Wuppertal, and Bonn; opponent of Nazi tyranny; convert to Roman Catholicism.

dogma might perhaps be valid. Instinctively, I did not want to proceed from it. Even less did I begin with the vulgar understanding of body as "corpus" or "person," toward which ancient documents could totally lead one astray. If on the basis of the idea of the mystical body the relation to the earthly reality of concrete persons as members of this body was to be interpreted only vaguely as a "poetic" type of expression, then in the second case it could not be clearly stated how many earthly corpuses or persons should unite themselves in one corpus or person of the heavenly Christ. So it also seemed to me to be problematic, in dependence on the famous fable of Menenius Agrippa,[4] to define the body of Christ constitutively as "organism." Then, in 1 Corinthians 12:12ff., only one metaphor would have been used which could be configured allegorically. Yet the text, immediately in the first verse, exactly as in Romans 12:4, insisted on reality and identity, not comparison and possibility. Accordingly, only where the mutual relation of the members is concerned does the apostle take to comparison and thus to the usual idea of organism.

One last thing must still be considered: in Paul, "body of Christ" denotes not only the church but, as in 1 Corinthians 10:16–17, the cruciform body of Jesus shared eucharistically. But again, from that point a relation is set up with the church and the union of its many members at the meal. Here I found the key to overcoming my problems, which offered me neither an exclusively christological nor an exclusively anthropological formulation of the question. For the apostle, "body" had to be more than something ready to hand or a type of existence in its individuality. At least in the text of the Lord's Supper it was the possibility and modality of communication. This gave sense to all the other passages. As body, the human person belongs to the earth with its gifts, necessities, needs, and sufferings. One can be joined with all creatures or be separate from whatever displeases or is hostile. One always has masters in everyday life and therefore is subject to the constraint of powers and forces, either becoming a servant of Christ or, as "flesh," a rebel against God or, in one's sexuality, even one with the whore. In his body, the exalted Christ is present on earth, through his members and the church as a whole, sharing himself with the world, just as he did previously as the Nazarene, as he claims on the other hand as *kyrios* the obedience of his own as well as of the world promised him by the Father. What connects Christology, anthropology, and sacramental teaching within this context is the understanding of corporeality as sharing and participating, viewed cosmically: the belonging to a world, be it of blessing or curse, of God or of demons. According to Paul, even the

4. Menenius Agrippa (d. 493 BC), a consul of the Roman Republic in 503 BC.

resurrection, which does not denote living beyond the grave in the modern sense, concerns bodies insofar as it sets them in the world in which God is no longer contested, is the only One who is there for what was created by God, and is "all in all," finally victor and liberator.

This interpretation assumes Bultmann's fundamental insight, to which I always held, that in general the concepts of the Pauline anthropology do not, in the Greek sense, denote a component but the entire person with one's various orientations, capabilities, and experiences. I have not understood why Bultmann, who singled out my dissertation without my deserving it, never directly opposed my analysis. He could not miss where we differed. He remained captive to the idealistic tradition when he found the concept of "body" as expressive of one's relation to oneself and maintained the possibility of distancing oneself from oneself. "Self-understanding" was decisive for him, and he was inclined to see in the body that earthbound existence that needed to be transcended in faith as well as in knowledge. By contrast, for me everything depends on the fact that existence in the body is and remains bound to another, that it may never be viewed in isolation and as independent, mature individuality, so that the possibility of self-transcendence also falls away. In a certain way, my interpretation was "materialistic." I did not want to miss the significance of "corporeality," but also for that reason the body's connection to the earth and thus to a "world" variously determined by creation, sin, redemption, and likewise to its various masters and conditions. From that point the notion of human autonomy was unthinkable. Conversely, the cosmic orientation of every individual is always a given, though differing in the particular spheres of power. One never really lives alone, not even in one's ideas. One lives eternally with, for, against, under, or as an authority, over some other, and with those closest, with enemies, lords, brothers, animals, plants, demons, good "angels," God, or Satan. So one always lives, and again in eternity, belonging to a world and its particular master. In sum, existence is participating and sharing, be it in blessing or curse, in obedience or rebellion, in pleasure or sorrow—manifold, but always "gifted," manifold, but always in the service of good or evil.

From that point, it was easy to see that when he comes to speak of the relation of various Christians to each other, Paul can connect the body of Christ—which he first of all describes as a worldwide earthly sphere of the lordship of Christ, thus representing it realistically, not metaphorically—with the organism idea of popular philosophy. One always lives in service under good or evil masters. When one is under the lordship of Christ, one arrives at solidarity with all, at fellowship in the church, as corresponds to an organism. This type of observation thus gives concreteness to the first of those spheres of lordship. Where Christ reigns his disciples live, as he himself on earth, in service to all, to whatever bears the image of the human.

With this we encounter again the other aspect of my dissertation, already indicated, which I later more sharply emphasized but have never given up: The body of Christ may not be confused with a religious association or an ideological community, as is possible only where, as chiefly occurred at the beginning of the century, one proceeds from the local community or the churchly institution. Also, the later alternative to institution, in Germany viewed as *Volkskirche* and event—and thus as missionary movement—is too schematic and phenomenological, not defined clearly enough from the outset by Christology, and it therefore does not precisely describe the ecumenical perspective. The body of Christ is the world under the sign of grace, in the lordship of the Nazarene as the *Pantocrator* designated by God. It is the new creation, which at the end of time points back to the old creation, wrests it from the power of the demons, and in the earthly present represents the inbreaking of the kingdom of the resurrection from the dead. Later, this will be dealt with in greater detail. Here it may suffice to point out that such an assessment was current in a time when our earth began to shrink and the ecumenical movement became gradually visible to us also in Germany. In two respects, then, I distanced myself from the liberal, idealistic inheritance of my school tradition, which in the end, at any rate, was current in Germany: I replaced the idea of the individual with that of the member within a sphere of lordship, which rendered categories of "autonomy" or "maturity" as well as "self-understanding" meaningless and actually incompatible with reality. The members of the body of Christ are never independent, never mature, and cannot realize themselves and need not attempt to do so—because they are identified by their Lord and have become distinctive. In the same way, I could not be content with what is again a most profoundly idealistic ethic—that of the I-Thou relationship. The world is Christ's arena, thus the church also, right up to the seemingly limited mundane existence of its members. The door to the ecumenical reality was opened for me.

The Priesthood of All Believers

In the struggle of the Confessing Church[5] our arguably most painful experience was the breakdown of almost all existing church leadership, which in any case allowed me always to be critical toward it. At the same time, we experienced the breakdown and more: the betrayal by those so-called officeholders

5. The Confessing Church, a Protestant confessional body in Nazi Germany, founded in opposition to government-sponsored efforts to Nazify the German Protestant churches.

who in their vaunted Lutheranism were so sharply opposed to the community, who were in fact almost totally responsible for the life of the community but often enough only drafted others for service to the extent that they had control over them and regarded the alleged "laity" more or less as the flock entrusted to them. For those able to think and draw conclusions from experience, the result was that the hierarchical structure of church order became problematic once and for all; it was in fact no longer acceptable. Even biblical instructions regarding the office—such as in the Pastoral Letters, but also the conceptions of Luther, Vilmar,[6] Löhe,[7] and many others, to say nothing of the Roman and Orthodox confessions—became implausible and, for our time at least, not useful. We were compelled to reflect back on the priesthood of all believers and to develop an order of fellowship, though perfection was not achievable by it, as we learned to our grief at our synods.

In my dissertation this development was prepared for theoretically as I discovered that, for Paul, the body of Christ encompassed the fullness of the charisms, on earth expressed precisely in the fact that all Christians have their particular charism. To that extent all Christians are "officeholders," and of course not merely in the closet as intercessors but in the worldly, daily routine. What had been in force regarding ordination since Judaism, and had been binding, was superseded by the apostle, who, by no means accidentally, neither recognizes nor wants to recognize ordination. The charism is established with the calling, and thus already in the baptism—as 1 Peter 2:5ff., doubtless on the basis of baptism, addresses the "chosen race" as a holy priesthood. Then, when introduced against enthusiasm—which proves to be necessary, as it was in the post-Pauline generation, but merely as an equipping for a particular, local, and temporally limited function of order—ordination is not at all to be glorified with theories of succession and legitimized as unique. We are all in apostolic succession, insofar as we are in the discipleship of genuine disciples. Otherwise ordination is a construction of those who would secure the church with ineffectual means, who above all would lift the dignitaries in it out of their proper role of *burden bearers*. Every charismatic has their own rank and authority; each one, in carrying out the capacity given them, is set over against the rest of the community, and is to be respected by it. This respect may be due in a special way to the most vulnerable: prophets, preachers, and teachers. "Laity" exists only in the sense that we all are such as members of the people of God, and we are also all "priests." Whoever

6. August Friedrich Christian Vilmar (1800–1888), professor of systematic theology at Marburg.

7. Johann Konrad Wilhellm Löhe (1808–72), neo-Lutheran pastor and leader.

pits the two against each other, and blasphemously or ridiculously displays
that in public by wearing the cross on his or her chest, sins against the honor
of the elect of God who, according to 1 Corinthians 6:2, will someday judge
the world, and who even today should supervise their functionaries in church
administration more critically than cautiously.

Such polemic is not far-fetched. It grows out of that dispute which the
Confessing Church had to undergo respecting the office of vicar in 1941–42.
At that time, a sturdy commission of theologians gathered at Halle in a total
of five meetings, each of which, under the leadership of Ernst Wolf and Julius Schniewind,[8] went on for two days, often long into the night. At the very
beginning, it became clear that the impending problem, which had become
urgent through the loss of many pastors due to the war, could only be solved
when the nature of the church office as such had been thoroughly considered
beforehand. Though the participants were conscious of being otherwise intimately connected, stormy debates immediately ensued. Representatives of a
traditional Lutheranism could not grant women a function that 1 Corinthians
14:34 expressly refused them. They were willing to recognize diaconate in the
widest sense, in cases of necessity—that is, to authorize exceptions. For them,
to concede to the vicarship, the office of public proclamation as such, spelled
interference in the *jure-divino*-legitimized order that had been sanctioned by
ordination. Into this situation, drawing on my dissertation, I threw the Pauline
teaching concerning the charisms, in order to loosen the inflexible fronts. First
Corinthians 14:34 is a time-conditioned prohibition in the apostle's struggle
with enthusiasm. It construes particular spiritual gifts as a divine distinction
given to individual members of the community and allows ecstatically gifted
women to play a dominant role in the worship services. Paul meets the imminent violation of the rest of the community by countering the enthusiasts[9]

8. Julius Schniewind (1883–1948), professor of New Testament at Halle-Wittenberg.
9. A clarifying note on Käsemann's use of the word "enthusiasm": It is not exactly clear to what
extent Käsemann intends to draw a connection between Luther's polemic against the Anabaptists
and the enthusiasm he sees at work in various parts of the New Testament. In English translation,
this is often the word used to translate *enthusiastisch*, and other times it is used to translate *die
Schwarmerei*; in the latter case there would seem to be a strong correlation with Luther and the Lutheran tradition. But if there is a connection, it is quite tenuous—and almost certainly not directed
toward any real denunciation of historical Anabaptism. If Käsemann has in mind a contemporary
Protestant manifestation of enthusiasm, it is often connected with his qualified criticisms of pietism.
While Käsemann may indeed be drawing on a common epithet from the Lutheran theological
tradition against Anabaptists, he is clearly not preoccupied with actual Anabaptist theology in his
use of *die Schwarmerei*. Instead, Käsemann understands such enthusiasm to be a characteristic
mark of much of early Christianity, both in Jewish Christian and in Hellenistic Christian circles.
For Käsemann, enthusiasm is characterized by a sense that the new age has already dawned
in the present and that the Spirit is charismatically at work. Indeed, though Matthew and

with another concept of church order and declares that it alone is constitutive and legitimate in the Christian sense. He agrees with his opponents that the Spirit rules the community. But he asserts that, as Romans 8:9 formulates, every Christian is given a share of the Spirit, that no one can be a Christian without the Spirit. The Spirit is thus not a power who awards privileges to persons, but rather the active presence of Christ on earth and his grace that blesses all disciples. This grace calls to mutual service by simultaneously sending and enabling one for it through its gifts. But mutual service is only possible when Spirit and grace are not given wholesale but differentiated, when each receives from the Lord their own ability and special task.

I may have been first to introduce the concept of charism into theological language, thus to use it technically, in order to set forth the fact that charism is the projection of *charis* into individual life—that it is, as it were, the individuation of grace, which enables each in their place and in their own way for service, and precisely by such differentiation allows the way of the Christian to permeate the entire everyday life of the world. None are ineligible and superfluous; none sit idly and without responsibility; all are sent for this attack of grace on the cosmos in its most hidden nooks and crannies! This is the order of the church as the body of Christ, which truly never sanctions a status quo. This is likewise the reason for the universal mission to serve the

---

Paul are both said to bear an "anti-enthusiastic stamp," Käsemann makes it clear that insofar as they maintain an ongoing indebtedness to and connection with Jewish apocalyptic (as he argues they do), their theology also bears within it a certain kind of enthusiasm, even if it is of a deeply critical nature. Despite his criticisms of enthusiastic tendencies within the New Testament and those that he perceives in every epoch, Käsemann also understands enthusiasm to be characteristic of all forms of apocalyptic expectation. Significantly then, for Käsemann, enthusiasm is *not* necessarily a pejorative designation—though often it is framed precisely in this way. It is important to highlight that Käsemann thinks there is much to be praised about aspects of what he will call enthusiasm—not least in the early Christian doctrine of *charisma* and the priesthood of all believers—but he will generally seek to take up Paul's sharp warning against the enthusiasm characteristic of the Corinthian church and all realized eschatology.

Indeed, Käsemann understands Paul's warning against a certain kind of enthusiasm to be rooted in apocalyptic. David Way understands Käsemann to use the word enthusiasm in a few different ways. Way observes that, after 1960, Käsemann understood enthusiasm to be the belief in the "direct operation of a transcendent spirit in an individual or community" in response to a divine epiphany. In early Christian circles this is characterized by the belief that salvation has already arrived for Christians in the present, and so too the resurrection has already occurred. As a consequence, enthusiasts are those who believe themselves to be removed from the trials of this world and transported to a heavenly realm. Way argues that Käsemann understands Paul's appropriation of Jewish apocalyptic to be in service to Paul's anti-enthusiastic theology. Way observes that, according to Käsemann, apocalyptic is not a "backward step" in early Christian theology (as it was for Bultmann and the liberal tradition) but rather a "permanent contribution to Christian theology." For a full discussion, see David Way, *The Lordship of Christ: Ernst Käsemann's Interpretation of Paul's Theology* (Oxford: Clarendon, 1991), 142–45.

gospel publicly all over the world and, from whatever particular situation of the individual, publicly to proclaim it—thus it is the office given with baptism, *jure divino* [by divine right], to every Christian. Nothing and no one may limit it; it may never be left to others, allowing one to retreat to private life. Love and understanding are joined in resisting disorder, in not denying what is temporally expedient in the community, because mutual service remains the norm of grace received. In this fashion, then, the invisible church becomes visible in the priesthood of all believers and yet is invisible by the fact that no administration, no book of laws, but only grace holds this priesthood intact and alive. Without the Spirit there is no genuine Christian or church order. A hierarchy of values and ranks does not replace the Christ, who indeed gives himself to all but gives privileges to none.

Our discussion found its written deposit in the 1947 Tübingen dissertation of F. Grau, "Der neutestamentliche Begriff Charisma," prompted by Otto Michel.[10] It should be noted that since the third edition of Gunkel's[11] *Die Wirkungen des Heiligen Geistes*, in 1909, this theme had no longer been dealt with in Protestant theology. This indicates how little the dominant liberal camp and the conservative Lutherans, following their orthodox tradition, had heard and understood Paul wherever an ample treatment of the problem of church office was at issue. In that connection, in his famous and still uncommonly interesting *Kirchenrecht* of 1892, Rudolf Sohm[12] had set the course for a needed investigation—which, however, was only first recognized by Erik Peterson for the concept of charism. Just as in all scholarship, so also theology is blind as long as acute interests or loners do not give it a jolt. But if in some unexpected spot a stone is thrown into the water, it spews up masses of literature, as is shown right now in our theme. Likewise among the surprises is that a teacher on the way toward conversion unforgettably impressed on me the concept by which the Roman hierarchical ecclesiology could be overcome in the Reformation sense. For Peterson, the charisms were of course only auxiliary functions belonging to the "laity" for the sake of the episcopal and ecclesiastical teaching office, allegedly in apostolic succession.

This may have had its effect on the course of our discussions during the war years, with the result that we could finally agree to public proclamation on the part of women. Of course, there was talk only of the vicarship. Of female pastors, more yet, of female parish priests, none dared to think, or

10. Otto Michel (1903–93), professor of New Testament at Tübingen.
11. Hermann Gunkel (1862–1932), professor of Old Testament at Göttingen, Giessen, Berlin, and Halle-Wittenberg.
12. Rudolf Sohm (1841–1917), professor of canon law and German law at Göttingen, Freiburg, Strasbourg, and Leipzig.

at least did not speak. At the urging of Schniewind, against the objection of Hermann Diem,[13] it was decided that women should not be allowed leadership in the administrative organ of the presbytery, and thus 1 Corinthians 14:34 should at least be conceded. In the course of time this proviso was forgotten or shamefully concealed. It is probable that the conservative members of the commission did not want to oppose the view of the universal priesthood, but at bottom they regarded public proclamation by women as merely an auxiliary service during wartime, a measure which later could at least be kept under control, and could perhaps again be restricted. They could support themselves on the New Testament witness: Paul too makes clear that there are more important and more hidden, less significant charisms, though according to 1 Corinthians 12:22f., he wants the latter to be esteemed by the community. Ephesians 4:11f. sharpens this view and with emphasis names only the differing varieties of proclamation. Finally, in the Pastoral Letters, at least in my opinion, only the monarchical episcopacy has validity as bearer of the charism handed on through ordination and in apostolic tradition. Against enthusiasm, the function of control over the sermon is now the most important task in the congregation, and here all other services are viewed as supports for the leading voices. Obviously, in the dispute with enthusiasm, Pauline church order on the basis of the charisms could not be maintained. Out of historical necessity, the hierarchical idea replaced it. But historical necessities, if we have respect for realities in other situations, always have theological relevance. This of course does not mean that they would thus be inviolable and irreversible. Also of theological relevance is historical criticism—which, by recourse to central views of the Bible, corrects, conditions, and authorizes that which has become sterile and misused; or, where circumstances dictate, it eliminates them. Otherwise we would forget that Christ remains Lord of his church and the Holy Spirit a critic even of the Christian congregation and its orders.

We have to admit that women's full share with us in the pastoral office has prevailed only amid difficult labor pains and in a situation favorable to it. We cannot ignore the fact that it is still contested in other church fellowships and that an end to this dispute is not in sight. We must finally assert that Paul, as Peterson formulated it, has in all of church history remained an "apostle of the exception," most misunderstood and continually trimmed. The priesthood of believers is usually spoken of only in edifying fashion. It is practiced in a radical way mostly by sects and only occasionally in the great churches. And we have not been able to realize the attempts of the Confessing Church to organize congregations and the church as a whole on the basis of

13. Hermann Diem (1900–1972), professor of systematic theology at Tübingen.

fellowship. Rather, a form of administration has been restored corresponding to the authoritarian state, and often allows fellowship to appear illusionary. Just as in the Catholic Church, Vatican II was very quickly tempered in reactionary fashion, the German Confessing Church—incidentally in contrast to the Netherlands!—has remained without lasting results for community and church leadership. In the last analysis, our struggle has only left scars behind and many open wounds as well. Thus, in protest and resistance to the status quo, let the universal priesthood be posited as the current indispensable form of survival in which Christianity turns away from the idol of a *Volkskirche* and resolutely accepts the reality of a minority.

The Wandering People of God

Long tempted by my teacher Bultmann and his Marburg school to assume the "Redeemed Redeemer," as Richard Reitzenstein[14] presented it to us, I believed I had to understand the Christology of the Letter to the Hebrews from that perspective. That had to have consequences even in ecclesiology; and these were put down in the book *Das wandernde Gottesvolk*,[15] which appeared in 1938–39. In three years of very arduous labor as the pastor of a large industrial community, I gathered the material together that enabled me to write down, during four weeks of imprisonment in 1937, the first sketch for the version developed in the following winter. The war prevented me from hearing a wider echo. When it happened, the situation of the Nazi period was already past, so that my religious-historical concept nearly hid the—to me, more important—theological concern. Since I described the church as the new people of God wandering through the wilderness, following the Pioneer and Perfecter of the faith, I naturally had that radical Confessing Church in mind, which in Germany resisted tyranny and had to be called to patience so as to continue its way through the endless waste. The reprint of 1957 was at least to allow for reflection on what we had experienced. Actually, since then, the church has almost as a matter of course been proclaimed as the people of God of the end time. Vatican II in fact took up such a concept, unfortunately seeming only to bring its hierarchical structure into relation to the so-called lay apostolate. For it is clear that we cannot speak seriously of

14. Richard Reitzenstein (1861–1931) was a German classical philologist and scholar of ancient Greek religion and Gnosticism. Along with Wilhelm Bousset, he is considered to be one of the major figures of the *Religionsgeschichtliche Schule* (history of religions school).

15. Published in English as Ernst Käsemann, *The Wandering People of God: An Investigation of the Letter to the Hebrews*, trans. Roy A. Harrisville and Irving L. Sandberg (Eugene, OR: Wipf & Stock, 2002).

the people of God within the conditions of Western democracy if we do not make precisely clear the importance of the alleged laity. In its greatest need, German Protestantism had experienced that all structures can be shattered, but Christianity can continue to live on and even become a refuge for the oppressed, a voice for those who have been silenced, and a sign of evangelical freedom for those in bondage. Of course, it will not remain so if Christianity relies on its authorities, its professional theologians, and its spiritual leaders. Certainly, all that should not be dispensed with in ordinary times—but in times of danger, those who experience suffering may function as a substitute, pointing us in the right direction. In the Christian community, it is the little people at the grassroots level who go for the jugular and decide what is worth fighting for and who, provided they do not bow down to Baal in everyday life, clearly prove themselves to be Christ's placeholders and ministers in a hostile environment. They represent the people of God as a whole and demonstrate the glory of their Lord, where those who formed something like a church upper class fail, fall, and are eliminated. Just as in the life of Christians in general, church hierarchy (if it may at all be formulated in this way) should prove itself through steadfastness in suffering and the ability to resist temptation from the world around it. For the people of God on earth are the multitude of those who are only allowed to wear the cross on their chests if they have previously carried it on their backs.

The merits of this concept of the church are clear. For too long and too earnestly it had been discussed in ecumenical circles whether church should be understood more as *institution* or, on the basis of its mission, more as *event*. But this is a false alternative, because an institution can only be a relic if it does not have a vital effect on its environs. It was also quite abstract and formalistic, since neither was Christ's lordship expressed appropriately and decisively by the expression nor did it become clear that the church as institution and as event is not determined by structures, and even less so by a mass movement. In both cases it is "we," that is to say, people who can be classified into diverse groups, who are united under the sign of the discipleship of the Nazarene. Personal relationships to the Lord, to the nearest and the remotest, to the congregation as well as to the world, remain determinative.

Of course, like all theologoumena, the concept of the church is dangerous, because it can be misunderstood, then lead to error. Above all, it is necessary to see that the people of God can be called "people" only in a figurative sense. Because there was no precise thinking on this point, there was a continual falling prey to ambiguity and false theology. There is already evidence of this when in Germany there is apparently ineradicable reference to *Volkskirche*. Everyone knows that in all countries, especially in those of the White Man,

Christianity must remain a minority, and in our regions it is becoming such more and more. Nowhere does it come together with its respective host people. It is insane to defend oneself by pointing to the missionary intent to penetrate the national sphere most intensively and unitedly. In 1931–33 the German Christians tempted us to become Nazis with such a device. For the rest, every sect and party has such an intent from which we would clearly have to distance ourselves. The origin of the concept lies in the fact that since antiquity there have always been national churches, but today this regional division has been romantically made the basis for an ideology in which Christianity and nation are regarded as associated with each other. From this, as from every ideology, necessarily emerges distance from reality and the combining of mission with usurpation in the political and private sphere. It would be a significant theological step forward if the idea and concept of *Volkskirche* finally disappeared from church language.

Only Israel could call itself "the people of God," with the result that the religious federation was at the same time a national one. Yet not even Israel as "elect people," assembled by God's revelation and command on Sinai, could simply be set on the same level with other nations. In the course of its history both components of its national tradition broke apart, resulting in talk of the "sacred remnant" and the "dispersed tribes." "Israel" true to the Torah could no longer be identified with whatever the original honorific "Jew" could lay claim to. Conversely, in no way did all "Jews" still want to be members of the covenant people. Community and separation were always together on the scene and have remained so to this day, even in a reestablished state. The New Testament assumes this dialectic and sets Christianity within it by allowing "old" and "new" to appear against a seamless continuity of the divine covenant, just as in "Israel" as the people of promise the "true Jew" is distinguished from the defecting, unbelieving, hardened one. Unfortunately, to a great extent such a dialectic is no longer understood in Christianity. Just as in the periods of liberalism, church and synagogue, and frequently, Old and New Testament, were regarded merely antithetically, so today, especially since the persecution of the Jews in the Third Reich, the opposite is often uncritically arrived at.

This is not merely done in Germany. Let two characteristic examples be singled out. Clearly, the Latin American theology of liberation, which in its context, entirely appropriately and necessarily, allows the gospel to be heard by the oppressed, rests on an unreflective identification of Christian rebellion with the Old Testament people of God. As a result the historicity of the exodus from Egypt becomes the center of proclamation, as, incidentally, likewise occurred in earlier times and on other continents. A certain theological

legitimacy to it is not to be denied. As the Sinai covenant loses its meaning
without the narrative of the exodus, so there may be the necessity for a radical exodus in the wake of Abraham. Recalling, for instance, the Letter to the
Hebrews and apocalyptic, the theme of radical exodus remains true for the
disciple of Jesus and so should not be suppressed in Christian preaching.
Baptism as a change in lordship already calls every individual Christian to
radical exodus, and today evangelical freedom should be spiritualized even
less than before. If evangelical freedom does not show itself as resistance to
and separation from every power, even of secular tyrants, then it becomes an
opiate. Conversely, the freedom of the believer may not cry out "*¡Venceremos!*"
without considering that the people of the exodus perished in the wilderness,
and Golgotha was not an unfortunate incident or final barrier on the attackers'
path to victory. As gentile Christians we are not promised that we shall arrive
at the promised land while on earth, as bitter as this may be to all who have
gone on the way without turning back. Seen from the outside, Christians as
well as churches may, in fact, normally be the losers. Success is not in their
vocabulary. The hermeneutical key to the New Testament, indicated in 2 Corinthians 3, as in Revelation 4–5, and also the difference between the gospel
and ideology, is the question whether the New Testament is interpreted on the
basis of the Old, whether Golgotha is interpreted on the basis of the exodus,
or vice versa. In our world, Christian conquest occurs *sub contrario* [beneath,
by way of the opposite], that is, as an awakening from the dead, at times, of
course, already occurring miraculously on earth and producing amazement
as well as fear. The Christian people of God remain a people under the cross,
though enthusiasts do not like to hear this, more yet, refuse to believe it.

The second example of churchly abuse of the conception of the people of
God was offered by the territorial synod of the Evangelical Church[16] in the
Rhineland in 1980, when it attempted to set in motion "renewal of the relation between Christians and Jews" by way of a solemn resolution. Whoever
belongs to the German generation that, burdened by an undeniable collective
guilt, is responsible for the persecution and murder of Jews will raise protest
against this resolution with a heavy heart. Conversely, no one will be allowed
to be silent, as are, unbelievably, almost all territorial churches and evangelical
faculties, still cowardly ducking out of the field of fire. This is not the place
to enter into the entire problematic of that resolution, supported by no other
German territorial church, to say nothing of the *oecumene*. But precisely

16. The Evangelical Church in Germany (EKD) is a federation of twenty Lutheran, Reformed, and United Protestant regional and denominational churches in Germany, collectively
encompassing the majority of Protestants in that country.

when one would like to improve and—as expected, vociferously!—"renew" the relation between Christians and Jews, one should not so light-footedly deal with the exegesis of Paul, initially cited as witness for the prosecution, as some of the grandchildren of Barth give themselves permission to do, and as Reformed federal theology seems to provoke. It is not true that, for example, "new" and "old" in 2 Corinthians 3 is to be historically rather than eschatologically understood, thus merely describing different epochs, not a separation at the end of time. The New Testament, particularly its Gospels, would have to be rewritten if the witness of the church toward the Jewish people may not be perceived in terms of its mission to the world of nations. If we speak of the abiding election of the Jewish people, we must at least consider that the prophets, and certainly Qumran, and Jewish Christianity, which speaks of the "remnant" of Israel, did not speak in such sweeping fashion, to say nothing of the deviant attitude in Zionism. But what is most important for me is to reject the formulation "that the church, through Jesus Christ, is taken into the covenant of God with God's people." Obviously no orthodox Jews will accept that. For them, only the one who is circumcised and keeps the Torah belongs to the divine covenant. That Christians as a whole do not embrace circumcision and Torah separates them from the proselytes. Whoever is "taken into" the Jewish people is necessarily a Jewish group or sect. Though in the first century many Jewish Christians may have seen it in this way, the circle around Stephen, according to the accusation against him, did not. Our faith in the Messiah Jesus exceeds the boundaries which are drawn for a Jewish group or sect. Gentile Christians can call themselves "the people of God" as Paul does, most of all in debate with the old covenant. But they are not members of the Jewish people and can never be such without circumcision and obedience to the Torah. Here a synod has made a historical misrepresentation and created not reconciliation but rather confusion.

Not by chance was it always difficult for the church to integrate the Old Testament into a "biblical theology." As often as the New Testament and later periods have tried on the whole to claim as Christian what in fact was taken from Judaism, the less was a suitable theory found for it. No more than a mutilated text was to be used, even if one allegorized. The scheme of promise and fulfillment helps only in part when violence is really done to it, and historically cannot be justified. With the Reformers, we may confront law and gospel here also, but we must be conscious of the fact that it is possible only from a quite particular—that is, a Reformation—interpretation of the New Testament. Historically and theologically, continuity as well as discontinuity are ascertainable from a later perspective. There is no unbroken tradition. These connections are to be observed where there is reference to "the people of God." We need the concept in order to denote that community in which the election of Israel is continued, and in which for that reason the holy book of Judaism does not make known God's will and grace in vain. But we can no longer connect national, territorial, judicial claims with this concept. Its legal tradition is reduced in Christian fashion to the commandment of love.

For us Christology is the hermeneutical key to the Old Testament. This statement may not be theologically reversed, as certainly as the terminology of Christology and soteriology, as well as the view of eschatology, stems historically from Judaism. This is the meaning of the famed distinction between "spirit" and "letter." The Nazarene, believed and proclaimed as the Christ, makes everything new and allows us to interpret the Old Testament history in a materially critical way. The wound which painfully separates church and synagogue must be left open on earth. The pains felt on both sides, however, indicate that we cannot be separated from each other and that we exist in polemical fellowship. Easter is not the prolongation of Sinai. Yet it reveals that God's rule, once proclaimed as liberating to a people on Sinai, in the new people of God, as the sphere of rule of the Messiah already come, lays claim to the whole world—thus allowing the covenant and the fellowship of a new creation to be recognized.

Confession and *Oecumene*

The Bible, as well as history, demonstrates that at all times Christianity featured an abundance of various theologies, confessions, and church affiliations. This may not be trivialized by romantically construing the obvious differences as the structure of an organism in which there are many functions and nevertheless everything is related to everything else and thus forms a comprehensive unity. Bitter disputes, mutual condemnations, faith struggles cannot be ignored. Contradictory contrasts cannot be swept under the table. In the new covenant as well, division and heresy accompany the way of the people of God wandering in the wilderness. A generation ago Rudolf Bultmann shocked the widest circles with the catchword "demythologizing." What concerned him was the interpretation of texts that conceive human existence from out of a mythical worldview. In the conflict surrounding demythologization, I always took Bultmann's side, since I too would not see the ancient mode of thought repristinated and made obligatory for us. On the other hand I have never been able to share Bultmann's concrete understanding of existence. From this split I arrived at a radicalization of Bultmann's thesis. Texts must be demythologized because and insofar as both humanity and the world require a continual demythologizing. Always, only in the best instance, only fragmentarily and "as in a mirror," can humans and world recognize themselves. Normally, in defiance or despair, they will regard themselves idealistically or be blinded by skepticism. The gospel reveals to all who they are, where they stand, what they need. The gospel demythologizes and de-demonizes earthly conditions, thus also our views and the texts that make them known. We find ourselves on a battlefield between God and idols, continually tempted not to let ourselves be formed by Christ after the image of our Lord, but to form ourselves and the world around us to our own will.

The church does not remain unaffected by this. Harmony has never been characteristic of the church. It too battles with all its members on changing fronts, not at all infallible, but often erring, with limited horizons, prey to the currents of any given time, omitting what is necessary, defending what is questionable, forever needing justification of the godless and healing from possession. Demythologizing of the church is one of the most important tasks of a proper theology. The theme of confession actually invites a questioning of bizarre situations regarding their abiding sense. Up to the Second World War and in many places beyond, in German Protestantism confessions were church forms of organization, beside which others were not even considered. Of course, their significance for members of the community was admittedly meager when confirmation instruction was completed with its indoctrination in the Lutheran or Heidelberg Catechism. This was almost never noticed when a union catechism replaced the two classical textbooks. The hymnbooks with their treasury of song from every religious provenience characterized the reality of worship as well as of the Christian daily routine. Naturally, there were traditional enclaves of the Lutheran or Reformed confession, in which the "pure doctrine" was tended to and pastors, educated by strict confessional professors, were still capable of conflict speeches. Finally, there were church officials who unambiguously or in proper proportion preserved the traditional teaching agenda, and there were certain conservative classes at the highest levels of the prefecture who felt firmly entrenched, though in detail they were inferior or not at all knowledgeable. In sum: confessional structures and relatively few confessionalistic propagandists hid the fact that members of congregations in general no longer had an inkling of the old doctrinal conflicts in Protestantism and—frequently also only in peripheral matters!—clearly could only distinguish themselves from Catholics and sects.

Such a development had begun in the Enlightenment and Pietism, insofar as both turned away from the stiff dogmatism of orthodoxy—whether toward a humanistic idealism or toward a personal piety in terms of the discipleship of Jesus. It was continued in Prussia by the royal enactment of the union on a broad, state-government basis, which obviously gave particular definition to the fate of the theological faculties, and in other lands actually radicalized the development, so that there Christianity became the prevailing form of a religious worldview. Only where Pietism (the filter of the Reformation as it were) had not gained a foothold or where (as in the so-called old Lutheranism and in the correspondingly strong Reformed circles) the orthodox tradition had been preserved—did this aspect, ultimately a worldview, not dominate conservatives and liberals. For the proletariat and the intelligentsia, the churches were almost entirely nothing but refuges, inheritances, like-minded groups of a religious understanding of self and the world. Confessions were taken to be medieval scaffolds of these views, and Protestantism, actually and precisely with its pluriformity, appeared as a relatively progressive characteristic of the religious enlightenment. When, in its official program, National Socialism described itself as the representative of a "positive Christianity," it assumed this aspect and, by the predicate "positive," emphasized that it was concerned with the practical consequence of this view of the meaning of life. This very aspect is still decisive today, when "basic Christian values" are everywhere emphasized. These values do not at all exist in genuine Christianity, since faith in Jesus as Lord and the resulting solidarity with all creatures cannot be described as "basic values," or be set within the chain of the ancient cardinal virtues. Christianity understood and accepted as worldview is the secularized remnant of a dogmatic whose christological and eschatological center is no longer accessible to the enlightened modern human.

As the name already indicates, through the Confessing Church, countering assault by the Nazis and the wholesale secularization of faith resulted in a reversion to confessions in the church. Work in advance for it was done chiefly by dialectical theology. Without its mighty influence on the young generation of Protestant pastors, the church struggle and the Barmen Declaration[17] of 1934 seem scarcely thinkable. But in this regard we may not forget what was at least sometimes linked (especially in the beginning) to this theology: for instance, the so-called Young Reformation movement and the liturgical movement, both sturdily rooted in the youth movement. The Reformers, in their own writings, were zealously studied by probably most students. The students had vividly emphasized not only the origins of Protestantism over against the later epochs but also that "confession" had first to be understood

17. The Barmen Declaration, or The Theological Declaration of Barmen, written to oppose the *Deutsche Christen* (German Christian) movement and adopted in 1934, rejected the subordination of the church to the state and the subordination of the Word and Spirit to the church. The declaration, which became the chief confessional document of the Confessing Church, was in large part written by Karl Barth but underwent modification.

as an act of actual confession before something like a *regula fidei* was visible in its documentation. We may not assume that before 1933 all this had decisively determined the theological situation. In that case, apart from hard-core liberals, conservatives and a small group of religious socialists actually bound to the confessions; and almost all Protestant theologians between 1931 and 1934 would not have been totally confused if a vote on the national question had been unavoidably required of them. Among the older ones, this vote for the most part fell to the advantage of the German nationals; among the younger ones, just as unequivocally for the National Socialists. In our entire career we had been too strongly marked by the romanticism of a national idealism, and in the university the history of the fatherland, nation, and home had been glorified for us as the nonnegotiable gifts of the orders of creation. This legacy decided the issue for us and relativized or actually repressed the horror over the absolutely unmistakable hatred for the Jews that confronted everyone in the village as well as in the great city, and worst of all among the bourgeois of the small cities.

For this reason it can only be said that we were not without alternatives when, in the summer of 1933 and onward, the Nazis more and more brutally revealed their true nature and consciences began to prick among all who were not totally fanaticized—late and timidly at first, but soon pitilessly facing them with a public and open decision. The choice was between nation and gospel, even when many up to Stalingrad and beyond would or could not separate the two. The more time went by, the more clearly each of us was asked whether one, by oneself and with one's congregation, would replicate Abraham's exodus from his father's house and his friends—as Fritz Graeber, as early as in his sermon at the Barmen Declaration Synod, had actually required of the pastor's wife as a modern Sarah. The Confessing Church began stormily and in no way united and, over against all earlier church organization, declared that it alone was legitimate. In every instance, except in the so-called intact territorial churches, it no longer recognized any church order as binding whose remnants the Nazis had allowed to live on. Quite suddenly we were faced with the theological problem: legal or legitimate? The solution "congregation under the Word" was the answer to it.

With a bold thesis I would maintain that something occurred here that Protestantism had not experienced since its founding—at any rate, not in Germany—and that actually deserved to be called a new confession. At issue was not merely a religious group movement such as, for example, in the various periods of awakening since the eighteenth century, or in the so-called moral rearmament. From the expanse of existing confessionally and regionally separated church communities and their congregations arose a new organization—not recognized by the state but led by "office holders" and leading authorities of the until-then-legal church structures, an organization supported by a more or less strong congregational basis, which claimed to be the true church and (altogether in terms of the Protestant tradition) appealed to "Scripture and confession" for its legitimation. In a single stroke, confession became up-to-date again—and indeed, as a public protestation against falsification of the gospel and assault on the community of Jesus, in appeal to the Bible and teaching of the fathers, and in the witness to the freedom of the Christian and to the right to life of all creatures. Christianity and world were clearly separated. Characteristically, in these years the intra-confessional conflict paled. At least at the grassroots, both Protestants and Catholics felt involved and obligated to resist. The new front ran right across all previous obligations in family, vocation, party, societal level, and every ideological or religious position. More cannot be required of "confession." Discipleship had become more important than theological or secular dogmatics, and fellowship replaced ecclesiastical structure.

The period of first love did not last long. State acts of force—which, naturally, immediately set in—did not dampen the spirit, though they moved many, who felt they were too widely exposed to be cautious, to retreat to the rear of the struggle (and this happened, of course, in both the lower and the upper ranks). It was conceivable too that different conditions; a better tactic; stormy temperament; and, most of all, harsher or more pliable opponents never allowed for a straight alignment of the front. The Prussian Union, earlier held to be highly questionable, was the chief target of attack and, as early as 1934, was a "ruined"—that is, a foreign-managed—church, for which reason the Pastors' Emergency League was first formed there. All this could not be unexpected by realists. But what totally surprised us was the refusal of solidarity, especially on the part of the Lutheran territorial churches outside Prussia, when consequences for the whole church were to be drawn from the declaration of the Barmen Synod. Structures previously without significance sometimes become bulwarks when new life is about to burst the encrustations of the past. Immediately, the Barmen Confession became merely a theological "declaration," since it had not comprehensively adopted a position on all the articles of faith. Whether this is ever possible, or whether what is attempted in this way is able to say anything to the people at the grassroots, was scarcely sufficiently considered. In the hour of need, what is simple becomes necessary. And in moments of brutal assault, all confession should be directed toward clarity about what is decisive. But this was of less concern to those whose necks the water had not yet reached and whose protective walls were, at least for the time being, still regionally kept intact; they become fixated on the idea that one must bring as much of the household goods as possible to safety. Confessionalists measured what the hour demanded by the legacy of past centuries, and so they ended up in never-ending compromises and allowed themselves to be moved more by the enemy than by friends. There must be demythologizing: The confessing German evangelical church never existed, only islands of resistance in the midst of the flood and a hinterland that the Second World War rescued from total destruction. Increasingly, the community in regional and local areas broke apart over this. What remained were nests of partisans and areas grotesquely called "intact" that screened the open space of a ghetto with walls becoming ever thicker and higher and that, immediately after the war, prepared for the initial restoration.

In the meantime, everything more or less swung back to the conditions of the previous century. Confessionalistic moves likewise failed as, on the occasion of the reestablishing of the Evangelical Church Confederation in Treysa, hope for a radically confessing church on a fraternal organizational form of the German territorial churches was not realized. The attempt by a reinvigorated Lutheranism at splitting the union into a Lutheran and a Reformed section failed. Earlier, the proposal of Pastor Girkon[18] of Soest, supported by the extreme Westphalian Lutherans, went down in the heated debate of a theological commission under the leadership of Praeses Koch.[19] Koch had in mind a high church structure of German Lutheranism with a corresponding worship liturgy, a right to vote bound to regular attendance at the Eucharist, and episcopal leadership with a German primate, which, hallowed in Scandinavia, was to continue the alleged apostolic succession. For eleven years a conversation was held over the Lord's Supper by theological representatives of both Protestant confessions, a conversation that finally led to the Arnoldshain Theses,[20] but they basically found only academic recognition. But, in addition, the protests against infant baptism, coming especially from the Rhineland by pastors of a particularly Reformed persuasion, could not prevail. What alone was effective was that the two confessions were integrated into a world council, each with its own imprint, in part following the ecumenical trend, in part rivaling the rapidly growing ecumenical movement. Finally, it can be said that, fundamentally, at all levels, only the ecclesiastical

18. Dr. Paul Girkon (1889–1967), pastor of the Evangelical Wiese-Georg-Kirchengemeinde in Soest, 1916–48; from 1946 to 1948, leader of the Office for Church Construction and Art of the Evangelical Church of Westphalia.

19. Karl Koch (1876–1951), anti-Nazi, Praeses (head) of the Westphalian Provincial Synod.

20. Eight theses respecting the meaning of the Lord's Supper submitted by a commission of Lutheran, Reformed, and United Church theologians of the Evangelical Church in Germany and approved in 1957.

bureaucracy regained and actually increased its standing. From that point a way into the open future was no longer visible.

On the other hand, the ecumenical movement offers such a way, though with many hindrances and in part with decisions that are quite problematic. It is a movement that took organizational shape after the war—globally, and in almost all non-Roman church communities. That the Orthodox churches were integrated into it as well, and that a bridge of goodwill and broad co-operation was thus created that existed nowhere else, belongs to those signs that allow the movement to become the most important ecclesiastical event of our century. The fact that in the ranks there is not only widespread interest but also readiness for personal and mutual assistance is surprising, despite the wide lack of understanding of confessional differences. It is most evident in the fact that Catholic priests and congregational members, strangely and in direct opposition to the Roman hierarchy at its upper level, are engaged to the point of participating in eucharistic fellowship meals inadmissible for them. It is also clear that unwavering adherence to confession is no longer the ultimate mark of faith. This fact deserves emphasis: Catholic theologians in all the world theoretically and practically support the union. Of course, what is most important is that for the first time since late antiquity, Christianity—indeed, without its largest community—is united worldwide. In a shrunken earth, shaken by so many political, economic, racial, religious, and cultural conflicts, this unity is more than expedient, it is unconditionally necessary if the sphere of Christ's lordship on earth is to avoid sinking to the level of a confederation of ideological groups. However indispensably the one church must be believed and represented ever anew, even more indispensable is the belief in the lordship of Christ yet to be demonstrated in all the world, upon which alone the church's unity is established.

This touches the theme that put me in connection with the ecumenical movement, so that now all my theological reflection is directed toward it. Totally unexpectedly I was invited in 1963 to the World Conference of Faith and Order in Montreal to speak on the unity of Christianity within the variety of its organization. It was clear that this invitation, not at all unanimously greeted in Geneva and elsewhere, was to test in an almost provocative way the voice of a radical historical criticism from the school of Bultmann for its quali-fication for membership in the great choir. Collision with the Anglo-Saxon tradition, which to that point determined the commission, was unavoidable (and even more so with Greek and Russian Orthodoxy). Clearly, the general staff assumed I would postulate the unity of the Bible as the basis of church unity. But just that was impossible for me as a critical New Testament scholar. To the horror of most among the almost five hundred delegates, I tried to demonstrate that the Bible establishes the plurality of confessions rather than the unity of the church. About three-quarters of a year later, however, one came to see that ecumenical plurality, already existent and recognized in the New Testament, must still be acceptable even today; thus the desired unity, as I had explained it, is not to be defined ecclesiologically but christologically. The Lord alone is the unity of all his disciples, who are, in fact and necessarily, different—which of course, even ecclesiologically, factually spells fellowship in the deepest and widest sense.

The same problem arose again and more radically for debate at the 1980 Conference on World Mission and Evangelism in Melbourne, where I delivered the keynote lecture on the New Testament concept of the eschatological kingdom of God. Now one could see with one's own eyes that whites no longer numerically determined Christianity. Theologically, of course, whites could still propose the thematic, but the treatment of the themes they could not organizationally control. Against the warning of the Jesus of the Synoptics, of Acts, and of the apostle Paul—at least as I was able to see it—God's kingdom on earth was spoken of phenomenologically and sociologically. Its visible signs occupied hearts and heads. Unmistakably, there was a broad current, as naïve as it was massive, that looked upon the revolutionary liberation of the oppressed as the central mark of the heavenly kingdom in which Jesus remained merely in the role of pioneer. The fact that the Eastern Churches, as a result, understood themselves as representatives of the onset of perfection— and that they could and wanted to see the West, at least among the whites, as on the way there—was not without its piquancy. I would in no way deny that all across the Bible the gospel of the kingdom and the poor are emphatically connected. For a long time I have criticized, as a Lutheran, the definition of the church in the Augsburg Confession because, alongside right doctrine and administration of the sacraments, a third criterion is indispensable—that is, the visible presence of the poor in the congregation and in worship. For liberation from earthly tyrants is part of the good news of the gospel.

Conversely, I have never allowed the gospel to be developed by a conservative, liberal, or revolutionary sociology of the Christian community or allowed the kingdom of God to be legitimized other than christologically, since signs and wonders also appear from the devil. Revenge is being taken in the ecumenical movement today for the fact that reconciliation, even in the world of humanity, has continually been referred to, but never the problem of heresy in the church. Heresy, along with reconciliation, has grown absolutely wild there. Proof of it is that no business may be transacted beyond the limits of the church community. Here confession must be recognized as an indispensable corrective of ecumenical development, and Christology as the norm of all ecclesiology (and also precisely in its function of judging). In any case, no community is Christian for which Jesus is only a model of proper behavior, thus always replaceable by other models. Everywhere in Christianity nothing is needed more than to clearly separate the gospel from ideology—be it the one, of the bourgeoisie, or the other, of revolutionaries.

If I see correctly, this is the present crisis of the ecumenical movement. It has incorporated whatever was urged upon it. It cannot withdraw from the world-historical situation in which West and East politically and culturally collide and in which the Christian churches at times are swept along into the suction caused by that collision. But above all, it is learning that in the long run the North-South conflict is becoming more dangerous and that while the White Man is, of course, still technically and militarily superior, this superiority can no longer be exercised everywhere without conjuring up a cosmic catastrophe. Time is blowing a storm into our faces. Our supremacy is tottering all over. If the politicians refuse to believe this, the churches should challenge the provincialism still entangled in the conditions and criteria of the previous century. Only for this reason people are not aware and do not dare to say that the class war our forefathers fought, nationally and at most continentally, is in worldwide motion today. Technology and military armament in reality serve the preservation of property and the accumulation of capital, inevitably resulting in the exploitation of nature and dependent people all over the world. Anyone who owns even the least amount of things lives from the sweat, hunger, torture, and murder of those who must fight back to defend themselves in a revolutionary way so that their children may grow up in dignity. In this worldwide class war, Christianity must, because it is on the side of humanity, stand on the side of the revolutionaries. Otherwise it must belong to the exploiters. It must do so out of love, so also out of reason and sense for reality.

One does not leave a world congress without experiencing the reality that nonwhite Christians are also oriented theologically to freedom movements. This means that their leaders are no longer able to grasp the Western tradition of the history of dogma and do not at all accept it as binding on them. This is true, as surely as their Western education (in missionary schools, for example) still holds back their emancipation, functioning as a substitute for what was earlier deliberately taken over and did not simply sprout up from the ground. World religions meet in friendly or hostile fashion and are enticed by syncretism. If politics does not do it first, the ecumenical movement should open the eyes of every Christian worldwide. Christians must see that from that point the destiny of their children and grandchildren will be decided. The human is the only creature who is able to shut eyes, ears, and nose to reality.

In fact, conversion means openness to a new world, acceptance of the most distant brothers and sisters, exodus from the houses of fathers and familiar sites. Yet conversion does not often dawn, or dawns too late, on those who everlastingly want to gain converts and dream of heaven instead of giving themselves to the earth as did their Lord. And, against our will, we will have to learn to become poor and to serve in the midst of mistrust and contempt, precisely where we earlier once played schoolmaster or the special elect of God. Much will go overboard, for that which is dear to us will appear to others as the property of the privileged. The question of the indispensable emergency ration should be put and most radically answered if we are to join the *oecumene* as it really is, without succumbing to the enthusiasm of religiously camouflaged freedom movements. What confession still is and can afford must be considered under this viewpoint of the emergency ration. In this regard, discipleship of the crucified Christ should be the most important good of the Reformation confession that we have to bring as our dowry to a future Christianity. In reality it is perhaps the only absolutely indispensable thing we can bring.

Resistance Movement

Earliest Christianity understood itself to be a creature of the end time. Not one word of the New Testament is correctly interpreted if we are not reminded of this. But this means that it was not by accident that the first Christians used that concept to describe their life, a concept expressive of the situation of the Greek citizen of the polis and the attitude taken toward it. *Parrhēsia* is the right to be allowed to appear and speak publicly in the political sphere, not merely to be exposed to the public eye, but also to the problems of the commonwealth, to make known one's own opinion without fear. Figuratively, the word then takes on the meaning of courage, trust, and joyous freedom. Those who are free are those who are "open." Because they feel they are citizens of the heavenly city as well as its earthly representatives, Christians have appropriated the Greek concept in order by it to characterize their situation made possible by the end time and their attitude resulting from it. For them, openness also signalizes freedom. With and through them, there is already breaking into all the world today something of the light of the last day. They see and are certain that even the graves will open for them. And since Pentecost, they live under an open heaven. The earth cannot set unconquerable hindrances for them. Their mission bursts bars and walls and encampments. No ghetto binds them to a fixed place. They are those who go out and wander as the free ones, bound to none and never entrenching themselves behind all sorts of dugouts, silencing their message, fearful of ruling traditions, prejudices, worldviews, and power structures. They have not forgotten their task to cry from the rooftops what they have heard in secret, that they must go to all the nations and everywhere accept those in need. In 1 Corinthians 4:9–13, Paul compares the apostles—obviously as models for a congregation puffing itself up and, in its enthusiasm, denying Christian existence—with the condemned, who find their death in the arena, a spectacle to the world, to angels and those looking on. Ephesians 3:10 takes up the theme: princedoms and the powers of heaven now see in the community the revealed gospel as God's wisdom. And 6:12 draws from it this consequence: "For our struggle is not against enemies of blood and flesh, but against the rulers, against the authorities, against the cosmic powers of this present darkness, against the spiritual forces of evil in the heavenly places."

The joyful freedom of Christians is evident as discipleship of their Lord in the struggle with the demons of the earth and in a suffering that on earth keeps watch over the image of the Crucified. Bultmann, presumably, would not have regarded this last passage as a central text for that self-understanding at issue in his theology. In any case, he would have demythologized it in a Kierkegaardian sense—that is, allowed it to stand as a description of Christian existence in encounter with one's everyday environment. That would not be false, although it involves a reduction. If one, however, recognizes that the demythologization of texts is only required because one's view of oneself and the world normally springs from being possessed by ideologies, dominant forces, or enticements, then we will learn to understand demythologizing only as a component of the de-demonization of humanity, relationships, and the earth. The Bible draws attention to this when it refers to our being entrapped in stupidity, blindness, deafness, and bondage—in brief, to what is not quite happily termed "original sin." Whoever, as an exegete, does not take seriously and transfer to the present what is told in the Bible of the might of demonic powers, and does not, with Colossians 1:13, see evangelical freedom as established in baptism—that is, as deliverance from the power of darkness and transference into the kingdom of the Son—will be able to do justice neither to antiquity nor to our own life situations. The Enlightenment of the eighteenth and nineteenth centuries no longer suits the one or the other.

It was extremely meaningful for me—may actually have been the last step available to me in my ecclesiological reflection—when, eventually led by the reality I experienced, I discovered the relevance of salvation as healing and de-demonizing. After the war my friends and I, totally unprepared, had to leave the pastoral office for the lectern. One of the most brilliant generations of German New Testament scholars had been lost. Could we be more than temporary bridges between yesterday and tomorrow? Under the most difficult circumstances and only half prepared, we began in Mainz, hungry, freezing, during the winter months sleeping on a cot in the university, mornings without breakfast, washing ourselves from the toilet, without literature except for whatever we ourselves owned. Five mission libraries from the Rhineland Palatinate did not contain one single newer commentary. Because I had never taught a course with lectures, over the course of five years I had to work through the entire New Testament from Matthew to the Revelation of John, at times only a half day ahead of the students and needing nine hours of preparation for each single-hour lecture. When things gradually got better, we were swamped with a torrent of Anglo-Saxon literature of which we could make use when—as "humanists," but by no means experts in the language!—we learned English together with our children. At the same time an extremely tiring scientific exchange was initiated with the Netherlands, Great Britain, Scandinavia, and Switzerland. Besides this, as Germans we moved on tiptoe, and as pupils of Bultmann and existentialists we were most often met with total ignorance of our radical criticism, due in part to dialectical theology, in part to the way of thinking defined by Heidegger.[21] In addition, for a long time accent on the eschatology of primitive Christianity remained a terrible hindrance. Apart from loners, it was first of all American colleagues who broke open a wider breach for us, so that around the middle of the 1950s we became presentable conversation partners. I am telling this in such detail to make clear that each of us in his own way was totally involved in being integrated in academic work and the internal structure of the German university. This should make abundantly clear that little time or energy was left to us to be concerned with the world around us, where in politics and in the church the restoration of the preceding centuries was being undertaken everywhere. The war in Korea, which brought us back to the Western alliance system, allowed our industry to grow massively, made possible an export boom, and almost overnight established our affluent society. This context is almost totally forgotten or deliberately concealed. And in general it has not become clear to us. Indeed, at that time, with the overpowering majority of the German people, we protested against military armament. The fact that, after the most horrible catastrophe, restoration and a distant war helped us to climb so rapidly again to the side of the victors did not, for the most part,

21. Martin Heidegger (1889–1976), German philosopher, acknowledged to be one of the most original thinkers of the twentieth century, best known for contributions to phenomenology and existentialism.

touch us deeply—since, as all others around us, we were too occupied with our work, happy over the fact that no one in particular disturbed us, that what was lost could be replaced, and that what was longed for could finally be realized. The initial timidity and shame faded away to the same degree success increased at all levels.

Not all were so naïve and merely concentrated on what lay nearest. In 1947 the so-called Darmstadt Word of the Council of Brothers of Evangelical Churches was a truly prophetic voice, which of course suffered the fate of many a desert sermon, and actually in the territorial churches had no resonance. At least decades later it would be admitted that there was a call to repentance there, to refuse that which delivered us completely to the demons of this present world. Here and almost here alone Christianity in our country reflected on its public responsibility, recognized its political guilt and the peril resulting from it. The fact that, in its egocentricity, the church in our country had not appropriately fulfilled its social obligation led to the statement that at that time was, and indeed still is, mostly felt to be outrageous: "We have denied the right to revolution but endured and approved the development toward absolute dictatorship." In this way the gauntlet was thrown to the capitalism of the small and large middle class, prettied up in the catchwords "free market economy," "Western culture," "free world." The fact that the class war broke out of national boundaries and broadened internationally to the limitless exploitation of the weak or deprived in the world was experienced at a time when beyond an "unresolved past" we saw that once more all the paths were open to the White Man and not least to ourselves. The tumult later raised by the Eastern Memorandum of the Evangelical Church in Germany failed to materialize because alleged fanatics and stubborn agitators neither could nor would be taken seriously. Once more, German Christianity had missed a decisive hour, did not stand the test as witness to its Lord.

Twenty years later the invoice for this was delivered when rebellious student youth first began to inquire into the role of their fathers and teachers in the Third Reich, almost everywhere got no answer, and now, in the open and rampant as a brush fire, have switched to revolts against all institutions and more or less everything older. Their ingratitude, their inability justly to judge the performances of the postwar period, their frequently infantile impulse to provoke and with slogans to drown out every substantive conversation will not be forgotten by those affected. Many a soul was inwardly broken by it. It is clear that the bourgeoisie, which until that moment was more or less invisible, now resolutely entered the fray and, since this time, continues to support brutal procedures against all the outsiders of society. The polarization that earlier, in essence, defined only the parties was broadened everywhere. That church leaders and synods silently tolerated them or actually furthered them in their own sphere had to be felt by all Christians to be a disgrace. Hate ate its way as far as into families. But when we have given all this its due, we may, as it were, be permitted to state that for those who were at all ready to learn and see, these rebellious youths were able to open their eyes to a bitter truth: like Israel, we had gone out of servitude under criminal tyranny into the wilderness and rubble of the postwar period to end with a dance around the golden calf.

In a certain respect, in those years, drawn into the vortex of daily disputes, and confounding almost all of my old friends as well as my colleagues at the university, I let myself be converted by the youth and never regretted it. This gave my theological work an unmistakable and most concrete goal. The presuppositions had long been given: Christian life is never a private affair. Our mission leads into the world just as into everyday life. We must proclaim eschatological freedom from the principalities and powers and, in suffering, witness to it with our existence. Our gospel has a political dimension that, to cite Barmen, leaves no earthly realm autonomous, or to its own legality, but sets everyone under the promise and claim of Jesus Christ. The idols have become visible with which we must now deal today and to which, even in Christianity, knees without number bow—namely, those privileges that the White Man fiercely defends with science, technology, weapons, and exploitation of creation as well as its creatures—though the White Man's supremacy stands on clay feet and is doomed for a downfall. Demonic possession rules our middle-class, affluent society when it lives at the cost of unnumbered millions of the hungry, factors atomic war into its politics (a war that no one can survive, to say nothing of being able to win), and at best leaves the meaning of the Crucified Nazarene's Sermon on the Mount to household usage of those pious folk who still claim eternity for themselves. Where this occurs, the true church must be the resistance movement of the exalted Christ on earth. The following essays and lectures should make this clear and, in so doing, lead us back to the watchword of Isaiah 26:13, for the sake of which the Gestapo came for me in 1937: "O LORD our God, other lords besides you have ruled over us, but we acknowledge your name alone."

✛ 2 ✛

Early Christian Conflicts over the Freedom of the Congregation (1979)

Preliminary Remarks

At the outset, I would like to define precisely a few facts that give basis and scope to the historical statements that follow in the second part.

1. Remarkably, none of us will deny that freedom is indissolubly connected with the gospel. But normally, in the church, this scarcely leads us to describe freedom with Galatians 2:5 as simply the "truth of the gospel." For the most part, the motif appears on about the same level as love, hope, reconciliation, and piety (to single out a few); it appears relatively seldom in our hymnals, for instance, and is then usually oriented to the individual. Liberation from guilt, weakness, anxiety, and sorrow is in the foreground. Put crudely, influenced by Old Testament research in the last fifty years on the exodus of Israel, emancipation movements of the Third World were the first to create a liberation theology, which has led to an ecumenical debate on this theme. The German climate was never particularly suited to it. Luther's finest writing, *On the Freedom of a Christian*, led to effects in poetry and philosophy, but less notice was taken of them in the church since the shock of the French Revolution, to the extent they were not nationalistically secularized. In general, while the theory was retained in academia, it was left to the enthusiasts [*Schwärmern*] and sects to make up for the deficit in the congregations.

A contribution to the discussion at the Loccum conference "Gospel, Church, Institution," March 19–21, 1979. First published in *Loccumer Protokolle* 10 (1979): 92–104.

2. Theologically, in the last generation it has sometimes been disputed whether the New Testament deals primarily with "freedom from" or "freedom for." Bultmann was indignant over the fact that Schlier, in the *Theological Dictionary*, and altogether correctly, inclined to the first—thus emphasizing freedom from principalities and powers such as law, sin, and death and, in the Synoptic narratives, from possession. In idealistic tradition, the orientation of discipleship to preserving faith in the freedom for particular types of behavior was more important. As a side effect of this view there sprang up, on the one hand, the demythologizing of ancient ideas concerning the lordship of demons and, on the other, the more severe individualizing, thus whatever was anthropologically dominant. To this I opposed the thesis that from the usage of its ancient environment, in the New Testament, freedom has a political and, precisely due to its relation to principalities and powers, a cosmic dimension. Individual liberation is a reflection and promise of the worldwide lordship of God broken in upon the earth. Only where freedom is experienced by the believer and further handed on is the message of the kingdom without illusionary effect; only there is the *status confessionis* credible, which can be characterized in an entirely different way; and only there is it for Christians truly the bearer of salvation.

3. Evangelical and church freedom are appropriately differentiated, insofar as early Christianity is not yet aware of those privileges that were granted to the church and its structures in later centuries and that we still possess, defend, and lay claim to. Only in the shadow of Judaism could Christianity appear for a period of time as a *religio licita* [lawful religion]. The New Testament congregation is recognized neither by organs of the state nor by society. It is tolerated largely because it disappears in the welter of Hellenistic mystery cults. Following the local Neronian persecution, it is only under Domitian that it comes into conflict with the authorities, though of course from the outset there were ordeals and sufferings in family, places of work, and the immediate environs. In our context, however, the aspect of Christian freedom together with its non-Christian environment will not be taken up thematically.

4. Of course, something must be said about the concept of "congregation," which in the Bible does not, as in our current usage, single out the individual congregation from the larger church communities. For the most part, of course, wherever Christian community is mentioned, such individual congregations are actually involved. This reflects the situation of the earliest missions. Conversely, every congregation represents the totality of Christianity. It is thus the church, the people of God, the body of Christ, without a deficit over against emerging larger unions. It was not the number of its members or its connection with a regional city such as Jerusalem, Antioch,

Corinth, or Ephesus or a particular leadership and constitution that constituted the congregation—but only the presence of Christ manifest in the proclamation of the gospel and its administration of the sacraments. The definition of the Augsburg Confession thus touches upon what is decisive, though we must ask whether or not it gives short shrift to the reality of the church's social condition—namely, that an unforgettable and eternally significant characteristic of the early church is that it was a congregation of the poor in terms of the Sermon on the Mount. As long as the imminent expectation of the parousia is still dominant and Christianity does not yet—as in early Catholicism!—begin to establish itself on earth, based on our categories, the visible, tangible form of organization has no constitutive significance. Individual congregations live, loosely connected, alongside each other, as appears to be the case in Rome and is assumed for Galatia or Thessaly. Wandering preachers communicate information with each other, apostolic or prophetic writings are exchanged, perhaps also material aid is made available. Synods and higher-ranking administrative organs do not yet exist. The distances separating the congregations are too great, the phases of development are not alike, personal influences and changing currents compete. In general, nowhere could a more fixed order beyond the local dominate.

Now, of course, this should not be understood from the schematic contrast between institution and event. Each congregation bears institutional features, insofar as it gathers for preaching and the use of the sacraments, even exercises church discipline, and cannot do without functionaries. It is just this that is not to be understood on the basis of our conceptions of canon law. One lives within the eschatological horizon and with the aid of charismatic services and on that basis also recognizes fellowship in distant congregations that leads, perhaps, to trade and association. However, the doctrine of an ecumenical church, virtually sketched out since the Antiochene mission, is not yet verifiable.

Early Christian Conflicts

In what follows, without entering into details, and for the most part referencing the probable results of research, I will sketch those debates encountering us in the New Testament or to be inferred from it, and in which what is at issue is the freedom of the Christian congregation. As early as after Easter there broke out in Jerusalem a severe and most consequential dispute between the genuine Palestinian Jewish Christians and the chiefly Greek-speaking emigrants from the diaspora and their descendants. The Lukan tradition in Acts

6:1–7 trivializes and paints over the event in edifying fashion. The mutual care for the Christian widows and their followers at best allowed already existent tensions to become acute, and the appointment of deacons was certainly not the means for alleviating them. Later, the alleged deacons work as missionaries and evangelists and are recognized supporters of the circle of Hellenists who, under the leadership of Stephen, begin the path toward the gentile mission. Research thus extensively records that the conflict concerned an independent congregational leadership of the Hellenists in which the Seven were set alongside the Twelve of the Palestinians. The most important difference between the two communities, and at least their protagonists, concerned the question whether mission in the Jewish diaspora should be limited to Jews and the circle of Godfearers—that is, whether gentiles might be received into the Christian community only after their reception into the synagogue or whether one might be allowed to convert and baptize them without preconditions. This virtually involved the decision as to whether Christianity should remain a messianic Jewish sect or, instead, basically ignore the Mosaic law of cult and ritual, engage in world mission, and be a church of Jews and gentiles— sociologically put, a new religious community. A more important theological decision has scarcely ever been made. At its center was the problem of freedom over against tradition and, of course, at its most critical point, the problem of freedom over against the pre-Christian tradition of revelation, especially in the Old Testament.

The accuracy of these historical statements will be corroborated by the trial of Stephen, in which the charge had to do with despising the temple and the law, resulting in the persecution of the Hellenists and their flight to Antioch. With its strict adherence to the law, Jewish Christianity was not affected by all this. Judged theologically, from the two communities in Jerusalem, in a certain way rivaling each other, there resulted something like differing confessions with a diverging dogmatic and severe limitation of fellowship. This is the background for the so-called apostolic council, for the peculiar position of the Pauline congregations, continually threatened by Judaizers, and for the thrust of Pauline theology.

Galatians 2:2 makes clear that Paul was not drawn to the apostolic council by his own decision. Very probably, the congregation in Antioch wanted to ease the growing separation from Jerusalem, thus to come to a theological reconciliation. The revelation of which Paul speaks in Galatians 2:2 might have been a prophecy during the Antiochene congregational worship. Barnabas, the first to fetch Paul to Antioch, was of course a leader of the delegation, while the central dispute actually had to do with the Pauline mission as the most aggressive and successful form of the Christianizing of the gentiles.

Jewish Christians, strict adherents of the law, who for a long time had already spied behind Paul's back, and in essence gathered around James, complain, repeating what in fact was the charge against Stephen but now with a Christian variation. For this reason they are described by Paul as false brethren. The majority at the council, led by the pillars of Jerusalem and especially by Peter, were so impressed by the successes of Paul and naturally by the plea of the Antiochenes that they agreed to reconciliation, contrary to the radical minority, and attempted something like a separation of the spheres of interest. This allows us to describe this outcome as an expressly ecclesiastico-political solution to a profound crisis.

But it is just this that allows the solution to fail, as is proved by the conflict in Antioch, carefully detoured by Luke and reported by Paul in his own way. The intended separation of interests could not be carried out in the diaspora. There the parties collided again after Peter, for reasons unknown, was relieved in Jerusalem by James, the brother of the Lord, and plunged, together with his wife, into missionary journeys, which led him perhaps to Corinth and probably, finally, to Rome and martyrdom. Attached to the groups in favor of reconciliation, at the common meals (the *agapē* feasts!) of the community, he transgressed the Jewish ritual law, not fearing contamination by intimate converse with gentile Christians. What had been conceded to Paul and practiced in Antioch without hindrance was and remained an offense to Jewish Christians according to 1 Corinthians 8–10, and indeed Acts 10:9–16, an offense for which the prince of the apostles was indicted by the people of James keeping further watch over the diaspora scene. We should note that Christian espionage and denunciation at the highest level occurred as early as fifteen years after Jesus's death, that at that time conflict over rank hounded the principal apostle out of Jerusalem, and that even later he was not spared surveillance. The secularization of the ecclesiastical institution has early roots. Peter was not a representative of evangelical freedom. If at first he had undogmatically consorted with gentile Christians, now he groveled, submitting himself to the Jerusalem discipline, whereupon Paul accused him of hypocrisy. Barnabas, pillar of the Hellenists, allied himself with Peter. Paul no longer mentions Antioch, makes his mission independent of this city. He now becomes head of a church fellowship flourishing in Asia and Europe, of course only for some fifty to sixty years, still on record in the Pastorals and 1 Peter, weaker in Polycarp, and with an echo in Ignatius. If Luke is its first chronicler, the Apocalypse, perhaps contemporaneously with it, will know nothing more of it. Even in the first century, Christian freedom movements had no long life.

In the case of the Pauline community, two factors, independent of each other, provided for evangelical freedom. The apostle, of course, had been officially recognized by Jerusalem. But in Antioch it had been admitted before the council that the mother congregation enjoyed a status that could not be ignored. At the dispute over the community meal, Jerusalem's authority had probably contributed to the outcome. Paul himself knows by revelation that he will run in vain without the approval of his work by the "pillars." So he is passionately involved in his community's collection for Jerusalem. Romans 15:25–31 shows that even at the end of his life the connection with the mother congregation hangs over him like a fate. Enemies await him there who are not merely among the Jews. He is not at all certain that the collections will be accepted by the brethren. He designates it only as a gift of love, while in Jerusalem it may be regarded as a sort of church tax. Paul would not regard it as so important if it were not really so, and would not need to bring it in person if his apostleship and work would not have to be accepted once more and for the duration by Jerusalem.

From Acts it is clear that Jerusalem actually raised claims to primacy in Samaria, and all of Palestine as well as Syria. For this reason the newly founded congregations are separated and authorized, so that from that point the visits of the people of James in Antioch become more intelligible, perhaps even the emergence of strict Jewish Christians in Pauline congregations, as for instance according to 2 Corinthians 10–13. The detail remains problematic. It can scarcely be doubted that in the history of the church it was first postulated by Jerusalem that Christianity would legitimately exist only in connection with a center. If this postulate was made regulative, but not finally enforced, it is due to the effects of Pauline theology and mission. They held that no principle can theologically justify the dependence of Christian congregations on a city. No hierarchical order is allowed to shrink evangelical freedom, though this remains a permanent temptation. Dignitaries are to be respected, not to be fixed ideologically and legally.

Also, and from the very beginning, the Pauline congregations were threatened by an eschatological enthusiasm. In Hellenistic syncretism, Christianity was understood as a kind of mystery religion that conveyed a sacramental share in the divine nature and liberation from cosmic constraint. Second Timothy 2:18 formulates this in terms of a resurrection that has already occurred. As early as in 1 Corinthians 15:12ff., the apostle's polemic is directed against a similar view that inevitably challenges future eschatology. In glossolalia, one speaks the language of the angels, of the healing of the sick and possessed, announces the breaking of the divine in upon earthly reality. The emancipation of women, who prophetically reveal their inspiration, as well as of slaves, who at least feel equal to their Christian masters, attracts attention and points to the nearing end of all earthly orders. The case of the incestuous person in 1 Corinthians 5 is especially dramatic. The intimate connection of the baptizer to the one baptized creates a pneumatic relationship which becomes the culture for forming parties in the community.

The authority of the apostle pales or is actually criticized. The so-called weak, perhaps those members of the congregation determined by Jewish law, are despised and violated. Through ecstatic carryings-on the common worship services lose their genuine meaning. I am going to break off with the description here, though it would be relevant to pursue it further. What is important is how the apostle reacts where evangelical freedom is disturbed through enthusiastic arbitrariness. What is unusual is that he does not appeal to the need for order, even where he seeks to set disorder aside. For him the idea of order plays an undeveloped role, as can be learned from a comparison with the first letter of Clement. The motif of the freedom of the congregation and of individuals is held to by relating everything to membership in the body of Christ and the need that irrevocably follows from it of adding to it through mutual service. This renders typical the right of the stronger, a right basically recognized, but limited for the sake of care for the weak. Peace, more than freedom, is the goal.

At this point occurs a post-Pauline reversal in the expanding great church. The enthusiastic danger continues. The Pauline congregations, to the extent they do not fall under new leadership and then borrow from the equally expanding Jewish Christianity, appear more or less to be subject to this danger. As the ardent imminent expectation of the parousia diminishes beyond the enthusiasts, and there must be strict adapting to the earthly, the consciousness grows that the universal priesthood of all believers represented by charismatics cannot, in the long run, do away with false doctrine and enthusiasm. Prophets are frequently carriers of infection, for which reason leadership of the congregations may obviously not be left to them. The legitimacy of a functioning congregational leadership becomes the most pressing task, as the Pastoral Letters in particular indicate. In the Pauline communities (against the Lukan view) not-yet-existent presbyters take over the responsibility, from whom monarchical bishops very quickly emerge. These leaders, still understood as charismatics, but through ordination retaining a particular status, and linked to confessional formulas taking shape in the meantime, conduct the oversight of the individual congregations, supported by deacons and other functionaries. To this organization Jewish Christianity was godfather. This follows particularly from a theological fiction according to which the bishops are heirs of the pupils of the apostles and, in this regard, put crudely, enjoy apostolic succession. Apostolicity is now the mark of the legitimate church, and this motif appears gradually to conquer the looser association of individual congregations in favor of catholicity. If the Pastorals still do not assume any recognizable regional units, they still advocate identical forms of congregational organization in regional areas. The claim to leadership over Christianity that was raised in Jerusalem may not be forgotten. It is transferred to Peter in Matthew 16:18ff.; to James in the Acts of Thomas, aphorism 12; and, in Ephesians 3:1ff., to the Pauline tradition. In this tradition, Paul is still understood merely as representative of all the apostles and their common tradition. What is most sharply outlined is that, in the post-Pauline period, the enthusiastic currents growing and taking hold of the entire field of mission urge toward reflection on the oldest (termed "apostolic") proclamation, in order to use it as church doctrine. Functionaries are entrusted with its retention in the congregations. Still viewed as charismatics, they are nonetheless equipped with fixed mandates and rights and, with the *depositum fidei* [deposit of faith], retain a place separate from and superior to the rest of the congregation.

Over against sectarian opponents, the development aims at unity in doctrine and organization. This is best characterized by the letter to the Ephesians, in which, at the outset, the church is treated thematically, and not by chance set independently at the side of its Lord as the bride of Christ. The church's signature is the ecumenical expanse composed of Jews and gentiles, apostolicity and charismatic structure, in which the leadership falls to the ministry of teaching. It appears all the more noteworthy that this conception remains ideal and is not converted into structures of a worldwide organization. The earthly reality is still oriented to the congregation, in the best instance to the congregational unit, not to a hierarchical order of the whole or of individuals. The same applies, of course, in an unmistakable uniqueness to the Johannine community. Its peculiarity lies in its allowing the sacrament to retreat in favor of proclamation, and precisely in this way—in the shape of the beloved disciple!—in relativizing the significance of what is apostolic, and actually the significance of every office; it views the presence of Christ in the Spirit and in the Word continually renewed by him as sufficient leadership of the community and guarantee of its continuance. This probably indicates an organization distanced from the tendencies of the worldly condition in the great church, a pietistic form of community, structured in terms of a fellowship and thus still defamed in the middle of the second century.

The immediate future, of course, belongs to a church organized strictly on the basis of the episcopal office and gaining at least regional equality from it. The conflict in 3 John indicates that the bishop prevails over wandering preachers as dangerous troublemakers. The letters of the Revelation of John are issued to an association of Asia Minor churches at war with prophetically led sects. Not without good reason, describing the reading of Paul as problematic, 2 Peter abandons the charismatic constitution of early Christianity and declares the interpreting of the canon, now regarded as norm, to be the function of the officially recognized office. Now there are "laity."

Summary

1. From the very beginning there are profound conflicts over theology and practice.
2. From the very beginning the constitutional structures vary. Only from the beginning to the middle of the second century is organization in the great church formed by way of administration through a presbytery and episcopacy under the watchword of catholicity.
3. Associations prophetically led and organized strictly on the basis of a universal fellowship are retained alongside, though shoved to the periphery.
4. The ecumenicity of the church is theologically conceived early on, organizationally visible chiefly in the Pauline sphere of mission.
5. The congregation and the loose congregational unit represent the church.
6. The decisive question for the future: Anxiety in the face of enthusiasm or an order become bourgeois?

⊹ 3 ⊹

On the Ecclesiological Use
of the Key Words "Sacrament"
and "Sign" (1974)

Critical Preliminary Considerations

Ecclesiology was, is, and, of course, by necessity, remains the basic theme of the discussion in the *oecumene* as represented by "Faith and Order."[1] We can expect nothing else when Christian unity is ultimately involved. Nor can it be ignored that from out of this center occurred thrusts in the most varied directions, that the danger of an "ecclesiocentrism" was often emphasized and attempts made to avoid it. Numerous explanations indicate, however, that correct perceptions and good resolutions toward prevailing trends are of little use as long as they have not been effectively formulated or do not lead to discussions of fundamental importance. For this reason, I introduce my contribution—which, shaped as critical preliminary considerations, deals with the ecclesiological problem as a whole and determines my following argumentation.

1. Dogmatically, it is perhaps widely recognized that the doctrine of the church must stand in the shadow of Christology and be identified by it. It

---

1. A reference to the World Council of Churches "Faith and Order Commission," for which this essay was written.

First published in *Wandernde Horizonte: Auf dem Weg zur kirchlichen Einheit*, ed. Reinhard Groscurth and René Beaupère, World Council of Churches: Commission on Faith and Order (Frankfurt am Main: Lembeck Verlag, 1974), 119–36.

can be put somewhat brashly that in that case ecclesiology necessarily always points beyond and away from itself to Christ, just as, according to the Fourth Gospel, John the Baptist does as witness and archetype of faith, and as for the most part occurs in the New Testament. It is no doubt offensive, but scarcely to be denied, that the gradient in ecumenical documentations has been extensively reversed. The ecclesiological problematic is in the foreground to such an extent that christological problems are almost no longer apparent alongside it, apart from speculating, say, on the relation of the Cosmocrator [ruler of the world] to the world. That Christ as Lord of the church is also its judge is drowned out by the applause more or less given everywhere to the idea of the *unio mystica* [mystical union]. And with this we are once more in the sphere of ecclesiology—that is, involved with the motif of the body of Christ. If we read what is discussed concerning the sacraments, apostolicity, catholicity, the offices and services of the so-called laity, or what is said of late concerning organic unity and conciliarity, on careful review we are amazed at how little christological arguments are needed for it. Old dogmatic-historical traditions and modern sociological types of observation combine in an ecclesiological navel-gazing. We often have the impression that the theological problems dealt with exist only because Christology is not sufficiently brought into play. In the course of its history, and in all its varying shapes, the church has continually stood in the way of its Lord instead of preparing his way. It does so when it does not in fact and constantly call its members to be aware of his dogmatically recognized priority, which is in no wise to be relativized; thus, for example, the church stands in the way of its Lord when it legitimizes the "signs of the church" from him as source in such fashion that without them he is no longer clearly recognizable or their marks clearly recognizable as most profoundly his own. To formulate it provocatively, all ecclesiological questions are to be discussed under the christological aspect, and only from there are they genuine and do they require answering. If we shift the weight here in the slightest, we displace everything; everything becomes problematic.

2. To the current observer of ecumenical history it appears that consciously or unconsciously, cleverly or anxiously, in just about every phase a theme has been bracketed out that in conversation about the church absolutely cannot be bracketed out if we do not intend to postulate ideals and practice ideology but to serve the truth and give place to reality in theology. It cost us much labor and time till it was no longer contested that the one, apostolic, universal church did not or does not continue to exist without tensions, conflicts, and even schisms, that theological and historically and socially conditioned pluriformity within it is possible and unavoidable, and that its solidarity grows out of manifold complementarity on various levels. Recently its structures are

precisely encouraged to find and develop their own identity in order mutually
to supplement one another. They are summoned, as it were in a family or an
organism, to recognize that they stand in the same truth with one another.
The extraordinary progress on the way toward fellowship is unmistakable. But
the price for it is that the problem of heresy is suppressed, without which the
questions concerning the limits and genuineness of Christian community cannot be answered. Pluriformity is not a slogan that hides arbitrary separations
from the Christian fellowship, gives free rein to ideological and religious indi-
vidualism, or hinders or neutralizes theological debate. The formula implies
that discipleship of Jesus is always lived in a specified historical space with its
specific possibilities, problems, and bottlenecks. It does not recognize a self-
satisfied group that maintains its identity at the cost of the entire fellowship,
without being prepared for a critical testing of its right or lack of it, or where
possible actually feels comfortable in its isolation. Pluriformity is the reflection of the ubiquity of Christ and the way toward concretizing our service,
not a license for sectarianism with a self-fabricated theology and arbitrary
conduct of life where the necessity for repentance is as little regarded as solidarity. The variety of gifts can also rupture fellowship. There are thoroughly
inadequate forms of Christian expression, and against the perils of syncretism
in theory as in practice one must be on guard as against plagues. There is no
biblical God without idols, no Christ without antichrists, no apostles and
prophets without their deceiving counterparts, no doctrine without temptation to deception, no true church without its satanic caricature. It will not do
to trivialize the indispensable discernment of the spirits by proceeding from
associations, debating the greater or lesser instances of catholicity, and to hope
for a gradual overcoming of the ditches that separate. There is a heresy that
renders fellowship impossible. Silently ignoring this theme and treating it as
taboo indicates once more that Christology is no longer the measure of all
ecclesiology. The nature of heresy as well can only be grasped on the basis of
Christology, to the extent that it is fundamentally determined by kenotic or
docetic views. Only where Christ remains the decisive criterion of every church
doctrine and all its individual expressions can the limits of church fellowship
be sharply defined, limits that otherwise become blurred metaphysically or
sociohistorically so as to give access to ideological speculations.

3. The last assertion needs explaining and grounding. In general, confessions and denominations appear as surmountable hindrances on the way
toward ecumenical reconciliation. Church leaders as well as theologians actually encourage such an opinion. Still, it is becoming more and more clear that
vast circles of Christianity—especially of the youth and the young churches,
but well into the most loyal retinue of the traditional associations—are no

longer interested in the differences that characterize them and, in great measure, can neither name them properly nor understand them. Meanwhile, we have long become aware of the significance of nontheological factors in this regard. Yet it still might not be clear or everywhere recognized that ideologies are more and more obscuring the confessional ditches that separate and—with the powerful participation of the theologians!—pave the way, at least intellectually, for new separations.

In the last decades, New Testament scholarship, accompanied by much clamor on all sides, took up the problem of demythologizing and, in the ecumenical movement, earned little understanding for it or agreement with it. If we intend to make progress in the future, we will really have to repent over this matter. What began in the scientific sector with the discovery of ideological factors in the early Christian proclamation will soon, if theology is at all still seriously done, have to be continued on a broader front as the unmasking of modern ideologies. It will have to lead to serious reductions of speculative theories that substantially find their favorite playground in the ecumenical movement. In Germany, my generation has some experience with the slogans of church unity as forms for provoking syncretism in every shape and hue, from metaphysics to politics. It would be odd if the *oecumene* did not come to sense that more and more strongly. A few walls could gradually be thrown up against such a danger, and today a few Trojan horses would still be relatively easily transported out of the walls again. I use this as an example to indicate what at the moment is the most dangerous threat facing us from an enthusiastic theology of history. Coherent with our situation and its manifold global aspects, the themes of the one church and the one humanity make contact and beset us in common and at the same time. But we would do well not to attribute this from the outset to providential intent. Rather, it needs to be stated quite soberly that never in fifteen hundred years has in fact all of Christendom been more forced to be on the defensive, and solely for this reason has occasion for unity, and also that, in the period of atomic weapons, the entire earth can be destroyed, and humanity's survival hangs on the balance of its antagonists. It is obvious that, in such a situation, religious associations must give particular support to the most comprehensive and just peace possible and must call for mutual reconciliation. Reason and love require this of us. What is totally different from such an insight is an ideological combination of the parallel necessities. To get immediately to the center of things: it is absolutely unbiblical, for example, to see in a united Christianity the anticipation of a united humanity when homage is not paid to an *apokatastasis* doctrine in which sin finds merely a reversible depravation of origin and forgets that, at least in the Apocalypse of John, something like a humanity united before the parousia under the sign of the antichrist is affirmed, and from which only Christianity is excepted. By speaking of unity, nothing is yet won so long as nothing is said of the mark that characterizes it.

The eschatological unity of the new creation in biblical proclamation has nothing in common with the dreams of utopian futurology but the concept of the unity of humanity. Entirely apart from the fact that the continental, political, social, economic, cultural, and ideological contrasts of our world are at best pressing toward a polarization by two or three powers, and that the specter of the Apocalypse, like Orwell's *1984*, knows of a world unity only in the antithesis, whether of Christianity or of humanity, the new creation of the Bible is related to the people of God under the lordship of God, not to a restitution of the world before the fall. To the extent the motif of restitution actually emerges, it is related to the fact that God becomes Lord again over what God created, not to the restoration of a paradisiacal condition, in which humans no longer injure themselves and others. The new creation of the Bible assumes a crisis that also denotes judgment and separation of the redeemed from the damned, not the resumption of a temporarily disturbed and failed development. According to the Bible, sin is more than the interruption of a normal growth, the breaking out from an order that remains intact. It is a rebellion of the creation against the Creator that creates a universal fate, rendering everyone guilty. Thus salvation is not the correction of an error and the purging of consequences resulting from it, but the pardon of sinners solely through judgment and as an awakening of the dead, thus in a totally new beginning of life from the grave.

If this is correct, we must decidedly separate ourselves from the idea of a process of development involving all of world history, which in its structure renders faith transparent and could highlight its present phase. Whoever really comes from Golgotha and Easter must know that God's activity is not calculable but, against our expectations and moods of despair, operates in an area that for humans is offensive and unforeseen. If we attempt to trace out this path within the sphere of immanence, to set it forth in its continuity and consistency, we must close our eyes to the fact that on this path a "No" is always uttered before people are helped. The continuity of the faithfulness of God is not evident in a logic of history. Unlike theosophy and anthroposophy, faith does not have to do with evolutions but with a Lord who, according to 1 Corinthians 1:18ff., destroys the proud, the wise, and the scribes with the foolishness of the cross. Only the one who relativizes the scandal of Golgotha—that is, allows it to become a stage on the pathway of the divine love—can rationalize world history in such a way that only fools cannot read the triumphal procession of providence from its pages and see in the church the goal planned from eternity and the beginning of a reunited humanity. An ecumenical movement that surrenders itself to such a theology of history and regards itself as a vehicle of such a development is in greater peril than a Christianity separated by confession and denominations. It is lost in ideology, for which Christ is only a means to the goal and a cipher of a utopian program of world renewal. Or, more pointedly put, it is not that a universal church—that does not actually exist but is very rashly postulated from many sides—employs a futurology to compete with secular ideologies and to carry on a politics anchored in metaphysics. Salvation is first of all a radical de-ideologizing in the name of the first commandment and the prohibition against images, and thus of the Crucified Nazarene.

"Sacrament" and "Sign" as Ecclesiological Slogans

When summoned to take a position, the exegete who does not deliberately speak to the problem of such terminology and its ecumenical use immediately suffers a painful embarrassment. Since the concepts just named in the New Testament have neither directly nor by implication any equivalents of an ecclesiological sort, the exegete will do the work of an interested systematician or conceive the task assigned, if not with the suspicion due to a glowing hot iron, then at least from a critical distance. This remark can be disposed of as an expression of prejudice by countering it with how often nonbiblical concepts have opened new horizons and perspectives for the use of theology and church. This is correct, and so it is necessary to investigate whether it is true in this instance as well.

A second objection to the exegete's discussion of the problem at hand derives from the fact that the slogans involved owe at least their thrust and extension, if not their origin, to the Second Vatican Council. In *De Ecclesia* it was asserted that "the Church is in Christ like a sacrament or as a sign and instrument both of a very closely knit union with God and of the unity of the whole human race."[2] If this is conceived as being worldwide, so as to find an echo even in South American liberation theology, it still should not be forgotten to what extent the characteristic self-understanding of a particular confession has found fascinating expression here. It is by no means agreed that it can be taken over elsewhere without limitation or at least according to

---

2. This quotation is from the first article of the Second Vatican Council's Dogmatic Constitution on the Church, commonly known as *Lumen Gentium*. The full English text can be found at https://w2.vatican.va/archive/hist_councils/ii_vatican_council/documents/vat-ii_const _19641121_lumen-gentium_en.html.

its intention. The competence of exegetes respecting this dogmatic question cannot transcend that of an emergency aid drawn in for counsel. The reason why these critical preliminary considerations are laid out in such detail is that in order to cast their votes exegetes had to be conscious of the premises and implications of their task.

Church as "Sacrament"

1. As cautiously as Protestants, likewise moved by the theme of catholicity, would like to express themselves here, so little can they altogether suppress indignation at the statement cited above. To describe the church as a sacrament will appear to them to be almost frivolous, in any case infinitely provocative as long as ecumenically, regionally, and locally we have not yet arrived at intercommunion and at recognizing others who seriously want to be Christians standing under Jesus's word, but deny them our full fellowship. A double game is being irresponsibly played here, one that is theologically inconsequential. For even logic, to say nothing of dogmatics, requires the obvious conclusion that if the church is a sacrament, based on this judgment there can be no church that is excluded from concrete participation in the sacrament. What is denied each other in part cannot possibly define the fellowship as a whole. Aside from the slogans "organic unity" and "totally obligated fellowship," "separated brethren" cannot even be sensibly spoken of when participation is not conceded at the point where fellowship is constituted and renewed in the biblical sense. Here, again, in thoroughly unbiblical fashion, Word and Sacrament are separated from each other. Within the horizon of this view, the actual and universal church is described by the sacrament that clearly outbids Jesus's call. This can only occur on the basis of a confessionalist claim that at bottom reserves the predicate "church" for itself and elsewhere at best catches sight of fellowships with Christian characteristics. Since, within the ecumenical sphere, no one really wants to state this in any definitive way, we may be permitted to speak of a lack of reflection within the framework of theological project formation. For all who are forced to such a conclusion but cannot enter into compromises for reasons of faith without compromising themselves, the project as such is of course defeated, agreement with the proposed slogans unthinkable, and any interpretation justifying them excluded.

2. If at all possible, theologically relevant formulas should not appear as formal and sweeping. According to what was said earlier, ecclesiological formulas are to be determined christologically. But neither is the case where one speaks of the church as sacrament and sign. Still hidden behind such language is a familiar christological tradition from the Western history of

dogma, according to which Christ is regarded as *sacramentum* [sacrament] and *exemplum* [example]. On that basis, does not the formula become more acceptable, since with such a transfer of predicates ecclesiology is clearly overshadowed by Christology, though not clearly stated? Of course, we may ask whether with such a transference of predicates a church that understands itself as universal does not blur the irrevocable distance from its Lord, because only he, if we want to use the word at all, is the "primary sacrament"—that is, the "effective sign" of the covenant entered into by God with God's creatures, and affecting both. A securing of the *solus Christus* [Christ alone], however, is essential, precisely on the part of believers, if, say, the church is not taken to be the *Christus prolongatus* [prolongation of Christ], or at least the repository of salvation representing its exalted Lord, now on earth dispensing God's grace and in this respect participating in the divine nature. Does this not assign to the church something forcefully taken from its Lord? Cannot such an assumption merely be dismissed by the fact that it constricts the motif of the body of Christ in terms of a *unio mystica* [mystical union] in which there are only different aspects of the same reality but no longer a qualitative difference between head and body?

In this regard the dogmatician would have to ask whether at this point— represented in such ecclesiological fashion and with the transference to the church of the predicate "sacrament"—Christ to a great extent falls into the chain of objective facts and, for example, loses the function of judge even of his church. The member of the *oecumene* will naïvely ask what church and denomination would dare to raise this claim as long as the body of Christ must in any case appear to the world as divided, and will ask whether here, say, the fiction of an obviously nonexistent, but postulated or yearned for, universal church justifies the dogmatic view. The pragmatist will finally—and, considering the inescapable realities, not entirely without reason—call to mind the formula of the *Corpus permixtum* [mixed body] and will actually be able to appeal to the Bible for it. How does this relate to the other formula of the sacrament? As long as these questions are not even thoroughly considered, much less answered, the *oecumene* can only be urgently counseled to avoid this dangerous slogan that in no way furthers dialogue.

Church as "Sign"

1. In the Vatican declaration, "sacrament" and "sign" were not set over against each other in complementary fashion, as appears to have been the case in the interim, but were rather coordinated as explanatory. For this reason there was talk of an "effective sign." This means that the character as

"sacrament" was the decisive definition of the church, and the predicate following was not in any case to weaken the first. Differentiation was made only in the matter regarding the purpose—that is, the mediating function that the church assumes between God and humanity as the instrument for effecting an intimate unity with God and for uniting the entire human race. Both details are meaningful only if the church, as the slogan "sacrament" already implies, is regarded as a heavenly entity. This corresponds finally to the odd formulation according to which the church exists in Christ. If we look for a New Testament basis for such an ecclesiology, we will first of all recall the Letter to the Ephesians, which localizes the church in a sphere above the earth and allows it to grow in heaven. But we should not miss the ambivalence of such an expression. According to Ephesians, precisely in this sphere, which no longer belongs to humans alone, there are also demons, the reign of Christ colliding with the reign of Satan. Here, the heavenly is paradoxically involved in the most extreme conflict, a paradox we will be permitted to call more or less constitutive for all the ecclesiological statements in the New Testament. The elect are the persecuted, the despised, the dying. They fall and must be raised up again, they doubt and need the comforting macarisms, and they come into conflict with each other and are called to reconciliation. The warnings of the letters in the Apocalypse execute judgment before the promise is renewed. It is clearly no different with the history of the Old Testament people of God: God's faithfulness alone supports and carries on God's work. Grace holds together what on earth always appears to come apart. Christ dies for the godless, to whom, according to the Gospels, also the devout of Israel and even the fleeing disciples belong. This is the scenery in which, as in Rembrandt's paintings, heavenly light falls in the midst of earthly darkness and allows room only for the *Soli Deo Gloria*. With this then can be connected our present experiences with all churches and denominations—experiences in which the generations oppose each other and in which political hatred, social exploitation, racism, and, of course, theological conflict are continually ongoing.

But to speak here of the sign of unity with God means "without all our merit or worthiness";[3] it is to confess an experienced forgiveness. If, in view of our external and internal disunity, we still dare to speak of the sign of reconciliation among men and women, it is so contrary to all appearance that the world's scorn for it is unavoidable. Following the statements made earlier, the ideology that sees in the church a stage in the process of the reunification of all no longer needs discussion. At issue here is to describe the exposure with which the picture of an *ecclesia triumphans* [church triumphant] covers and

3. Martin Luther, Small Catechism, art. 1.

suppresses the earthly reality and in so doing must necessarily be incredible. But in view of such claims, honorable people can scarcely do other than take the side of the unbelieving Thomas and demand that they really get to see with their eyes the "sign" that is proclaimed here or they will not believe.

2. It was already indicated above that present ecumenical usage appears to use the slogans "sacrament" and "sign" in a complementary way against their original intention. Perhaps we may assume that the christological two-nature doctrine is in mind here, and as applied to Christianity. There is a heavenly and an earthly side of church fellowship, and only where both are in view do truth and reality not split apart. Here, then, the church, in its earthly reality, other than according to the predicate "sacrament," has chiefly the character of a reference to what is incomplete or to a shading of the hidden glory of the kingdom of God. Its function is seen in a more strictly pedagogical function. For the variety of its concrete forms of appearance at various levels, and for their complementarity in an "organic unity" and its conciliar construal and fellowship, room is gained for development. But included in this are also possibilities of bolder experiments that, for the present, would give better access to the Christian life or, in locating the identity of the young churches and transconfessional groups, would help to describe the impulses in the socially, politically, and racially contested space. Ecumenical growth and Christian engagement beyond the boundaries of traditional offices and diaconal tasks can be furthered by the ecclesiological slogan "sign." Symbols of the kingdom of God are already to be found today, wherever there are disciples of Jesus, where God's reconciliation with us is carried out on earth in mutual reconciliation, where the exodus from an old world is always occurring anew and the new Adam separates himself from the old. Thus understood, the new slogan is a good watchword, though we must be aware of the obvious weaknesses attached to it. The alternation that was asserted between the original and the intention later insinuated from it indicates that the formula as such is ambiguous. It is also too sweeping to be acceptable without further ado, since anyone may appeal to it who absolutely feels no obligation to set an example answerable to the church. Again, the christological determination is lacking that at least could check misinterpretations and is conscious of the confusion over anti-Christian "signs."

3. In the New Testament, signs are, on the one hand, connected with miracles and, on the other, with offenses—and both characterize the eschatological background of the ecclesiologically oriented slogan. From the available records it is hard to see that this aspect was sufficiently noted, though it is essential. For the Western world, at least, though by no means limited to it, the fact is that the church function of being a sign was lost in the same way as

its abstraction denoting offense. In general, the Christian community has so accommodated itself to the world around it that secularization could be and actually was regarded as a sign, and itself as instrument of its political society, whether explicitly in the bourgeois, in a Marxist or nationalistic sphere, or even in dictatorial regimes. In view of such perversion of the church's task, it cannot be too strongly emphasized that the cross is the true sign of the church and is nowhere in tune with it where the church is not involved in the scandal of its crucified Lord, known to all. A church that has ceased to be suspect and offensive to the world and its political authorities, economic managers, system ideologues, and even to the champions of stolid social conventions and religious tradition in its own midst is no longer a church—because it is no longer stigmatized from Golgotha as the arid no-man's-land outside the camp, factions, and empires. At this point there must be emphatic reference to the *ecclesia visibilis* [visible church], in which the kingdom of God and the heavenly *ecclesia invisibilis* [invisible church] are manifest on earth. Christianity participates in the glory of its exalted Lord and authentically announces his glory when it bears the cross after him on earth and in this way distinguishes itself from the miracles and signs of the antichrists. For this reason it cannot possibly reveal the developmental process of a reunited humanity. For on the cross, and in the disciples of the Crucified, the spirits divide; last fronts emerge; the struggle of God with a fallen and rebellious world for God's right is continually taken up; and the anti-church, which replaces the cross with power, competes for the destruction of the true church. Ecclesiological use of the slogan "sign" is suitable to the extent that it implies this state of affairs and occurs for its sake.

4. Used thus, the concept should clearly not weaken the meaning of the church theologically, implying that what is imperfect in it must be excused and is a mere sign of an unidentifiable hope. Where, in the shadow of the cross, Christians no longer allow themselves to be forced into line on earth and, before the earthly authorities, witness to the God and Savior of the weak, another world has appeared out of the chaos of spite and despair. There is a new creation and conquest of the demonic, promise for all the lost, and worship of the One who alone deserves the title Cosmocrator. Not entirely without sense, the oldest miracle stories have preference for reporting the healing of the possessed. Therein is announced the promise and authority of a church of the Crucified to a humanity more and more ideologized. Piously navel gazing, we have too long spoken of the *unio mystica* by leaving aside the propriety or impropriety of the formula. It is time for Christianity to arm itself ecumenically for war against possession and take exorcism to be the most important function of its diaconal work. The idols of our time hide

behind ideologies, and they have more to fear from the Crucified than from rationality, since reason too often falls prey to yearnings and anxieties and achieves nothing against blindness. Christianity is promised and demanded by the first commandment to break through the fata morgana, or fog of illusions, and uncover the truth of God, humanity, and the world in the sign of the cross of Jesus. Where it succeeds in this, just as its Lord himself, it is the sign on the horizon of the awakening of the dead and a new day of creation.

Church as the Kingdom of Christ and Fellowship of the Disciples of Jesus

Other than the slogan "sacrament," that of "sign" can be used ecclesiologically. Of course, it is too formal and sweeping without first being made unequivocal and clear by giving it theological precision. We would do well to look about for another signature and with it an alternative model that more sharply sets forth the meaning of the criticism offered thus far. In any case, this criticism coheres with a christological determination that leads out of the isolation of ecclesiology and the use of mere ciphers. This can assume the dual aspect of connecting and mutually explaining the heavenly glory and earthly lowliness of the church. Finally, we should look about for slogans—taken, as much as possible, from the New Testament itself—that are intelligible to all of Christianity and do not too intensively reveal the patina of theological tradition. This may justify the proposal that ecumenical unity be viewed by way of the ecclesiological formulas of the lordship of Christ and the fellowship of the disciples of Jesus. Naturally, no detailed ecclesiology should be developed from it. It is necessary to show first of all that there are basic motifs here, and then set forth their relevance to contemporary conversation.

1. The church is constitutively the *Regnum Christi* [reign of Christ]. This appears most clearly when in Romans 5:12ff. the spheres of the lordship of Adam and Christ are compared, or in 1 Corinthians 15:24ff. In the present, Christ as the predestined Cosmocrator interprets the final lordship of God— that is, according to the context, wherever faith recognizes him as *kyrios*. The enthusiasts have gone even further and, as hymnic material indicates, have already proclaimed the subjection of the cosmic powers and forces, whereas Paul in so many words allows this to occur only at the parousia, and for the time being (as in Romans 8:31ff.), he limits it to the sphere of the believers. This corresponds to the preaching of Jesus insofar as he also, through his activity, saw the inbreaking of the future *basileia* [kingdom] in the struggle with demons and thus set his hearers under the Beatitudes. These few remarks open a perspective on the entire New Testament and suffice for the thesis

that, in its members' situation of inner conflict, the church—as the *Regnum Christi*—is the earthly realization of the coming rule of God and, naturally, in opposition to worldly power. Described in such a function as the body of Christ, to this extent the church reflects the image of the One exalted since Easter for his earthly sojourn to the cross, as is summarized in 2 Corinthians 13:3f. Clearly, not only in a complementary way but in a way that precisely implies its truth, such an understanding is related to what is in fact the oldest Christian self-predication, as disciples and followers of the Nazarene who was enthroned as Son of God. The lordship of Christ is not merely proclaimed but lived by the community, and of course in opposition to a threat from the side of a hostile, demonically inspired world around it. The cross becomes the criterion of discipleship. Word, baptism, and Eucharist are structured and maintained in such a lordship and discipleship because the Spirit is mighty through them.

2. The sketch just given is intended to recall New Testament contexts that no Christian and no church fellowship can ignore and that aid an ecumenical movement in a way scarcely sufficiently exhausted until now. Here too, since an alternative model is at issue, only hints are given, though now the problematic of the *oecumene* as a whole can be taken up. At its center has always stood the question of unity, the necessity of which, as biblically promoted and universally recognized, can only with difficulty and in part be connected with reality. The dilemma grew as did the number of members, because it continually made clear the dogmatic, cultural, historical, social, and political divergence. It was significant progress to learn that pluriformity, tensions, conflicts of various sorts (as in all of life so also in Christianity) are to be regarded as unavoidable and actually indispensable to mutual service, from which point unity was understood as solidarity that, with respect to organization, led to the concrete postulate of conciliarity. Nevertheless, this involved taking a position that of necessity could not be sharply defined so long as the question of the demarcation of heresy was not discussed and discussion of the otherwise immediately threatening collapse of fellowship was not allowed. These difficulties were now to be minimized. If heresy is, at bottom, of a christological sort, then it expresses itself as bursting church fellowship by contesting the royal rule of Christ and denying the discipleship of the Crucified. It should scarcely need to be made clear that other differences, at whatever level, were not allowed to be tolerated as long as agreement existed on these two matters. Conversely, up to severe tensions and conflicts, pluriformity is necessary if the kingdom of Christ is to penetrate every corner on earth and discipleship is to bear the unmistakable mark of a disciple—a mark that, in the concrete situation, is not to be borne by others. The ubiquity

of the *Regnum Christi* is impossible without contrasts, and even shockingly extreme forms of behavior (something much too seldom recognized). Solidarity is not an end in itself, but the basis for worldwide service to the same Lord and the creation that belongs to him. As long as it is served, there is unity. Oddly, different types of behavior only prove that the Christian is conscious of the breadth and unavoidable linkage of one's service to the situation and for this very service may expect the agreement of the community.

3. No less significant is the insight that the unity of Christianity treated here, in view of its manifold supporters, will of course always be newly sought, discussed, fought over, and found—as a result of which failures are unavoidable. Still, despite these events on the human level, it is not the result of a process of development, but rather prior to all the indispensable effort on its behalf and all the errors resulting from it. The reigning Christ is its truth and reality. He does not allow this unity to be totally destroyed, but through his Spirit is at work in it by gathering together again the separated and divided. Finally, it is lost only where he is no longer allowed to be Lord and discipleship is denied him. Since the situation is such in the New Testament, the local community is more often described as church than is the Christianity of a region or Christianity as a whole. Where the lordship of Christ and discipleship are the criteria of the church, catholicity is not preeminently a spatial and temporal category but a situation by which the entire earth is summoned back to the obedience of the creation, even if this summons occurs from a prison cell. The fact that the world is summoned by the gospel and is in the balance between God and Satan is of universal significance because this summons is an eschatological event and leaves its imprint on history as a whole. It is no different with apostolicity, inadequately grasped by the problem of historical succession, because its dimension is world mission, its founder the Cosmocrator, its organs all those who are called and sent out by the Nazarene and thus follow the first of his disciples. To sum up this section, the *notae ecclesiae* [marks of the church] are already given us with the church itself, not tied to our norms and organizational forms. They are marks of the reign of Christ, under whom, in the chaos of the fallen creation, a community is readying in departure for a new world under a heaven no longer closed. This does not mean we would be relieved of responsibility for validating and announcing the *notae ecclesiae* but, indeed, that we must regard ourselves mutually as members of the same body and give priority to our belonging to each other over our differences.

4. Under this aspect, the current acute dispute over whether the church must be established "vertically" or "horizontally" seems senseless. Where the kingdom of Christ is confessed, the divine deployment is addressed, the

state of being in the service of the gospel and in universal mission. Where discipleship of the Crucified is at issue, it cannot be ignored that his pious contemporaries were his worst enemies, that throughout history the doctrinaire and the conformism of the churches have obscured his portrait more than all the slanders of anti-Christian movements. His first community grew from the poor, the outcasts, sinners, and even zealots, and from the beginning his action was determined by a helping and healing diaconate. Whoever is not just coining tasteless slogans here, in order to judge one-sidedly, but is tearing fellowship apart, whether from a thoroughly anti-Christian spiritualism or a social humanism, sets an ideology in place of the One who allowed the message of the gracious God to be concretized in help for the needy and in fact for the unworthy. Where everything is reduced to a single digit and rendered uniform, the wealth of gifts coherent with the abundance of existing necessities is despised. Where the intention is just to make the pious more pious, one follows the Pharisees, scribes, and the people of Qumran from whom Jesus separated himself at this very point. Where one's earthly salvation and eternal salvation are in mind, and it is forgotten that both can be hindered by inhumane structures of society, sacrifice is offered to the idol of the status quo, and discipleship is refused the One who, in the Old and New Testaments, calls his servants into the exodus of the wandering people of God. The leading aspect can perhaps be described as pointing in this direction: where the reality of the world is that of a jungle of a fallen creation, the kingdom of Christ can be preserved in discipleship of the Crucified only in such fashion that every individual Christian, small groups which cannot be doctrinally fixed, and confessional associations at all levels of their effectiveness penetrate the jungle with their characteristic capabilities and in view of the possibilities offered to them, in order there to model their service to their Lord and his creatures. So far as this is possible, everyone owes them counsel and help without thinking to impose one's own opinion on them or to determine their path. They represent church unity by carrying out their service in the name of Jesus. For church unity does not mean universal and mutual control but the granting of freedom for service on behalf of the same Lord and his own in the various situations, and in the use of the various gifts and possibilities. Unity is at hand where the kingdom of Jesus and the fellowship of those who follow him are provocatively visible to the world. It needs no other marks.

$$\dashv 4 \vdash$$

"Jesus Christ Frees and Unites"
(1975)

Before entering upon the substance of our theme, it should be stated that its formulation should not mislead us into pronouncing a sentence beforehand. At issue is not a universal truth accessible to everyone of goodwill. Indeed, by an unrestrained and absolutely certain statement, universal validity is claimed and its ability to be experienced worldwide attested. Nevertheless, from the outset we must be conscious of the fact that the echo of our theme is a worldwide skepticism and contradiction, typically recorded by religious propaganda and Christian provocation. What is actually at issue in our statement is a confession for the truth of which, first of all, only believers can vouch. Believers must vouch for it because the Christian message does not coincide with appearance and on earth remains contested. Brought paradoxically to a point: our theme loses its credibility in the same measure as it is presented from out of ideological security, an activity widespread even in the church, and as a postulate. Where Jesus Christ is at work he allows his disciples to be sensitive to ideologies and radically frees us even from religious illusions. All that follows, using our theme as an example, will verify this statement in the face of much resistance.

The Good News Discredited in the Church

If we take seriously our assertion that Christ frees and unites, we immediately get into the deepest embarrassment. Has ecumenical theology considered what

A meditation on the theme of the Fifth Ecumenical General Assembly of the World Council of Churches in Nairobi. First published in *Ökumenische Rundschau* 24 (1975): 129–42.

a colossal provocation it has formulated with this assertion and how rapidly it must turn on itself? The danger of church triumphalism is always close by this theology. Incontestably, there is fear of obscuring the glory of Christ when it is not projected as powerfully as possible in the ecclesiological sphere. Naturally, we do not deny that various distresses and human imperfections characterize church reality. On the other hand, we do ourselves much harm to look on and carelessly give in to all the stupidity, cowardice, arrogance, self-destruction, and violation that leap out at the critical observer from past and present. Our theme, however, if it is to be appropriately discussed, allows for no disguising. It is rightly confessed only by those who not only are aware of their part in earthly poverty, transitoriness, weakness, and distress but also admit to a lasting guilt attaching to themselves and Christianity. It is harsh, but scarcely unfair, to state that more than anyone or anything else, the churches and their members take cover, hinder, and disavow the work of Jesus when they take it under their own control. There may be nothing more difficult for Christianity and its groups than to allow its Lord a free hand, so that the Spirit might blow where it will and be able to defend itself against all domestication. The world around us, which critically measures the rightness of our message by the credibility of its messengers, will notice whether at least we ourselves are stigmatized by our Lord. Conversely, the world finds it to be discrediting when we set a goal and limit for him and administer his cause as if we could be anything else than his servants and instruments.

What can be seen as most conspicuous about us is disunity in thought and action. This has its deposit in the plurality of confessions and denominations, in the forming of parties among them, and in many cases in a sectarian turning away from fellowship. The color scale is at least as variegated as that of the differences in the secular sphere. Added to it in our generation is a polarization of old and young, conservatives and liberals, of fundamentalism and historical-social criticism that spares no community and is even reflected ecumenically. Nothing here can be spared without hypocrisy. We should all be ashamed, should contribute to reconciliation above anything else. Present conditions may in no case be derived from the necessary pluriformity of the church as organism, and be trivialized. Indeed, God gives to each their own, but not the same. Along with the possibilities of individuality, God also sets limits. From various social commitments, we learn that we are structured for mutual complementarity and aid. By God's differentiating activity, the One who created us and calls us to salvation is the One who separates us from conformism, which is a flight from a responsibility that cannot be given to another, and legitimizes indignation at what is stereotyped, which, unfortunately, all too often violates Christian everyday life. Solidarity assumes those who differ, each of whom—by environment, history, and the front in which they are integrated—unmistakably bears their own impress. All this is perverted where confessionalistic obstinacy, speculative arbitrariness of theologians, suppression of conscience by institutions or majorities, and the intolerance of minorities rule. They destroy fellowship precisely because they do not sufficiently respect the variety of gifts and services available. By making belonging to Christ a matter of uniformity with a party, they attack the Lord himself, who established the criterion of discipleship as love of neighbor. The nature of this world—a world with its religious variety and in Christian guise, whose end we are to proclaim and represent (just as did Paul)—flowers in grotesque theater when, for the sake of differing views and types of behavior, we assert ourselves against one another in things great and small, instead of being engaged for one another. If our theme is not superficially treated, piety must be seen as a possible source of dispute, hate, and disloyalty toward the fellowship. Only then is it shown that Christ must be greater than our Christianity and must actually conquer our piety if the unity willed by and glorifying him should appear on earth.

It is here also that our freedom must most profoundly be made known. In it, though this is almost unknown and sounds blasphemous, what is not in the least at issue is the liberation of the pious from their homemade piety or conventional religiosity. The debate over freedom, obviously a particular characteristic of our time, is conspicuously encountered everywhere in Christianity. It has become complicated because in it the most varied motifs and goals appear that are incompatible with church and gospel. Nevertheless, what is clear is that our theme finds a soil already prepared and meets open expectations. Here then, more severely than elsewhere, the intensity, breadth, and peculiarity of our engagement would have to allow itself to be concretely tested. Stamped with the signature of freedom, Christianity as a whole, as well as in its individual members, would nevertheless instigate a continual sensation and provocation to all the world because it would be near the yearnings and needs of humans and of the earth and would speak to them merely by being there. This may even apply elsewhere. In view of our conditions, we will indeed be allowed to assume that the hopes placed in the churches are, to a great extent, no longer fulfilled and that the secular freedom movements of our time regard us as more their enemies than their allies. From our history it is of course clear that we ourselves once appeared as a freedom movement. But the storm floods have long since drained away and, in any case, given place to greater or smaller rivulets. Then too, the intrachurch debate over Christian freedom is conducted altogether by minority opposition to ruling currents and institutions. It therefore signals unfinished business, opportunities missed, discipleship crippled, and fellowship with the oppressed is betrayed on earth. And it no longer points to a characteristic mark of the community.

Christological Interpretation

Our record is not looking good. Our theme is scarcely covered by it. If we inquire into the reasons for this, we should not ignore the fact that a questionable theological development has considerably contributed to it. In a really inexcusable unconcern, Christian unity today is being combined with the utopia of the unity of the human race. I enter into this because there is evidence here of how heavily the humanitarian aspect displaces the christological. This is no less the case when more and more often in dialogue with the youth, the representatives of the Third World, or political ideologies, emancipation replaces the concept of liberation. Admittedly, Christian freedom has had and may still have emancipatory implications. And emancipations in society—whether of slaves, women, youth, or other national and social strata—are justified on the basis of the gospel. It would be worth something if one could limit the catchword *emancipation* to the social realm from which it emerged. But it has long been transferred to individual existence. Emancipation now means the arbitrary emergence from conventional paternalism and thus follows the postulate of idealistic tradition that, since antiquity, has promised human beings the right and power to realize themselves and therein find the meaning of life. Christian theology, which by no means needs to be hostile to violent changes in social structures on the part of political groups and classes, must fundamentally resist the inclusion of such a tradition. The New Testament offers no room to a pedagogy under the sign of self-realization and a self-liberation derived from it. For this will necessarily attempt to overstep the limits set for the creature and lead to a sublime sage in service to the law. None of us are ultimately there for ourselves. On the contrary, where the Crucified reigns, each will give oneself to death that Christ may be praised and the other's life preserved. Every desire to model one's own image and undergo education in character resists the correction of Galatians 2:20: "It is no longer I who live, but it is Christ who lives in me," a correction coherent with the dialectic that, in discipleship, whoever will find life must lose it. None know others and themselves to the extent that they could expect from that knowledge a guide for behavior, or in fact read from it a moral law which obligated all. No power, wisdom, or piety on earth can cope with the might of sin and the end of death such as illusionists imagine in godless ignorance of their capabilities. Salvation is received, not wrested on a Herculean path. Christian freedom is first of all and forever a liberation through an alien power and grace.

For this reason, in theological usage, the slogan "emancipation" is altogether unsuitable to the extent it does not merely descriptively characterize particular social upheavals. Christian freedom does not even lead to autonomy, but rather marks that position under the lordship of Christ wrested from the force of other powers. In a paradoxical dialectic, it is thus the reverse side of Christian obedience, which can scarcely be connected with the idea of emancipation. It need not be explained that the motif of self-liberation has no place in such a context. Biblically, even the aspect of responsible action—in which we engage in support of subjugated people and fight against enslaving conditions—will be more a consequence of our liberation as the primary and constitutive expression of the *libertas christiana*. Otherwise, as an idealistic interpretation always does, the New Testament viewpoint is set on its head. What it does not take seriously is that the New Testament regards the loosing from demonic bonds to be the content of its message, and it understands our help for others from that perspective. Unequivocally stated: for the New Testament, freedom happens within the realm of earthly possession. For this reason, Colossians 1:12–13 classically praises the heavenly Father, who "has rescued us from the power of darkness and transferred us into the kingdom of his beloved Son." In our addiction to demythologizing such statements and adapting them to our reality, we too easily overlook the fact that here human existence and community are not determined by social or political contexts. Reason and human dignity are not the measure of all things. Freedom manifests itself as an eschatological miracle.

What is decisive is not that we find the way to our real nature (to our identity) but that, according to 1 Corinthians 15:24, Christ rules—and thus all other powers lose their force; all fetters, walls, prisons lose their horrors; all ideologies lose their fascination. We can then formulate it thus: first of all, at issue here is not one's right but the keeping of the first commandment. The Godhead of God arrives on the scene and eliminates the deception of the idols and their service, but in so doing, God reestablishes respect for the creation, responsibility for our fellow human being, and a life under the open heaven. All this must be explained in more detail. The result of our discussion until now may be summarized thus: counter to the slogans currently in vogue, the Bible does not exclusively speak of freedom under an anthropological-social aspect, but rather defines it christologically in order to unfold its meaning for anthropology from that point, and only from that point.

Whatever others may think of it, for Christians freedom is strictly and solely this: that Christ has drawn us into his victory over all forces and thereby given us a share in his rule (and, naturally, also in his service). In discipleship of the exalted Nazarene it becomes true and real that God does not leave this world and his creatures to the idols, but is there for them in a lordly way, opening the living space of the first commandment to every creature. Conversely, from openness toward God, loosed from entanglement by egoism and the ban of earthly powers, we can serve the one Lord and all the others. According to 1 Corinthians 3:21ff., only that one is free and set within the unity of the *Regnum Christi* [reign of Christ] who listens to this One. But how is it with the reality of such statements when we recall the discrediting of our message through and among us? Not that we are asking for the divine perfection of Christian life, which on earth will never overcome its weakness and continually needs forgiveness. We are asking for an existence and community that, despite all their failures, still do not merely demonstrate the defeat of Christianity but witness to the actual lordship of Christ—thus for the right to our message despite the grotesque theater of so many defeats.

These questions require two answers. First of all, we must make clear to ourselves that no one belongs to Christ who does not give him their heart and with it the disposal over their will and life. The radicality of the first commandment may not be infringed, a commandment that forbids serving two masters and wanting to compromise with the forces laying claim to us. Clearly, the Christianity we have in view to a great extent hides from this radicality and, with all kinds of slogans and norms, attempts to avoid the first commandment—the commandment that alone is decisive for it. In this way, it becomes a hindrance instead of an instrument for its Lord. Second, it holds true that no one avoids the first commandment without also being in debt to it. Promise and claim must be gotten from elsewhere if both are not allowed to be given from this source. Our heart does not get along without something to which it can be linked, by which it can let itself be bound. It is difficult, if not outright impossible, to break loose from religiosity. There are also Christian forms of false piety. There are many redemptive features that can simply be transferred to Christ, as already occurred in the New Testament and grows rank throughout church history. In this way, the possession referred to already comes into play and, with particular pleasure, mixes itself with piety.

The essence of human possession lies in the fact that, out of lust for life and fear of death, it forms everything after the pattern of its yearnings or nightmares, from all of which it does not exclude its Lord. Our religiosity then creates him after our own model and is thus ruled by what it has invented. The fashioning of idols never ceases on earth, and it actually gains in intensity where the gospel has taken root. In this world God is always wrestling with the idols, cannot be conceived without this conflict with them, and is known only in separation from them. The disunity of the church, its lack of freedom and authority, are not to be overcome organizationally or in edifying fashion, not to be compensated for by an intensified piety. We must learn to be suspicious precisely of our piety, so that it does not determine who Christ is and draw from itself images of him that suit it. For this reason, our piety must be assigned limits so that, as our Pentecost hymns state, it learns to pray and hear through the Spirit who Christ really is. Only then is there a breaking out into the freedom and community united in the *Regnum* of God. All churches are inclined to take lightly the question as to who their Lord is, and they are inclined to answer it by pointing to the risen and exalted One. This does not suffice, because there are also false saviors and revealers. What marks distinguish the true Christ from the projections of our piety? Only where this question is precisely answered can it become clear where there is truly for us freedom, unity, and the *Regnum Christi*.

Here as well, I will content myself with two points. The fact that in general Christ is still seen only as the exalted Lord of the church can absolutely be connected with the need of the natural human to think of God under the category of power, thus in a metaphysical sense like an *Übergott* [over-God]. Actually, neither would we want to nor would we be allowed to dispose of the aspect of power. What is decisive, however, is the paradox with which this occurs biblically: in the Bible, God is the almighty Creator in precisely such a fashion that God binds Godself completely to God's human creature and thus descends into a history of suffering, enmity, disappointment, and blasphemy. According to the oracle of 2 Corinthians 12:9, God's power is at work within the area of weakness. From that point is already indicated what is involved in Jesus's way. It is the experience of the Easter community that Christ had to suffer and die according to the Scripture, and that community holds fast to this experience in its message of resurrection. The Nazarene shows us who our God really is in distinction from all the idols. God would remain unknowable to us, without a face turned to us, if, as the Exalted One, God did not also bear the features of the Crucified. At the peril of arousing resistance and passionate contradiction, it should be clearly stated that the freedom and unity of Christianity cannot be real or be maintained where the reality of the humiliated Christ is forgotten or relativized and weakened. The disunited community tearing itself apart over doctrines and types of behavior develops where, instead of the One called Father from the cross, appears the metaphysic of our ideals and nightmares about God, and where the story of the man of Nazareth disappears under the golden gleam of a Christology of glory. Those who do not allow themselves to be drawn into the passion by the Master are not free of illusions about themselves and the world, and they exchange the *Regnum Christi* for those spheres of lordship in which unity is forced and every party supporter achieves their truth and right at the cost of others. Then our fellowship must become a playground for our personal insights and ideals, the earth a field of propaganda for our conventicle piety, the church a school for a religiosity and discipleship to be furthered in opposition to unwanted groups. Then, in the name of Jesus, as the history of Christianity proves on its innumerable pages, in the universal war of competition between those who are wise in the faith, the new world under grace and the commandment of God is made a variant of the old world with a modified hierarchy of values. Privileged and oppressed, knowledgeable and instructed, rulers and conformists, heroes and underdogs once again stand over against each other expressing in their antitheses that God is turned into an idol, the Nazarene is betrayed, and our fellow human beings have become material for our creative will to shape. Of course, this leads to rebellion in the form of emancipations, to squabbling over the right interpretation of the Bible, to a refusal of mutual recognition, to secession from the body of Christ, of which only fractional subdivisions remain. Our Lord, precisely as the Crucified, is a scandal to the world, becomes the instigator of a religious disunity, our freedom from the legitimation of a piety stamped by human beings and their caprice. This is a reality that can be verified on every hand. It allows me to state that the struggle over the validity of the first commandment is continued in the church. False Christology and ecclesiological guardianship continue the service to idols that contest the truth and lordship of Christ. Christian freedom and unity must now be realized from out of such conflict as well as within it.

No less does a second point deserve consideration. We are accustomed to defining the church on the basis of Word and Sacrament. Perhaps, on the basis of the gospel, we should add a third mark, in order to fend off spiritualism and on earth achieve a sharper profile. The Beatitudes at the beginning of the New Testament, and the Apocalypse of John at the end, do not allow the least doubt that the Father of Jesus is a God who resists the proud, bestows grace on the lowly, draws near to the outcasts, the poor, and the suffering. The entire history of Israel points in the same direction. But it is a matter of interest that in Christianity, apart from certain sects, ecclesiological conclusions can scarcely be drawn from this history, though the center of our proclamation—that is, the resurrection of the dead—must be set within this context. We have occasion to make a correction here if we really want to establish Christian freedom and unity and summon people to it. No community deserves to be named after the Crucified that does not turn to the least, the helpless, the abandoned, the violated, to those who are not strong, wise, or pious in themselves, and thus make clear that the justification of the godless is projected right into the social dimension. Only an abstract theology that, by way of the glory of the Exalted One, disregards the revelation in the earthly Jesus, a theology that removes the church from the time and distresses of the creature, that allows it to be the host of the triumphant instead of the conflicted followers of the Nazarene through a barbaric world—only such a theology can dispense with this signature.

There are places where there is great concern over mixing salvation with the well-being of humanity, the earthly with the heavenly. This is still to be discussed. But the incarnation of Christ would have to write in our heart and conscience that such concern is expressly spiritualistic-enthusiastic and may actually be heathenish. It pleased God to combine here what we separate, to connect salvation and healings, gospel and bread for the hungry, liberation from guilt and liberation from anxiety in the face of the powers—to keep corporeality no less than possession in view. The superpious separate what the Creator, Redeemer, and the One who raises the dead allows to be inseparable. Then fellowship is crippled, Christianity becomes one religion among many, needs of the believers' souls are tended, and one's back is turned to the world in its lostness. Then patience and solidarity apply only to playmates and the like-minded, until finally fire and sword—inquisition through doctrinal tribunals or mistreatment of conscience—create conformity. The path to Christian freedom and unity is always obstructed when the ravaged Nazarene is no longer in mind, the God of the godless and brother of the damned no longer confessed, and forgiveness not allowed to be the last word in the church. The space and nature and task of Christianity can only be appropriately defined on the basis of the Christ who was crucified.

The Activity of the Disciples

In this concluding section, we need to discuss what we must do and allow in order to confirm, in our own lives, the theme "Christ frees and unites." Members of a Reformation church should at least recognize what today threatens to be forgotten, obscured, and discredited, and need not be decisive in other confessions—that is, that the Christian and the community live from the hearing of the Word. The fact that realists have problems with this, that the youth far and wide do not understand it, since words have everywhere become emptied, ought not to lead us astray. The Christian will not let the cry for help be played off against the hearing of the Word if, apart from a piety of works, he or she does not intend to fall into the hands of agitators and organizers, into the constraints of ideologies, or be subject to manipulation. What discipleship is and how it establishes Christian freedom and unity are incomparably described in the call narratives of the Gospels. Jesus goes along the Galilean sea and says to the fishermen there: "Follow me." They let everything lie and follow him—into the lordship of heaven, into the great mission, into that openness no longer barred by fetters, walls, and graves. This is not to be verified by way of psychology. The risk, the offense, the miracle are not to be abbreviated. Conversely, our life would be poor if it were no longer engaged by a mere word, no longer like Abraham being without security, perhaps without seeing a path and goal, leaping out of a pious past into the future and delivering oneself to the Nazarene so completely just as love, likewise seldom plausible, will always do. More yet, whoever does not learn that at the crossroads we can scarcely explore with any exactness the pros and cons of the one or other direction and that the greatest decisions are ultimately determined by trust is deceived about the limits of understanding. Everywhere, not only in the area of religion, there is the word that gives and requires trust, sets existence and world within a new horizon, has power and actively, as promise or judgment, penetrates our life. The Word of Jesus and the gospel is of this sort; it brings redemption to the damned of the earth in the comprehensive sense, and it leads us into freedom and the community of the free. We must hear it ever anew, as it prophetically comes to us ever anew. To have heard it once is not enough. This distinguishes the good news from the information with which, in a period dominated by technology, many theologians confuse it, as well as from secret interpretation as the mysteries offer it.

Believers are not committed to a particular worldview in which the meaningfulness of being [*Dasein*], Philo's royal way out of universal guilt and transitoriness, is mediated in illumination and beatific vision. The gospel does not make us sages who have most profoundly overcome earthly conflict like the true Stoic and are ready and obliged to communicate their supernaturally gained information to the rest of humanity. This may be the type of observation by which to interpret other religions. For good reason the generation of dialectical theology struggled against such a "religious interpretation" of the gospel, an interpretation appealed to where the aspect of the informative is accented and the question of meaning is set at the center. The difference is chasmic whether the gospel teaches about life and death, God and humanity, about history as a drama of redemption, and thus has a primarily interpretive function, or whether there is heard from it the voice of the Lord without whose continual promise and claim we cannot remain in discipleship. Ultimately, all the meaning of our life lies solely in the fact that we must confess: *Regem habemus* [we have a king]. This is not a religious possession that we could have, distanced from this Lord, and have mastery over. Here I sense to whom I and the earth belong, what is said to me anew each day when I remain under the Word. This suffices for life and discipleship, sets one within the human's becoming human and in encounter with the Creator and Redeemer. To know to whom I belong frees me from idols and illusions; it unites the flock, which, along with forgiveness, has free access to God and humanity, and thus to blessedness. There cannot possibly be a disciple who fails to be stigmatized by the Word and to live out from it.

This Word, sounding with unremitting newness as the voice of our Lord, is, just as the call to discipleship, a commissioning for that service which in turn attests that we have truly become hearers and disciples. This does not mean that information occasions appropriate actions—that our inner attitude must be outwardly tested or that, however idealistically, we may formulate the priority of the event in the soul or mood prior to the practical involvement in the conditions of the world around us. From the outset, the gospel is turned to the whole person—not, say, to the intellect or conscience alone. Thus, together with the heart, the gospel immediately demands the entire will. Precisely in the sphere of corporeality is shown whether our heart and will were obedient. But if this is so, we are not addressed first of all within our private being [*Dasein*], where we, as it were, are most by ourselves, then only released for the conditions of public life. For the gospel we are a piece of that whole world to which its call to salvation applies. By seizing hold of us it has seized hold of the whole world, and beyond it with our service. This means that God as Redeemer remains the Creator and God's activity recognizes no other space than the political in which powers and forces collide and each maintains its own right. Here Christ will be Lord and erect his *Regnum* among his enemies. Here he calls us to freedom that, removed from the constraints of egoism, from the world's being possessed, from its norms and conventions, sees access and breakthrough on every hand, and the possibility of acting. Here our Lord promises to be present at all times and places, so that, except for the disobedient heart, there is no longer any taboo for disciples who can measure all the heights and depths of the earth to make visible everywhere the presence of their Lord. In a certain sense this takes up the command of the creation story: "Subdue it." For everything belongs to the one who belongs to Christ.

The intention here is to speak in substantially warlike language. On the basis of the Christian mission, we must point out the senselessness of the modish alternative between the "vertical" of the salvation event and the "horizontal" of our obligation. Clichés are seldom worth anything, and certainly do not speak for recent theology. The vertical and horizontal are separated in order to distinguish between eternal salvation and human well-being on earth, to separate our service to the gospel from the caritative diaconate. As to the concern last named, the question again is where it must apply without hesitation and where it must not—as, for example, among revolutionary freedom fighters. Protest has been raised against this entire way of looking at things in the name of the Incarnate One. Only in this way can druggists dispense and sort out their medicines, and only in this way can bureaucrats tell their files apart. We cannot assign more weight to the proclamation than when we state that we live from the hearing of the Word. This does not mean we lift such an event to the sphere of the individual being [*Dasein*], thus also abbreviate the lordship of Christ. This lordship is proclaimed by the gospel as its authentic content, so that our salvation is part of it. With the coming of the Nazarene, it is already established among us. Otherwise it would remain a utopia that not even the future could realize. Of course, in the present it is contested on earth and plunges every disciple into inner conflict. But we would have to betray it if we wanted to set it in a world above, to which only the spirits had access. Our everyday life and our corporeality will be determined by it, so that even the sip of cold water given the persecuted points to it.

So, according to the Bible, there is not only preaching but also healing and aid, and in such fashion that the worthiness of the person is not questioned and that all pious pedagogy is omitted. In the name of the history of the Nazarene we must guard against a doctrine of salvation alienated by a bourgeois ethic and schoolmasterish bookkeeping methodology. What our neighbor needs in a given situation, by which God now wants to aid him, is dependent upon neither our reason nor our faith. The New Testament criticizes Jewish piety that sees God's and humanity's affairs in conflict and thus inquires after the more pressing duty. It knows of no service to God in which reconciliation with the other would not be integrated. It points us to the whole person, so that in practice we refuse to deny not only the *humanum* [human nature] but also the earthly lordship of Christ and the future resurrection of the dead; so that we refuse to accept souls at the expense of bodies, not understanding and practicing diaconate in the social realm as charism, as a concretion of grace and a proffering of salvation; so that we refuse to bracket out from our task the altering of structures hostile to life, as if the world of economy and politics had nothing to do with the Nazarene. Where, according to the Baptist's preaching, every hill shall be brought low and every valley exalted when God makes entry, Christians cannot seriously regard the status quo as sacrosanct and simply look on human exploitation as though God's name were hallowed and God's will done in such fashion. In the train of the Nazarene, we cannot possibly respect bloodsuckers and instruct the violated in morality and discipline. To us and the world around us it would have to be clear where we do not belong.

Now, of course, the objection will be raised as to the purpose of such action and what it could achieve. It was already made clear that our reality does not correspond to our message. In conclusion, then, allow for a brief inquiry into the task and promise of good works. Disciples are not justified by them, but, conversely, without them they are no longer disciples. Not to be called to performance but to obedience, to regard service as a living in grace—this is the consequence of a proper listening to the Word, and it is Christian freedom as the unrest of an active life. We must be reminded of the fact that in the Bible work and freedom alternate—insofar as every *Dasein* is directed toward a yield—and at the same time must recall that signs and wonders accompany the revelation of God. My life should not drain off into the sand without a trace, and God does not speak and act without making known God's claim to lordship and leaving behind witnesses to God's victories. Combining the two, we may state that good works are required and produced by us as signs of our having been blessed by God. God has blessed us by setting us under the lordship of God's Son and has made us disciples. It is impossible that we should not answer and give thanks for it (of course in all our life relations and conditions) and that we should not, by our activity, witness to the presence and the *Regnum Christi* on earth. Instead of molding others and our earth after our image, we reflect with our works to whom we belong, and thus erect signs of his lordship (which has already broken into a world of idols and demonic forces).

Christ frees and unites. We have not avoided admitting how Christians and churches have discredited such a message. But our guilt does not allow us to deny Christ's lordship on earth, and in the present through all Christian organizations. Our guilt does not bury the Risen One again, not any more than the world's being possessed can outlaw the portrait of the Crucified. Nothing else remains for us but to allow ourselves to be called from out of our poverty and shame into his lordship, "so that we live under him in his kingdom and serve him,"[1] signs of the fact that he is greater than all that otherwise raises a claim and exercises power and that he has begun to create a liberated community from out of and among enemies.

---

1. Martin Luther, Small Catechism, art. 2.

✝ 5 ✝

The Presence of the Crucified (1967)

J esus Christ is the same yesterday and today and forever" [Hebrews 13:8]. With these words a formula is transferred to the Man from Nazareth that originally refers to the omnipresence of the eternal God. If this summarizes the entire proclamation of the New Testament, it also raises the decisive question regarding our proclamation. The reason is that the Man from Nazareth is the Crucified One. How does the presence of God rhyme with Jesus's cross? What is it that allows the Crucified One to be called omnipresent, thus godlike? This question gives shape to the secret unrest of every faith. Just as in preaching, so also in Christian life: it must continually be raised and answered. Our theology stands and falls with it. Everything else is prelude or postlude.

The answer seems easy. The first disciples already gave it after Golgotha first thrust them into collapse and flight—that is, the answer that God has made Jesus the eternally present Lord by raising him from the dead. This answer, however, is too facile if it obscures the cross with the message of the resurrection. To a great extent this already happened in early Christianity, and it has happened increasingly in the course of church history. The congregation at Corinth illustrates by example that the preaching of the resurrection can be

---

A lecture given at the German evangelical *Kirchentag* in Hannover. First published in *Deutscher Evangelischer Kirchentag, Hannover 1967: Dokumente* (Stuttgart: Kreuz-Verlag, 1967), 424–37. The debate following, in pages 438–62, led to vehement argument. The theme of the *Kirchentag* was "Peace is among Us." Lay members of the Evangelical Church in Germany founded the *Kirchentag* in 1949 as a biennial gathering to discuss contemporary issues in theology, culture, and politics.

just as misused as the name of God. This is what occurred at Corinth by deriving from reception of the sacrament participation in the glory of the exalted Christ, by declaring the way of the earthly Jesus as meaningless and setting the present possession of salvation in place of the future hope. Everywhere today Christianity faces the same danger. No preaching is protected from leading to superstition, and superstition is never more dangerous than when entrenched behind pious sentences and convictions. All Christian preaching necessarily awakens superstition when for whatever reason it neglects Jesus's cross. The cross was not merely a judicial error of Romans and Jews. It may not be made an interlude that through divine intervention was put an end to as rapidly as possible, an unfortunate incident in the history of salvation, the level course of which was restored at Easter. Otherwise, our God would be a plaything of idols, for which it is enough that they are proved to be mighty. And otherwise, the Christian life would be made the incessant search for miracles in which the supernatural breaks through our reality and the church is a community of the pious that in the last analysis is always right.

We cannot ignore the fact that Jesus's cross announces that our God in fact is and acts like no other, that victory was not promised to earthly piety, that faith may not be separated from inner conflict, or the church separated from the world, that salvation comes to us all only so long as we do not long for demonstrations of power but allow the word to be put to us again and again: "My grace is sufficient for you" [2 Cor. 12:9]. Indeed, cross and resurrection belong together. But for now, only the Crucified has been raised. If we ask in what way we participate in his resurrection glory, this is the answer: the exalted Lord makes us willing and able to bear the cross after him on earth, and in this way himself becomes wonderfully effective and present in his community. Christ reveals his lordship in and over the world when he ascends to the cross and calls us to follow him under its sign. In this time, there is no presence of the Risen One other than in the call to and service of the cross. Everything else is pious and dangerous enthusiasm.

We now have to consider what this means. We cannot begin any better than to recall the fearful cry with which, according to Matthew, Jesus died: "My God, my God, why have you forsaken me?" [Matt. 27:46; Mark 15:34; Ps. 22:1]. This should not be understood as an expression of despair, as has often been the case. Rather, according to this word, Jesus died praying Psalm 22, thus even in ultimate torment looking to the Father and realizing the mission delineated by the Old Testament. He died as he lived—that is, with God's word on his lips and in unshakable trust in the One who alone and always is the true help. The accent lies on the address: "My God." Nevertheless, the additional clause may not be ignored. The deepest distress of the One dying lies in the fact that from him too God has hidden Godself. Therefore, his prayer is a cry from hell. Both together show how Matthew wanted the cross to be understood: the Son holds to faith even when faith seems to have become senseless, when the earthly reality makes known the absent God, spoken of by the first thief and the scoffing crowd. And not without reason.

It is so extraordinarily important to begin with this passage. It frees us from the spell of edifying slogans and dogmatic theories. Naturally, we could have begun with speaking of Jesus's death as sacrifice, atonement, ransom, and then no doubt would have taken up a significant strand of the New Testament message. But in so doing we would immediately have landed in the language of Canaan, which can only be intelligible to the theologically initiated. By these stereotypes Jewish Christianity connected the new with the old covenant of God, in which the priestly sacrificial service was to guarantee the undisturbed fellowship of Israel with its heavenly Lord. As the true Mediator between heaven and earth, Jesus is regarded by this earliest Christianity as both renewer and fulfiller of the Old Testament order of salvation, and he seals it with his blood. At issue here, then, are the expressly theological and most time-bound interpretations of his death. The later community held to them in its liturgical-dogmatic tradition, because the connection between the Old and New Testament was important to it, and everywhere in the world around them gentile Christians could understand sacrifices and sacral atonements. As a result, Golgotha could be understood as superseding and replacing the entire ancient practice of religion.

If such a polemic made good sense, it is already clear from Paul's use of it that difficulties arose. Very soon, gentile Christians no longer felt they were proselytes of Israel, adding to the old people of God. Just as their mission penetrated the world and burst all national limits, they could only metaphorically and figuratively be described as "people of God," while Israel quite realistically and exclusively maintained that it was such. In place of the Sinai covenant, from which the gentiles are antithetically removed, now appears the universal covenant of creation, with which the ideas of atonement and sacrifice can no longer be easily connected. The church no longer has a temple, and its God is not reconciled by our gifts and performances, but by grace reconciles Godself with us without our effort. Thus, a new theology results from the worldwide growth of Christianity; it extracts from the assertion regarding Jesus's sacrificial death the contexts accounting for it, and with it the rationality immediately given in Jewish Christianity. What remains intact from it is only the motif of substitution, according to which Jesus died in our place and for us.

How then did it come about that in general today the idea of sacrificial death appears to be the central idea in the passion narrative? Religious traditions that lose their native soil frequently gain new vitality by settling in another place. That which describes a mystery no longer completely transparent attracts a new meaning. The death of the redeemer is also known to ancient mystery religions, and Christianity was always inclined, altogether in opposition to the New Testament, to understand God's righteousness as demanding and punishing performances. If both are connected, the dying Jesus becomes the founder of our salvation by taking our guilt on himself and bearing God's wrath for us. Innumerable preachers now torture themselves on Good Friday in order to make clear how this could be possible, without succeeding at it. Of course, people have continually died of alien guilt and for others. But we may not set Jesus among them, since he would then be only one among many. We must read the theory of satisfaction into the New Testament, since it can no more be found there than the doctrine of the punitive righteousness in Jesus's death. In doing so, we end by speaking of a mystery and make of the church itself, even in Protestantism, a mystery community. We have so accustomed ourselves to the idea that we see in it the core of our faith, and we think there is nothing to be defended more fervently. Almost no one thinks any longer of the price we pay for it. Now we can no longer make ourselves intelligible to the world to which we are sent, but must speak in oracles, not far from the path to speaking in tongues. The world is content with it. It can now set Jesus and his disciples among the religions, all of which have their peculiarities. Should we be content with it? Should we entrench ourselves behind the mystery when it is a matter of revelation? God's revelation is mysterious by running counter to our will and desires, not by urging us to regard as true what cannot be understood. Does the cross really remain the salvation of all when we cannot explain to everyone why it is so? Is Christ present among us when we can only stammer about him and when his face in truth hides more than becomes visible? Has not Christian theology, in its dogmatics and preaching, more often closed off than opened the churches' access to Jesus? The Man from Nazareth was intelligible to all. Why are Christians today no longer such?

Matthew shows us that we can and may speak of the cross other than with the theological formulas of sacrificial death and atonement. For the sake of mercy as well as of mission, should we not finally loose ourselves from the hallowed language of Canaan when it is really Jesus and his cross that are at stake for us, instead of dogmatic traditions and private convictions? Will we ever repent of the fact that orthodoxy has always violated and killed others in order to teach them the right faith or the edifying phrases recognized in church? Jesus did not die that we might be devout by way of formulas, and we will not be saved by way of proper dogmatics, but often only hardened.

Of course, religious fanaticism was also present at Golgotha, but on the side of the opponents who even then maintained they had to protect the weak community and the truth of God. In the unremitting alternation of theologies it is clear that God never allows Godself to be pocketed by us, that God's revelation remains living and inexhaustible, that it will be experienced anew by every generation and is never gained but in the enduring of errors. The history of salvation is no chess game whose individual pieces we could control or calculate. It is a worldwide war, altogether undecided on earth, in no way to be glossed over by us, and in our century more and more unfavorably shaped toward Christianity. It is easy to hand out victory slogans as losers, as we have always done to the bitter end. But in so doing we put ourselves to sleep, and we render ourselves, among other things, suspect of fraud. One thing is necessary, to know what it is for which we will live and die. We learn this under the cross, indeed only when we do not set it in a mysterious timelessness and edifyingly hide it, but set it within our own history. It is not the symbol of a religious ghetto, but God's truth in and over all the world, and thus also for our own time and for those now living.

What Matthew means by the last cry of the dying Jesus we have come to hear in Luther's Small Catechism with the word: "We should fear, love, and trust in God above all things." On the cross of Jesus the first commandment is raised up and fulfilled. Otherwise nothing happens there. But more cannot happen. Whoever has attempted it personally knows how difficult, indeed how impossible, it is to keep the first commandment. On Golgotha we see why this is so. To fear, love, and trust in God above all things—this is to occur within the brutality of our earthly being [*Dasein*], under the constraint of death, the shame of the humiliated and defamed, the murderous hatred of humanity, under the pressure of political forces, of religious impatience, of the despising of the weak, and over and in all of this in view of a hidden God. On Golgotha all of the history of salvation comes to its ultimate clarity. Here is tested what it means "to have no other gods before me." Is this our God, the God of the Crucified? Is this God our only comfort in life and in death, who will be called to and glorified on the cross, and by Jesus was called to and glorified? On the other hand, this event concerns Jesus, who in the hell of the supposed absence of God calls to the Father and witnesses to the Father as present. We know nothing of him if we do not know this, however many dogmatics we have read and however much we celebrate his resurrection glory. He is glorious on the cross and only for this reason glorious since Easter. According to Matthew, what happened on the cross forms the sum and substance of his life. We know of no one else who in the name of God did not want to make the godless pious and the pious more pious but, rather, went to tax collectors and sinners and said to them: "God is there for you." This was the path toward Golgotha. He died because he acted and spoke in such fashion and revealed his Father as the God of the godless. He brought the first commandment to the lost, not as law but as promise and salvation.

We must ask once more what this means. Why does such a path and this message lead to the cross? We need to understand that at this site the word about God includes a final word about human reality. Who God is can only be defined by saying what is at issue with human beings, as, conversely, humans in any given situation correspond to their God. The hidden God called to from the cross can only be the God of the godless. But hostility to the cross is the genuine nature of humankind to which this God is made known. One will live and survive, politically, religiously, privately, and in one's social conditions will always and everywhere present oneself in a thousand different masks and unveilings. Therefore one lives, if we may call it that, from the absence of the true God, however many gods one may make for oneself. We would not recognize this if, as in the portraits of Rembrandt, light did not fall into this darkness from the One who hangs on the cross. This One is different. His cry is not directed to life and survival, a cry for himself, but a cry to the Father. His cry is opposed to the reality of the whole world. Since Golgotha the profoundest question put to humanity is, Who is right, he or the others? This is the history of salvation at its inmost core: he or we; his cry, in which all his doing and saying are gathered once more, or our will to life and survival—thus Golgotha on the one or other side. We should not begin with the creation or with the hope in resurrection, or with the enumerating of the mighty acts of God. This can occur on either side of Golgotha, as shown by the Jews beneath the cross. And we should not begin with the idealism of faith in human goodness, or with the cynicism of the conviction of human evil. There is an even division where Pilate, Herod and Caiaphas, the incited mob, the two thieves, the complaining disciples, and the Roman captain are gathered in Jesus's passion. We must begin and end with the Crucified.

The Revelation of John praises him as the strangled lamb, who alone is able to open the sealed book of world history. Only from him does it become clear what is at issue with God and humanity and the relation of both. We need deeply to impress this point. The worldwide faith of an earlier time in divine providence, in the cause of all things and guarantee of human immortality, has everywhere begun to totter. Christianity as well has too long been in debt to the god of a philosophy, though it cannot be known whether this god is Yahweh or Baal. Unfortunately, the modish slogan of "the death of God" for the most part seems so blasphemous to it because it no longer knows about its roots in the Old Testament, where even Baal and the idols are called dead and nothing. This slogan would not be hurled with so much pathos at us today if we had not earlier spoken so carelessly of the God everywhere visible in nature and history while we masked the God of the cross with edifying veils. The time is irrevocably past that left to us in the so-called Christian West a monopoly on worldview. It would not even be a loss if over it we found our way back to the One whom the dying Jesus represents as his Father. Before we take the field against speaking of the "death of God," like the first thief and the scoffing mob, we must learn that God encounters us where we will not see and believe God. God must be looked for and found at Golgotha before we assert that God is everywhere. That our God goes into death with Jesus, that through Jesus God is even in hell, remains the decisive argument against the assertion that God is dead. We have no right to speak of the God of creation, of salvation history, or of the resurrection as long as we have not discovered the God of the cross. Otherwise we would not distinguish God from the idols, believed only because they are mighty. And otherwise, our message would treat of the One formed after our image and made serviceable to our will to life and survival. In creating, the God of Jesus and the cross penetrates the nothing and leads through graves where God will raise the dead. Wherever they occur, God's mighty acts are ignored, despised, blasphemed, not believed. God resists those who are always drafting their own heaven and making their own hell, ever forgetting themselves by reaching beyond themselves, yet assuming God's absence even in their religion, because they can only circle about themselves.

As Moses and the first commandment are fulfilled when Christ dies, so at the same time the call to Adam—"Where are you?"—receives its answer. The ancient church thought Christ died over the grave of Adam. This has deep meaning, for at Golgotha Adam is revealed and conquered as the lost son. This occurs from the second Adam, who—unlike the first, who even in paradise sought only himself and forgot the voice of his Lord in disobedience—obediently entrusted himself to the Father, even in the darkness of earthly distance from God, and therein remained the Son. Our God calls, creates, and preserves humanity, and in this distinguishes Godself from the idols by bowing to the lowly and being called to in hell. But God creates the new human by uncovering the nakedness of the old human, taking our salvation out of our hands and into God's hands. Christ must die so that we may live. His death cry is the new creation call. For he frees us from the two illusions: that God is absent where God does not reveal Godself in signs of visible power and that we of ourselves could ever be anything other than godless. Christ shows where God and the godless come together and remain with one another—there alone, where Christ does not let the Father go and dies for us, setting the world on grace.

Because this is so, the story of Jesus does not end at Golgotha. Indeed, the crucifixion was a once-for-all event. This is important because it prevents us from allowing an idea or a religious symbol to be made of the death of Jesus. Nonetheless, that God has not gone who was called to from the cross and gives us peace in God's grace. And there is no access to this God other than from the cross of Jesus, so that here the once-for-all and what abides are connected. For this reason, the Revelation of John describes even the end of the world as the revelation of the lordship of the Crucified: "Look! He is coming with the clouds; every eye will see him, even those who pierced him" [Rev. 1:7]. In what is almost more superb, Luke 12:37 describes the same situation: the returning Lord will once more do what he has done on earth—that is, tie the slave's apron around him and serve those who are his. His service is his glory and the only symbol of his lordship. This holds true even after Easter. As in the story of Thomas, the Risen One will and must be recognized by his nail marks. Otherwise he does not remain Jesus. However highly the resurrection glory is praised, nothing at all is gained by it, and only a false faith is awakened, when by it something else is meant than the remaining lordship of the Crucified.

At times we might despair when we see that the most bitter theological dispute is being carried on today over the empty tomb. Almost no one seems to realize how unfruitful and senseless this conflict is. Only a very few New Testament writings speak of the empty tomb. Since we can no longer inspect their data, we are really in dispute over what we take to be possible or impossible and whether every word of the Bible is reliable or not. By this means, faith is made into holding something to be true. But this leaves the matter to our discretion, to our ideological or scientific convictions, to the breadth or narrowness of our imagination. It renders faith helpless and mute before those who have different religious ideas and allows it to break down when not every word of the Bible is proved to be historically reliable. The dispute over the empty tomb also brings us into conflict with decisive statements of the New Testament and Christian dogmatics. In Paul we read, "Flesh and blood cannot inherit the kingdom of God" [1 Cor. 15:50]. If the tomb at Golgotha was really empty, this word of the apostle obviously does not apply to Jesus. But in that case, Jesus was not really human and his death was an apparent death, and his resurrection nothing but a continuing to live on after a brief interruption. Should this be our faith? Right here we have arrived at the heart of the problem. If the tomb was empty, at best this means the re-vivification of the earthly. This represents nothing specifically Christian, as Judaism indicates. In this case, Jesus merely exemplifies the extension of the human yearning for living on after death. Is that not a bit too little? Is Easter nothing but the fulfillment of our earthly yearnings, our urge for living on? For the most part, Christianity is preached in this way, and the passion of the dispute we are carrying on today indicates that nothing is more important to the devout community. Finally, in this way our human desires dictate what should be the central content of the faith.

I must go at this in such detail since it is against this background that the radicality of the early Christian Easter message quite shockingly stands out. This message also speaks of our personal hope and the promise given us beyond the grave. But it does so secondarily, and in the shadow of what is important to it beyond all measure: "God has made [this Jesus] both Lord and Messiah" [Acts 2:36]; "for [Christ] must reign" [1 Cor. 15:25]; "he disarmed the rulers and authorities and made a public example of them" [Col. 2:15]; "at the name of Jesus every knee should bend" [Phil. 2:10]. We cannot alter this series without everything becoming distorted. It is totally and absolutely unchristian when at Easter our own wishes and hopes are so pushed to the foreground that Jesus is only the guarantor of their fulfillment. From the Christian point of view, our future is a piece of his lordship, which reaches far beyond it. But because his lordship remains that of the Crucified, even after Easter, it is continually opposed to our own desires and longings. The voice of the Risen One has never gone out other than to call us to discipleship. It does so in the same words that the gospel reports of the earthly Jesus: "Whoever does not take up the cross and follow me is not worthy of me" [Matt. 10:38]. As if this were not clear enough, the next verse makes it an inviolable condition of our own resurrection: "Those who find their life will lose it, and those who lose their life for my sake will find it" [Matt. 10:39]. With the empty tomb this is absolutely not done, even if one were to prove it a hundredfold. It would be of no use to us at all if we have not stood in the discipleship of the Crucified. Today, we should rather argue over what discipleship of the cross means. Easter would be more credible to the world if it would see Christians not merely looking toward heaven but losing life on earth for the sake of their Lord and his own. It is so horribly cheap constantly to allow the Easter bells to ring instead of spelling and putting into practice what the apostle describes as the Easter journey of Christianity on earth: "I want to know Christ and the power of his resurrection and the sharing of his sufferings by becoming like him in his death" [Phil. 3:10]. This is what the presence of Christ in his community on earth since Easter is all about: "By becoming like him in his death."

How does this happen? The practice of all churches gives intensive answer with its worship services, especially during Passiontide and beyond, with symbols of the cross that it erects in and over its buildings and on cemeteries, spreads in art and kitsch, interprets in plays, music, and literature. It is not easy to avoid the call to reflection resulting from all this. In fact, we need to be called in this way. What cannot be forgotten and forces us ever again to remember and contemplate shapes our life. The danger, of course, is incontestable that we will become used to it, or be moved by it only in our feelings. Jesus's word demands more of us than devotion and emotion—that is, it demands our preparedness for acting and suffering. Above all, we must make clear that generally this contemporizing of the cross event does not penetrate beyond the church and that, where it does, it is understood merely as a characteristic expression of Christian religiosity. For some time, the presence of Christ has appeared to the world around us only in the mirror of a private or group piety. This should be intolerable for us. With the greatest emphasis, the Letter to the Hebrews asserts that Jesus died in the no-man's-land outside the camp, where there are no longer sacred precincts or cult and where profanity erupts on every side. The contemporaries of the Nazarene already found it to be so, because he associated with tax collectors and sinners. Not by accident, since the second century, early Christianity was charged with atheism because it removed the gods from the world. In our time it has become a matter of life and death that we break loose from the ghetto of one among many religions reserved for us as a pious natural preserve, having adapted to it under the influence of the mystery idea.

Everywhere today, Christianity faces the need for an exodus, such as may not have been more urgent since the days of the apostles. It has always faced such a need, since Jesus said to his disciples, "Follow me." The exodus, breaking out of settled camps into the earthly no-man's-land, is not the tragic fate of individual generations. It is the very mark and nature of the people of God, which otherwise does not exist. According to the Bible, exodus begins with the expulsion from paradise and the call to Abraham, the father of faith, who goes into an unknown land in order there to encounter his God. Israel must become the people in the wilderness when the first commandment is set up over it. The prophets all proclaim a departure, an exile and a return, thus a continually being underway. John the Baptist speaks of the exodus to the impenitent devout of his time. The Son of Man has no place to lay his head. He goes unresting throughout Palestine, instead of establishing fixed communities. The apostles are sent into all the world rather than allowed to remain in the Holy Land. All of church history should be read beneath the motto "Here we have no lasting city, but we are looking for the city that is to come" [Heb. 13:14]. The parable of the ten virgins sets even the last hour on earth under the word "Come out to meet him" [Matt. 25:6]. Naturally, there is the other side of the history of salvation, of the people that always long for the fleshpots of Egypt, grumble in the desert, and resist the prophets with the slogan "This is the temple of the LORD" [Jer. 7:4], even when it is the sanctuary of Baal.

In every period, there is a Christianity that has forgotten that the Lord commands, "Follow me!," that has fitted itself out religiously as a mystery cult, has struck the alliance of throne and altar, has sunk into middle-class mentality. And today, worldwide, along with the threatened white bourgeois, that Christianity defends the status quo, the inheritance of centuries, with ultimate passion. There can be no question where we belong. It is here that we should hear and learn the Bible. But the question is whether we will or can hear and learn here, though it is here and nowhere else that the decision is made, not merely over the letters of Scripture and confession but over their sense and nonsense. It is not theology, not even the best, but rather discipleship that makes clear what faith and superstition are. Christ's reign and glory become a pious ideology when his disciples are lost in the contemplation of his passion, when they set up and exhibit reproductions of his cross, speak about him in edifying fashion, set their hopes on him, but no longer take his cross on themselves and follow him into the earthly no-man's-land. Instead of transfiguring the church as the mother of the faithful and as the mighty fortress of God in this world, we should at last understand it as the host of Jesus in the final and continuous departure.

If we reply to this that these may be beautiful words but are much too general, that they would awaken unrest instead of joyousness, would use negative criticism instead of a criticism that builds up, would cripple the will for service in the church, would set the comfort of the gospel in the shadows and improperly forget how much sacrifice, loyalty, and honorable labor, how much readiness for reform and even experiments gained ground among us every day—I am far from demeaning such objections. From a particular perspective they are, to a great extent, justified. There is always that community which must be cared for, preserved, and increased and those without number who are committed and use themselves up within the sphere of proclamation, leadership, and love. But they also existed in Jerusalem when Jesus went to the cross and said, according to our Gospels, "Your house is left to you, desolate" [Matt. 23:38] and "not one stone will be left here upon another" [Matt. 24:2; Mark 13:2]. Are we certain that what happened to the old people of God cannot happen to us? If the gates of hell cannot prevail against the community of God, they have almost extinguished the flourishing Christianity of Africa and Asia under the onslaught of Islam. In our own lifetime, church institutions in whole countries have collapsed like hollow houses of cards. Only fools can close their eyes to the fact that the obverse side of the ecumenical gathering is a worldwide dying. One need be no prophet to be convinced of the fact that the organizational forms of Western Christianity will never resist the storm tide of secularism pressing in upon it. In the future, it might be advisable to open our worship services with the word of the Baptist: "Now the ax is lying at the root of the trees" [Matt. 3:10; Luke 3:9]. At any rate, in this year I can think of meaningful celebrations of the Reformation only as days for repentance under the theme: "Remember then from what you have fallen" [Rev. 2:5].

Such assertions are by no means made from an addiction to a criticism that, from the outset and without limit, turns against traditions and institutions, rebels against the complexity of modern existence, and thus disregards the necessity for a multilayered organization, even in the church. I am not at all speaking against recognized authority on the one hand or against an extraordinary measure of fulfillment of duty on the other. In general, attacks would be a manifest injustice here, as to how much remains to be improved in detail. All the more sharply, and precisely at a *Kirchentag*, may be voiced the disappointment, no longer to be suppressed, that German Protestantism has given in to restoration. What did we really learn from the struggle in the Third Reich, which anyway was largely carried out under the insignia of self-affirmation, which over the long run did not, at any point, bring us into an open field but instead ended with us in the rubble? That we have gotten free of a few national and social fetters ought not to deceive us about the fact that the Babylonian captivity of the church continues. That captivity is Babylonian in which the church is more and more completely involved in itself and finally becomes its own monument and museum in which its members are forever feeling their pious pulse, corporately and individually, in which offices and services are subservient to specialists and are measured by conventions, in which the sermon is in horrifying measure composed of clichés and spreads boredom, in which the confessions defend and enlarge their vested rights (though the normal visitor at worship no longer understands their meaning), in which the old in deceptive brilliance emerges from the rubble and must justify the appearance of actual existence. To life belongs provocation, passively and actively. A lifetime ago we learned that. When does Western, German Christianity challenge its environment again, conscious of the tremendous provocation that it meets with in open indifference and friendly toleration?

For this world, the cross of Jesus is and remains a provocation. But is this understood even if preached every Sunday? I conclude that the church no longer lives from and under the cross, that for this reason it lacks only one thing, to be called back to the cross. We live in a peace that is not the peace of Christ but the adapting and excluding of what is religious from everyday life. Yet everyday life is the area in which faith must prove itself, and worship services are nothing but an arming for the Christian's everyday life. In this way the discipleship of Jesus should be the dominant theme of all proclamation and the measure of all organizational work. What does not serve it cannot survive in the shrinking process of the church that awaits us. This means finally that for the first time in German Protestantism, we have to not only proclaim the universal priesthood of all believers but realize it and subordinate to it all the offices and functions of the church. In the future there will be only one form of Christianity—that is, the mission, as should always have been the case. Whoever does not share in the mission will no longer be regarded as a Christian. Religious needs may be met elsewhere. Jesus says to every one of us, "Follow me," and with that call gives the one office he has to bestow. Since each of us has our own peculiarity, abilities, and weaknesses, particular path and limits, this office will not produce equality but variety and will reveal a thousand vulnerabilities. It will be really uncomfortable for us and require incessant education. Those previously oriented to the organizational model must unlearn, no less than those who do not know their own limits and would push themselves to the foreground. But despite all the risks and inevitable failures, we must awaken, support, and stage the unrest without which there is no mission, participation in which, especially in a society urging conformity, is the presupposition and duty of every Christian. We have too many managers and too few partisans, and only by virtue of a Christian partisanship will we once more break out of the religious ghetto into the open field. Then the cross will appear quite on its own; and as with Jesus's, so with our own: it may exist in trouble, hostility, disappointment, and defeat. The beautiful legend of Saint Christopher is still true. Under the cross one goes deeper and deeper, to the depths, and finally must carry those for whom the burden would otherwise be too heavy. But in just this way the glory of the resurrection shines into our life. It allows the cross to be affirmed in all its expressions and makes the dying blest.

From this perspective, let us look now to the motto of the *Kirchentag*, which, like the Bible, connects the reality of our peace with the cross. Once more we must ask to what extent this can be held to. Does not the very discipleship of Jesus draw us incessantly into resistance to principalities and powers, a resistance expressed in the separation of churchdoms, confessions, theologies, and forms of piety? How can there be any peace at all when the cross leads and calls us to suffering? The answer, often enough, taken over from Stoic into Christian philosophy, would be dangerous. The peace of Christ must be a turning in suffering from the world and must be achieved in an inner concentration on what is essential and eternal. For the right of this peace ends in the universal human experience that our will is made firm and resolutely directed toward its goal only when trained by hard testing. Still, we are not allowed to flee from earthly conflict into a self-chosen solitariness and in this way create our own peace. Then we would separate ourselves not only from the world and our fellows but also from Jesus—who did not avoid the cross and who, since Easter, has become the object and bearer of a worldwide conflict dividing even Christianity. In addition, the peace of God is not a condition we would have to effect with our programs, actions, and powers, no matter how much as a movement of grace it takes our acting and suffering into its service. The peculiarity of God's peace is appropriately conceived only when we understand it as the power and space of Christian freedom.

For all the churches and every individual Christian, nothing is more necessary today than finally to live and learn that freedom is the most important fruit of the cross and its most convincing expression. More yet, it is the anticipation of the resurrection from the dead within earthly existence. Here, Good Friday and Easter come together. The fact that the disciple becomes willing and able to carry the cross after Jesus on earth marks the disciple as a witness to the risen Lord, who even now gives the disciple a share in his royal freedom and in the life of the future world. Over disciples reigns a peace that is higher than all reason and unshakable in temporal conflict. Disciples become free over against themselves, something piety alone cannot at all effect. If Jesus's cross has irrevocably shown us that our own strength, cleverness, and religiosity are nothing, that grace must die and has died for the sake of the godless, then we need no longer take ourselves so horribly seriously and can leave our earthly and eternal salvation in a childlike uninhibitedness to the care of our God. Then we need no longer count and measure out the rungs on the heavenly ladder and everlastingly inspect ourselves or others regarding our progresses or setbacks. No longer plagued by anxiety and high spirits, we can turn all our power toward becoming truly human and guardians of all that is human, an activity always basely betrayed since Adam and Cain, even in the churches.

Those who at Golgotha have heard the call of the Crucified to his discipleship are uninhibited by the world and its powers. They know that they owe not only to the creation but to God a daily dying in the service of the neighbor, before which both the blinding enticements of earth and the fear of its tyrants grow pale. Of course, settled camps of tradition or of the prevailing givens always try to recapture them. Still, no camp holds them for long. On the way with Jesus, we can associate with all who need love, and we are subject to none who would make us the instruments of their will to rule. The powers of this world no longer obstruct our view, no longer obscure our reason, no longer limit our discipleship. The disciples of Jesus live only "from God's grace." All that they experience must serve their salvation and remind them of their Lord. According to Colossians 1:10, we have only to consider "lead[ing] lives worthy of the Lord, . . . bear[ing] fruit in every good work." Ephesians 1:12 summarizes it even more beautifully: "that we . . . might live for the praise of his glory." This demands action of us wherever we stand and even when we can no longer stand. The passive, daydreaming, complaining Christians, not constantly moved to discipleship, are a disgrace to their Lord. Mere devotion to duty, however, is far too little. Happiness belongs to our service, as also does imagination, which, in a love that is inventive, continually allows something to happen to it. To it also belongs the civil courage of those who push ahead of the hangers-on and who, against the stream of time, are almost always found on the side of the "most loyal opposition." The cross revolutionizes hearts and minds. Those unable to feel anything of this cannot believe they hope for the resurrection from the dead. Nothing is achieved with the empty tomb, because at issue is the presence and lordship of the crucified Christ in our lives.

We do not do justice to this presence and lordship of the Crucified with theological convictions, pious hopes, and worship celebrations. His presence and lordship demand the service of the free community that overcomes the world in the midst of the world. It does so in obedience to the first commandment, which names the cause and right of Christian freedom. To have God as Lord is the biblical definition of freedom, of which only those are aware who experience inner conflict on earth. There are always and everywhere other gods that threaten freedom in advance of humans and circumstances. For this reason, according to Isaiah 26:13, the voice of freedom is expressed in prayer: "O LORD our God, other lords besides you have ruled over us, but we acknowledge your name alone." It is the same cry as that with which the dying Jesus throws himself into God's arms out of the hell surrounding him: "We acknowledge your name alone." But the Father answers, acknowledging the Son and bringing about Easter: "He . . . became obedient to the point of death—even death on a cross. Therefore God also highly exalted him" [Phil. 2:8–9]. Now we are called to allow ourselves to be given this freedom by the Crucified and to preserve it in his discipleship on earth. Peace is among us insofar as this freedom is manifested in and through us. Only there does the world experience the gospel. "Worthy is the Lamb that was slaughtered to receive power and wealth and wisdom and might and honor and glory and blessing!" [Rev. 5:12].

┼ 6 ┼

The Place That Cannot Be
Surrendered (1977)

For just as the body is one and has many members, and all the members of the body, though many, are one body, so it is with Christ. For in the one Spirit we were all baptized into one body—Jews or Greeks, slaves or free—and we were all made to drink of one Spirit. Indeed, the body does not consist of one member but of many. If the foot would say, "Because I am not a hand, I do not belong to the body," that would not make it any less a part of the body. And if the ear would say, "Because I am not an eye, I do not belong to the body," that would not make it any less a part of the body. If the whole body were an eye, where would the hearing be? If the whole body were hearing, where would the sense of smell be? But as it is, God arranged the members in the body, each one of them, as he chose. If all were a single member, where would the body be? As it is, there are many members, yet one body. The eye cannot say to the hand, "I have no need of you," nor again the head to the feet, "I have no need of you." On the contrary, the members of the body that seem to be weaker are indispensable, and those members of the body that we think less honorable we clothe with greater honor, and our less respectable members are treated with greater respect; whereas our more respectable members do not need this. But God has so arranged the body, giving the greater honor to the inferior member, that there may be no dissension within the body, but the members may have the same care for one another. If one member suffers, all suffer together with it; if one member is honored, all rejoice together with it. Now you are the body of Christ and individually members of it.

1 Corinthians 12:12–27

A Bible study held at the German evangelical *Kirchentag* in Berlin. First published in *Deutscher Evangelischer Kirchentag, Berlin 1977: Dokumente* (Stuttgart: Kreuz-Verlag, 1977), 62–71.

Y ou are the body of Christ." The last sentence of the text states the presupposition and summary of everything at issue now. It is just this that we have to hear today, to spell out, to learn—and all the more so since it no longer seems valid in German evangelical Christianity and is contested from the one side to the other. These words describe the place of the Christian on earth that cannot be surrendered. No one is seriously to be called a disciple of Jesus who is unaware of being called to be a member of the body of Christ. Conversely, the entire body becomes questionable, sick, and unfit when its members are changed into parties and are at war with each other. Our *Kirchentag* stands and falls with whether we hear, accept, and do not misunderstand: "You are the body of Christ."

How did Paul arrive at this word, and what did he want to say with it? Perhaps we should answer these questions only when we have been reminded beforehand that the important utterances of the Bible have motive and altering power. They set us in a situation we would scarcely look for on our own and point us to an exciting path from which people and conditions appear in an uncommon light. Under the Word we never remain what we were earlier. We are reshaped and—as with birth, youth, and old age—experience it for the most part as a painful process. The Corinthians to whom Paul wrote also had to learn this. The apostle was concerned for his community. It had already divided into parties, and its majority mistrusted even him and esteemed other teachers more than him. I find it comforting that in its weakness, at least, the first Christian community was not too different from us. As early as when congregations scarcely numbered more than a hundred, there were problems of faith and conduct of life. Even apostles were in no wise always united, not even respected without further ado by those they had converted. Paul endured almost as much suffering from the other Christians as from the enemies of his message. At all times Christians have often been on one another's nerves, and only too often made the way more arduous than light for one another. Not least for this reason we are told to "bear one another's burdens" [Gal. 6:2]. God's odd children must actually be admonished to bear one another rather than to strike out at each other. This usually applies where spirit and power and life are in rich supply.

In the first lines of his letter Paul expressly boasts of the abundance of gifts and activities in Corinth. As the story of Pentecost graphically describes it, heaven was opened over this community. Thus, according to 1 Corinthians 14:25, gentiles who may share in worship as onlookers learn that the divine Spirit descends among humans. Overpowered, they fall on their knees and noisily testify, "God is really among you." In this community occur healings, victories over possession, and ecstasies in which Christians are certain of their heavenly citizenship. Right here lurks a danger known to us from church history up to our present: the experience of heavenly citizenship can block the sight for earthly realities and necessities. Many worship services and fellowship hours alienate us from humanity, the neighbor, and everyday life rather than directing us toward them. For many professional theologians and numerous amateurs, the dogmatic and ideological system is more important than service. Many a faith measures itself by formulas and stereotypes and makes of the gospel, which is Jesus's call to his kingdom, a doctrine swung like a club over differing opinion. In the midst of religious emotion the old Adam is thoroughly engaged in jealously and in tyrannically shoving the other to the rear and blasphemously entangling God in one's own private affairs. Unfortunately, the evil slogan first directed at Christians that religion is an opium of the people cannot simply be shoved aside. Too many among us are actually on a flight from the world, do not endure the hard everyday life without drugs, and make use of our piety for it. Faith is not protected against falling prey to illusions. To resist them is rather its continual battle.

Paul likewise sees the disciple set no longer under a closed heaven but on earth, where the Spirit works mightily with signs and wonders and teaches us to accept God's Word and will and to do it. For this reason, from the great mission into the world connected with Pentecost, Paul draws consequences. There is no more time for navel-gazing and criticism of the errors of others. We are not called to enthusiasm. The ladder that Jacob once saw in a dream served the angels as a bridge to earth. But it should not tempt us to penetrate heavenly mysteries and neglect the bodily preservation of the discipleship here below. In time and on earth, heavenly citizenship now means that great mission that once came to Abraham, then allowed Jesus to descend to the depths of our world, and since the days of the apostles calls each of us to give to our life meaning, depth, and a broad horizon. For this reason we must energetically oppose that altogether unevangelical chatter that today, with its needlessly pretentious sloganeering over the vertical and horizontal dimension, tears apart God's salvation and service to human well-being. We know of such slogans from the time when the Nazis wanted to leave us and the sparrows to heaven but for themselves demanded lordship over the earth. Against such superstition, the Bible confesses that "the earth is the LORD's and all that is in it" [Ps. 24:1]. Here below and nowhere else is decided who our master is, over whom the disciple is not to be elevated. In our earthly state the form of spiritual, heavenly worship is manifested in discipleship of the Crucified on Golgotha or it remains a pious delusion. Faith is expressed in love that does not leave the world to the demons and their spheres of power to save its own skin. Salvation would not be healing and rescue if it did not include the well-being of our neighbor. The Creator cannot be separated from the creature. The Creator binds our salvation, now as formerly, to our not distancing ourselves from the creation, and thus we are merciful toward its bodily need in every possible way and raise visible signs of a redemption drawn nigh.

This said, we arrive at the center of our text. But we must be surprised at why, according to Paul, the exalted Christ needs an earthly body. We understand this only when we keep in mind what it means for us to have a body. To put it briefly, the body is our contact with the earth. We experience all good and all evil through it. In the body we feel all the enticements and dangers, desire and suffering, poverty and hunger, good fortune and success, work and longings, youth, age, and death. In the body we also encounter dependencies in family, vocation, society, people, and culture; experience the forces of tradition and convention, of tyrannical powers that violate us; and likewise experience the healing, help, liberation, friendship, and hostility of the people we meet, a common departure into an unknown future. With our corporeality the innumerable possibilities and realities of this world become tangible, visible, experienceable. When the exalted Christ has an earthly body, he is further in continual contact with our earth, into which he once descended as Nazarene, to which he gave himself even to the cross; and in its darkness, as in Rembrandt's paintings, he will shine his light. In his body he holds the world fast as the creation of his Father; he works, as before, among the sick, possessed, lost, and despised, still forever waging war against the powers that distort the image of the human and suppress the truth of God. He gives freedom to the imprisoned and salvation to the otherwise despairing. It is no accident that we are told at the Lord's Supper, "This is my body" [Matt. 26:26; Mark 14:22; Luke 22:19; 1 Cor. 11:24]. In our text Paul expressly refers to the fact that by baptism the Spirit sets us within the body of Christ and at the Supper confirms us in it again. In precisely this manner the exalted Lord creates contact with the earthly, establishes fellowship with himself and his mission, makes us his members and the instruments of his rule. His enemies were not rid of him when they dragged him to Golgotha. His disciples are not left alone on the way of discipleship. Resurrection from the dead does not first of all and exclusively mean hope beyond the grave. First Corinthians 15:25, rather, states that Christ must rule until all his enemies lie at his feet. His earthly body is the space in which he himself is present and effective with his Spirit, establishes his kingdom among his enemies and despisers, and rules graciously as well as in judgment. If we are this body and individually its members, then we are the means by which his will, his word, his deed, his presence seize a place on earth following cross and exaltation.

"You are the body of Christ." This is not to be heard as a theory and theological program needing to be realized in the course of time. It is an encouragement that sets us all and everyone in particular where we have to stand and fall. The emphasis here lies on the two words: "You are." We are not asked whether this suits us or not, whether in our opinion we are fit for it or not. All such discussion is cut off, and we may not allow ourselves to be led astray by human contradiction and doubt. The Lord has decreed it. The disciple would not be the one called to be such if the desire were to resist or allow something else to be true than the one voice of the Master. Paul refers the Corinthians to baptism, as the moment in which they became members of Christ, and to the Lord's Supper, where the Spirit says to the community again and again, "You are the body of Christ," thus custodians of his presence on earth, instruments to the praise of his glory. This is magnificently visualized in the legend of Christopher, who wanted only to serve the greatest and, as ferryman, found his Lord in the divine child. He finally had to be brought to the shore by the One he wanted to carry, and so experienced the power of grace. Each of us who has wagered with the Nazarene is called to be a Christopher, a bearer of Christ in this world. It is our service to carry the Lord from one shore to the other in the current of the time, of the changing situations and generations. But we will not be Christophers, Christ-bearers, by our own power without being carried away and swallowed up by the current. The enthusiasts in Corinth must learn that their Lord fetches them from the heaven of ecstasies to earth and sets them there in his mission. They must learn that grace becomes service and service persists only by grace. They must leave the roundelay of blessed spirits (where they imagine they are) for the area of corporeality, the everyday, the world—that is, for where their Lord suffered and where he sets up his lordship in the midst of his enemies.

What is being repeated now is what once took place between Galilee and Jerusalem. On earth, the presence of Christ will always be spoken against. For this reason, we pray for the coming of his kingdom and thus "that God defeats and hinders every evil counsel and purpose that would not let us hallow God's name and let his kingdom come."[1] There is also evil counsel and purpose in the community itself, not merely from without, and the community gives evidence of it by seeking to distort or cripple the body of Christ. In lively dialogue our text describes this from two opposite sides. There are those who compare themselves with others and are conscious of their inferiority. They state that they are not fit for any service and absolutize this as if they were totally useless. The foot doubts its right to be a member of the body because

1. Martin Luther, Small Catechism, art. 3.

it does not have the capabilities of the hand. The ear measures itself by the eye and resigns in turn. We are familiar with this event. There is a sloth that is not eager to make an effort when it is hot or cold and when burdens oppress. There is a cleverness that would prefer not to be tied down when someone will bind it. There is the genuine or false humility that entrusts nothing to itself, and therefore leaves precedence to others or trains in the corner for criticism of the other.

Always at issue is that buried talent of the faithless servant, of which Jesus's parable speaks. No doubt, today the graves of unused talents in Western Christianity and in almost all our congregations form the unfruitful land on which everything is only poorly growing or not growing at all. Pentecost and resurrection of the dead would coincide if these graves were ever opened. There is nothing more to be prayed for than to finally bring to light what Christians anxiously, lukewarmly, selfishly, and wantonly withhold when they allow their gifts to be buried. In addition, there is that other behavior illustrated by the text as a dismissal of the other members by the eye and head. Here, perhaps, it is not always said out loud, but only thought of. It may be simply practiced without thinking. Still, with us it often happens as though the talent received were embezzled. Authoritatively or in thoughtlessness that looks to one's own street, one's own goal, one's own possibility, the untested or undervalued abilities of others are suppressed and dismissed: "I do not need you." There was edifying talk of the priesthood of all believers. Yet, and actually among Protestants, the so-called laity were pushed by officeholders and theologians to the auditors' bench and regarded as juvenile. Sects and free associations could only run wild because the official church representatives for the most part feared that chaos would ensue if they were to give the reins and schoolmastery to others. In our generation the decision has still not been made whether a woman may be a pastor with full rights. Where are the migrant workers responsibly integrated into our congregations? Are not our gatherings outwardly mirror images of a middle-class society that more and more excludes itself from what does not suit its views and customs, which could plunge it into unrest, into new problems and changes? But must we not wish to be spiteful when we complain about how often our worship services are boring and musty, since everything runs according to a fixed scheme? At times, one senses bodily that resistance here is in reaction to everything not already known and chewed over for decades, that for this reason irreconcilable differences necessarily move out of the political sphere into that of the church.

Now, where one would have to pray and praise with others and hear God's Word, which is always new, where one would go with others to the table of the

Lord and be at one—there division is proclaimed and the front impassable: We need you no longer. We are qualified. We bear the banner. We are Christ's body. There is no place for you with us, no rights, no voice, no task. The battle cry has not only been heard in our time. Otherwise, there would not be so many churches and associations throughout the whole world. The orthodox have always spoken in this way to liberals and pietists, and, conversely, whites have spoken in this way to people of color, the old to the young, the established to the proletarians, the regular visitors at worship to those living on the margin, the provincials to the *oecumene*. What can be traced through the centuries is that cliques keep their own nests warm, that fanatics in Christian fashion demand marching in step and a uniformity of convictions, and that the alien servant of Jesus is subjected to our law, reshaped according to our image. But this is spiritual murder. Here there is always disregard for the good, gracious will of the Creator who gave to each their own peculiar face, their own way, a peculiarity that reflects the riches of the Creator's grace and makes possible mutual help for those who are different. The apostle declares with greatest emphasis: "God arranged the members in the body, each one of them, as he chose." The solution is: One body, but many members! Many members for the very reason that otherwise the body is crippled! We intrude upon the omnipotence of our Lord and his call when we do not allow ourselves to be set in our place and with our possibilities in his service or when we interfere with others in it. No one is superfluous. The sin against the Holy Spirit begins where people are encouraged to believe but are not given access to the freedom of Christ in order—in their special way—to be something to the praise of his glory and mercy.

Put pointedly at our *Kirchentag*: We must always, as here, create room for the market of possibilities. It makes good sense—and can be seriously defended theologically—to regard Christianity as the earthly marketplace of the possibilities of Jesus and his followers. For good reason, earlier in our chapter Paul describes the gifts of the exalted Lord as energies radiating throughout the whole world and found in a variety of services. The body of Christ as a field of energies awakened by Jesus is also the market of possibilities at which we offer what we have received from our Lord and what we must have in his mission for the salvation of the world and the well-being of our fellows. Each of us is asked, Where is your position there? What have you received and what have you to give, provided you do not hide your talent like the unfaithful servant? The universal priesthood of all believers does not merely belong in the chamber. However much this may shock us, it must be brought to the market, where others have something to do with it. Christ will be carried by us into the world, and he will be portrayed there in our time as Helper and Redeemer—there, where our distresses break out and cries of despair are ignored by an affluent society; where the poor, suffering, outcast, and exploited wait for salvation; where the will to power suppresses truth and honesty; where problems are trivialized or silenced; where the demonic powers are tolerated, respected, advanced for the sake of preserving our possessions and for the increase in economic growth. The Christian community is not charged with transfiguring what exists, importing deceptive ideals into an already dishonest society, gathering for festivals where the masses are benumbed with bread and games. Whoever comes from the cross of Jesus serves in worldly, everyday life, uncovers its reality and the abysses (which gape not only in its corners). There is no salvation without the offense and provocation that have always accompanied the way of the Nazarene. The sympathy that we for the most part enjoy among the mighty is dubious, because it may apply less to our service than to our capacity to adapt. In any case, it does not extend to those who have been disturbed by the worldwide rising tide of barbarism and whose hearts burn as did once those of the disciples on the road to Emmaus because they cannot separate the exalted Lord from his suffering fellows and a martyred humanity. If after Easter it is not merely a matter of our earthly and eternal survival but of Christ's kingdom in the midst of his enemies, in a world tortured by possession, Christians neither can nor may any longer be guards of an idealistic inheritance and the religious rearguard of a middle class sinking in affluence with body and soul. Then, at least in part, truly Christian service will not look particularly pious and edifying. It is said of the Servant of God that "he had no form or majesty" [Isa. 53:2]. It will indeed also be said of those whom this Master imprints with his image. Before he ascends to heaven, he leads into the filth and guilt and tears of an earth that still, as in his days, is a hell for most.

By virtue of the magic of technology we have learned how our world has shrunk and connects everything with everything else, even when our eyes are closed to it. The mass media tell us what happens in the most distant areas. To not take notice of it or to rapidly forget it is of no use to us. We are called, each of us, to our particular path. Our Lord becomes unworthy of belief when his body no longer portrays and holds upright his contact with the earth. His energies and gifts create a market of possibilities at which there are no unemployed or unworthy of life, and certainly not merely theological problems, pious and edifying experiences, a respectable and better society. In sharp contrast to the political and economic conditions around us the decisive motto here reads, "The members of the body that seem to be weaker are indispensable." This is scarcely meant pedagogically—that is, that we should learn from those who are weak to be charitable and not to live only for ourselves. The reference is to the divine will and action: God gives greater honor to the disadvantaged. There is no objection to charity spent from our superfluity. But there is much objection to seeing our neighbor primarily or exclusively as an object of charity. For good or ill, the earth too must see that weakness and misery are unavoidable. On the one hand, it will counteract this by tearing down the slums, as in India and South America, and by resettling its inhabitants far from the big cities, where they will no longer be seen and where they can hardly find their way out. On the other hand, given the circumstances, it will give alms in considerable measure, which in many cases of course help individuals temporarily but ultimately merely relieves a guilty conscience, justifying those who seek to defend against rioting and preserve the status quo.

We do not deny the value of humanitarianism wherever it has existed. But is it unjust to assert that, for the most part, humanitarianism was aristocratically set up, that it was occupied with the ideal man, with the beautiful, with the good automatically emerging? The one sacrificing, not the sacrifice, stood at center—the hero, but not the one dishonored. Who says, from the inmost heart, that the weak are necessary? Does this not occur only in the shadow of the One who was called "despised and rejected" [Isa. 53:3], who utters his blessing over the lost son, the tax collector in the temple, the thief on the cross, over all the tormented and waiting? It is the gospel that God joins the weak, will do so not only in the inferno of the earth but also, according to Luke 12:37, on the last day in the sign of a slave's apron. In the body of Christ, this gospel is held to, against human illusions and the deception of false gods, and we must reject the superstition that we can finally accomplish it by our own reason and strength. Our reality is given its due, and honor is given the God who descends and draws near to us on the cross. It is our nature and the signature of Christian fellowship to be weak and needy, directed toward salvation, help, and mutual service. From there it is clear that the apostle maintains that the body is not merely one member but many members. The troubles of earth, the cries of the damned and dying, the appeal to our feeling of responsibility and will to serve are innumerable and limitless, not to be stifled by individuals, groups, and confessions. There, in the shape of the body of Christ, a new world must ecumenically indicate that our God will help all, and indeed everyone in particular.

Paul demands that the body have many members. He does so, oddly, for the reason "that there may be no dissension within the body, but the members may have the same care for one another." This is understandable, because what is the same cannot help itself, cannot properly speak with the other, since each thinks and has and wills the same. This can only be boring for

both, since there is no taking the field in common against others. But how is it
with unity? In the German Protestantism of our time the apostle's argument
is stood on its head when what is called pluralism is condemned as unevangelical, unbiblical, more severely dividing the church than in the Nazi period.
We will, of course, have to respond to this that such a call to arms makes
a loud noise, and is obviously effective, but it remains remarkably unclear.
Anyone who has studied a bit of church history meets theological pluralism
everywhere on its pages. There are two testaments, which are not simply to
be reduced to a common denominator, since otherwise there would be either
only Jews or only Christians. There are four Gospels, which differ from one
another considerably, as even children can tell. Even in the first century there
are apostles, teachers, and missionaries at odds with each other. In Jerusalem
there is already separation between Palestinians and gentile Christians.

There never was a unified organization of Christianity, never a confession
in which the all-important articles would have been formulated and recognized
in agreement. How can this be overlooked? How will we unite the multitude
of churches and Christian communities other than by resolutely recognizing
with Paul the many-membered character of the body of Christ—or else by
just as resolutely, and then despotically, claiming a monopoly for a single
group and treating all others as ulcers on the body of Christ? But how long
will we be able to be unified in the one group, be able to follow the leaders,
able to lock the community of Jesus up in a spiritual barracks? The freedom,
service, and solidarity in the Christian community rest on the fact that there
is diversity in the whole and uniqueness in the individual. And, in addition,
we should not spitefully interfere with divine omnipotence. It has made the
creation rich and colorful and does not incessantly copy itself. Nor does it
allow believers, as the figures of the Bible show, to beat the drum over the
same achievements, though pious schoolmastery is not aware of it. On our last
and God's last day we will certainly not be required to recite the catechism,
as surely as that might have been most useful in the period prior. At the last
judgment, what matters is what the Risen One says to Peter: "Do you love
me?" [John 21:15–17]. Whoever orders the body of Christ according to other
norms and values lays hands on the temple of God, and that will be good for
no one. Conflict is irresponsibly carried on not only because we forget that
it is not we who establish the church and are judges of the alien member. It
is also irresponsible because political criteria are laid down here, such as are
deployed for the exclusivity and discipline of a party. A pluralism that tolerates extreme wings and oppositions has explosive power. But Paul emphasizes
that, in Christianity, God has bound such extreme opposites together. The
Jew is separated from the gentile by the law as by an unbridgeable abyss. For

the Greek, according to inherited ideology, the enslaved human being is a possession, not really a person like the free human being.

What separates heaven and earth was united in the body of Christ. There extremes have a place alongside each other, will tolerate opposites that exclude, as God now tolerates and bears the sinner. This may not be grasped and judged politically, but theologically. What is only ostensibly at issue here is the problem of pluralism, where the diversity of the body and its having many members are emphasized as in our text. What is actually at issue is that the exalted Christ will reign on earth and build his kingdom, that grace puts us to work together with it. To the gospel belongs the incredible message that the Almighty will not do without the weak in God's service and has need of each whom God has created, with their powers and weaknesses; God sends them as custodians into the earthly every day. If there were only the like-minded, the representatives of a particular piety, ideology, and morality, the representatives of a class, race, confession, and church, Christ would remain a religious leader. His promise and his claim would not penetrate every space and the whole world, as the mission of Pentecost intends. He would not come to people everywhere and be able to remain with them to the end of the world. Only when his body has many members and bridges all the contrasts of earth can he reveal himself everywhere. The omnipresence of Christ as salvation of the world requires the diversity of the body and the differentiation of its members. Under its sign there is no division but rather the care of all for all in unity. One is free for service to the other in that humanity which suffers and rejoices with the other. This is our place, not to be surrendered, pointed out to us by God and to be taken by none. We are the body of Christ and individually his members. Amen.

⊹ 7 ⊹

On the Way toward Abiding (1977)

If I speak in the tongues of mortals and of angels, but do not have love, I am a noisy gong or a clanging cymbal. And if I have prophetic powers, and understand all mysteries and all knowledge, and if I have all faith, so as to remove mountains, but do not have love, I am nothing. If I give away all my possessions, and if I hand over my body so that I may boast, but do not have love, I gain nothing. Love is patient; love is kind; love is not envious or boastful or arrogant or rude. It does not insist on its own way; it is not irritable or resentful; it does not rejoice in wrongdoing, but rejoices in the truth. It bears all things, believes all things, hopes all things, endures all things. Love never ends. But as for prophecies, they will come to an end; as for tongues, they will cease; as for knowledge, it will come to an end. For we know only in part, and we prophesy only in part; but when the complete comes, the partial will come to an end. When I was a child, I spoke like a child, I thought like a child, I reasoned like a child; when I became an adult, I put an end to childish ways. For now we see in a mirror, dimly, but then we will see face to face. Now I know only in part; then I will know fully, even as I have been fully known. And now faith, hope, and love abide, these three; and the greatest of these is love.

1 Corinthians 13

The Christian message does not always speak in simple fashion throughout. Just as the narratives of the Bible are often beautiful, so it has also preserved a wealth of songs (as, for example, in the Psalter) and

---

A Bible study held at the German evangelical *Kirchentag* in Berlin. First published in *Deutscher Evangelischer Kirchentag, Berlin 1977: Dokumente* (Stuttgart: Kreuz-Verlag, 1977), 84–93.

has actually appropriated the rhetoric of the wisdom teacher, as in the middle portion of our text. In the first three verses, the protases tower up like long approaching waves. They reach their height with the phrase "but do not have love," and then they suddenly break up in the brief conclusion. So, what everything depends on becomes clear. Nothing else has promise in heaven as well as on earth. Paul has not defined love so much as he has very precisely described its nature and function from contrasts and failures and other forms of behavior. Unfortunately, we have horribly sentimentalized this chapter, given it the tacky superscription of a "canticle," and used it preferably at marriage celebrations, as if a young pair's interlocked hands were the best illustration of our text. It hides the fact that here the Christian community is called to the trenches and that, at the beginning and the end, human, even Christian, conceits are laid bare with cutting sharpness. Again, as so often with reading and hearing Scripture, the fact remains that we learn only when we are also prepared to unlearn. To grow always means to leave behind what once seemed important to us. We are all underway. Whatever else may be involved with the love spoken of here, in any case it sets us in movement. Considering the beginning and conclusion of our text, we may actually say that love here means to be on the way to abiding. This must occupy us now under different aspects.

In general, goals are more interesting for us than ways that are often long and tiresome, begin with unsuccessful approaches, and can end in blind alleys or in wandering. In any case, disciples of Jesus should deceive no one over the fact that discipleship of the Crucified can be called neither inviting nor uncomplicated when measured by the usual earthly standard. First of all, strikingly, but deliberately, and in a heaping up that cannot be missed, our text describes the failed possibilities of our life. No mere dreams or longings are involved. Paul has in view what is given space in early Christian worship and felt by the Corinthian Christians there to be necessary and desirable. Clearly, the community there was most impressed by what we call speaking in tongues—to use a technical foreign term, by glossolalia—those stammering sounds of ecstatics that burst through intelligible speech in preaching and prayer as, for example, today in the Pentecostal movement. When it comes to experience in religion, the greatest increase of sacred feeling may be seen in rapture. Here, then, more than usual, one may see the Holy Spirit at work and, as the Corinthians clearly did, think one hears the language of the angels in heaven. Paul does not engage in direct criticism of this view or of the phenomenon of speaking in tongues. Quite the contrary, in so many words, he personally confesses that he too possesses this capacity, practices it, and regards it as a gift of the Spirit. If we do not note this, we will miss the crucial point of his argumentation.

Alongside glossolalia, the gift of prophecy is set at the beginning as especially important. The context indicates that, in doing so, the apostle is thinking less of prophetic interpretation of the future than, along with the Hellenistic world around him, of the spirit-filled exposition of Holy Scripture. In fact, we may say that the stress lies more on the diagnosis than on the prognosis. In contrast to the early Christian teacher, who hands on and explains the tradition, the prophet virtually has the task we assign to the preacher. The prophet preaches the gospel, often by reference to the Bible text of that time—that is, the Old Testament. Unlike the teacher, who, more than anything, keeps the past alive; and unlike the one who, as theologian and dogmatician, so to speak, has to do with the knowledge of the plan of salvation and the mysteries of the divine activity since the creation; the prophet directs his gaze toward the present needs. The prophet utters the good news in a specific situation—with its possibilities, dangers, and sufferings—allowing us to hear its comforting, demanding, promising, and judging message. Put pointedly, the prophet actualizes into the present what God's will is over and in us. In an expression current in Judaism for something impossible for human beings, Paul speaks of the one who in the power of faith can move mountains. The one who has faith performs miracles of healing the sick and especially the exorcism of demons, as is frequently reported in the Bible. The early Christian community sees in this a witness to its continual link with the powers of the heavenly world. Its representatives demonstrate the nature of heavenly citizenship. Finally, those who are named leave their possessions to the community, as Ananias and his wife pretend to do in Acts, or as later, Francis of Assisi, for example, shared his possessions with the poor. Early on, such caritative care actually surprised the gentiles to the point that they recorded it. On the other hand, the burning of Christians is spoken of in a clearly metaphorical sense since such a martyrdom scarcely occurred before Nero.[1] The reference is to those who are prepared to endure every bodily torture in order to bring others to faith.

Capacities and activities are listed here that, even in a religiously active community, have uncommon value, are admired, perhaps even envied, and are a special reminder of one's awareness of standing in an end time broken in. In a certain respect this sets us on the soil of a typically Greek perspective, which sketched the ideal of the perfect human and thus put the question concerning the highest values. In Christian Corinth this question still appears to resonate. Then Paul, with what he lists in our verses, gives the answer to it. His sentences clearly end in shrill discord. They attest to the capacities

---

1. Käsemann's Bible version of v. 3 reads, "though I hand over my body to be burned."

mentioned as existing in the community, that they have significance and can scarcely be dispensed with. But the apostle does not recognize them as the final and highest values. They are God-given gifts and, like all gifts of God, are liable to human misuse. That one has them says nothing at all. Everything depends on how one uses them. Put provocatively, the chapter to which we give the title "canticle to love" begins with a stinging criticism of religious talents and activities. Actually, we would suitably speak of demythologizing. To speak of highest values, virtues, and ideals is pagan. Whatever is called such reflects the desires and needs of a given society—at times, even of religious groups. Such types are interested in what the individual possesses or can possess, and they disregard or judge the one unable to impress them.

Conversely, in a Christian sense, one may never be measured by what one lacks. Here, guilt results solely from what we had and what made us strong, rich, and clever. Our God reproaches us for what we receive but have not used or used rightly. None of us has any reason to constantly feel the pulse of our inner life, or even to allow others to test it. No one needs to be put into competition here, to be compared with it, to be found inferior or superior to it. Our God is no umpire in the competition between the competent and the striving. What we are and have we owe to grace, which forgets no one, gives to each their own and never the same to all. But it is decisive whether we accepted and were content with what grace gave us, whether we preserved it and did not underhandedly turn it to our credit and possession. In this way, then, love comes into play, for it will maintain nothing for itself but only hand on what has been received for the use of others. It allows grace to remain a given kindness by not allowing itself to be moved to hoarding, and it does not egoistically use what is destined for consumption (as Calvin once beautifully formulated it). We said that love is in motion, and it makes this known by the fact that God's gifts lure those who receive them out of themselves, making them active and progressive, that is, urging them to the other and into a world in need of help. Love serves, sharing with others what it has received, not refusing it even to enemies, and allowing itself to be sent to every creature, instead of raising the drawbridge in front of the fortress of faith and, as it were, entrenching itself within as protector of the grail. By not hoarding grace but allowing it to be grace for others and for all, and thus to be fruitful, it becomes the measure of religious life as such and of every Christian talent. Whatever does not urge toward love and witness to it is sheer pretense, misused blessing. Paul recalls the instruments like the gong and drum, beaten with the hand, which in pagan temples create loud resounding sounds. The down-to-earth apostle asserts that they create nothing but powerful, empty noise. And precisely this is his charge over against those who speak in tongues, over against prophets, miracle workers, and ascetics, over against all the charismatics in the Christian community, if love does not urge them on the way to the other and into a world without hope. Like the gentiles, they make astonishing but empty noise. Up to the present day there is nothing but clattering and droning in all the churches and societies. But the smoke is without fire. There is nothing behind it worthy of life and effort, since, Christianly speaking, there is sense only where love is shown. Otherwise even faith, miracles, and martyrdom are child's play, a religious circus for those who, eager for intoxication, spread it around themselves.

If we look now at the central portion of our chapter, we must still be clearer and more focused. Up to now we have engaged in a criticism from which we concluded that love fetches us out of fairyland and urges us toward others. What love is at its profoundest is now indicated by what it does and omits. If we combine all the short sentences that follow, and are grouped about a center, then love is the energy that sets us on the way toward humanness—in which we live no longer for ourselves but with others, being there for the other. Let no one think this is obvious in the Christian community. Quite the contrary: With heavenly blessing emerges deadly peril. The religious person is so serious about dealing with God that the neighbor and the world around are lost from sight. Then the question is actually "Who is my neighbor?" [Luke 10:29]. Since only the like-minded friend and crony is taken to be such, the parable of the good Samaritan needs telling. Such an attitude leaves the world to the demons, and God's suffering creation is actually betrayed by the pious as if it had nothing more to do with us. Then we hear the message "love abides" in edifying fashion, as may occur, for example, with a young engaged couple or in a newly established friendship. Then it is said: this is eternal truth; everyone can know it, this love, and we have always known it. But in this case, what we call love remains for the most part a passing fancy. It suddenly blazes toward heaven and suddenly sinks back into ashes.

Christians must learn that what abides is never what is already attained but rather something that continues, a way on which we are to stride as far as into eternity. This way has no end because it is discipleship, thus not dependent on our will, our desires, our illusions, but on the Jesus who called us to it and goes before us. Because he knows the Creator and Father, he also knows the creature and the other, and he becomes human for our sake. Those who are not human in their discipleship deny their Lord and his mission. In a certain respect, the work of faith is nothing else than following the Master to be human, and to learn to be so ever anew. Dreaming of the superman who ascends to Olympus is pagan. The more science and technology furnish us with power in the universe, all the more a new barbarism is growing everywhere. It is that affluent society that in all its strata, for better or for worse, allows the securing of the position of wealth and the growth of the economy to be determinative, curses its victims in the Third and Fourth Worlds, victims scorned by us with our free-market economy. The fact that words, ideas, heads, and hearts are manipulable, that propaganda constantly conceals or violates the truth, that for the sake of power every demagoguery is allowed, that all agree to every sacrifice when others offer it, and that nothing can keep us from mutual self-laceration when our interests are at stake—this is something we experience in our country every day. Where, in view of this, we get the courage sweepingly to accuse other peoples and regimes of injured human rights is a question seriously to be asked. Not least, the justice and necessity of the accusations deserve contradicting. It is hypocrisy when, in all this, we forget to sweep before our own door and in our own house, as is the case not only in the political realm. In the churches as well, good sense and heart are suffering. To a great extent, we simply reflect the environment, and we force people and relationships under the yoke of abstract ideas. That the Nazarene was crucified as a rioter can no longer be grasped by a community that, in general, has become bourgeois. One is left with the impression that its majorities that are still gathered for worship fear nothing more than having to leave their traditions and habits, to follow their Lord into the no-man's-land beyond set camps and parties. From the outset, the call of freedom sounds like heresy, and it seems insane that the very obedience of Christ on earth should make rebels, though the history of the church is full of examples of it. Discipleship of the Crucified offers defiance to this reality of our everyday life as well as to our world, and can avoid offense less than ever. To be on the way toward the eternal in love means, offensively, to register, in the here and now, a turning away from the fleshpots of Egypt and the altars before which those grown fat pray in the hope that rest and order may further serve their greed and wastefulness. Our Lord directs us toward what is human and toward others.

This must begin in a small way. We must always be prepared, and not wait until all the great things take place. In the human realm, what is small, always preserved anew in patient faithfulness, is more important than what is praised by market-bartering advertising. Many single and small steps compose the way prescribed for us. And it is fitting that the new text begins with "love is perseverant." We know that in every race, in the last curves, it is perseverance that decides. In dealing with others it is needed even more, as can be seen and shown especially in the dealing of the old with the young and vice versa, but is chiefly to be learned in the family and the neighborhood, with colleagues and rivals. We are so impatient, have no time any longer for ourselves, cannot wait to allow for growth and ripening and thus so often harvest only bitter fruit from the tree of knowledge. When this occurs, the other cannot really finish speaking, reflect or gain trust, cannot become a partner instead of an object of our moods. We are often more concerned with our dog and cat than with the neighbor. Still, we can train for the long haul provided obesity and calcification have not progressed too far. Otherwise we aid the increase of inhumanity in and around us, and that we are on the way with the One who has gone to Golgotha becomes more and more incredible. Just as the earth is directed toward the sun and rain, so everything that lives, whether admitting it or not, waits for goodness. Wherever in impatient greed we chase after success and pleasure, the other for the most part stands in our way, or we push the other around until they have adapted to our desires. The other gets to trace indifference or aggressiveness among us. The aged, sick, children, and migrant workers know how to sing about this. We ourselves wither internally, and perhaps never note, or note too late, that only goodness blesses life and makes it fruitful, that intelligence, riches, and power never replace it, seldom make room for it, but that thankfulness and openness, sacrifice and suffering must form and ensoul it.

Goodness also makes room for fellowship, as the following sentences with their vigorous "not" make clear at the beginning. Perhaps something like a confessional mirror for the prudent has served as godparent here. It tallies up what hinders wisdom and thus renders solidarity impossible in the narrow and broad circle. Just how goodness is expressed is difficult to define. To it belongs spontaneous appearance and reaction to the given moment. In this way it is walled off as it were from every kind of evil as its counterpart. Those who love do not behave fanatically, because they cannot be led by principles and ideals that are able to see and pronounce only what is black or white, good or evil, friend or foe. The fact that, as in all our history, we are thinking abstractly again in our country—that is, preferring order in bookkeeping and the registering of welfare over life itself, which cannot be recorded bureaucratically—should, after all the catastrophes of our century, teach us to fear. At any rate, we have not yet learned tolerance. The flag is always worth more than the person who follows it, whether by force, blindly, or naïvely. At least among Christians, the word should still be heard: "And if you say, 'You fool,' you will be liable to the hell of fire" [Matt. 5:22]. Must doctrines, stereotypes, principles, and ideologies really divide the community, in which none can exist by themselves and which choke the word of the One who for us all radically refutes the self-righteousness even of the pious? Just as in our text boasting is connected with fanaticism, whether one boasts of merely imagined gifts—as does, for example, a theology of prejudices, or of the least intellectual efforts—or is puffed up over services having actually occurred, the community of the faithful is changed on the quiet into a religious game of meritocracy. Love does not need continually to feel its pulse or that of others, does not need to exhibit certificates for orthodoxy and heresy, the reception of which in heaven is at least doubtful.

Conversely, it is no mark of freedom when, as the enthusiasts, one is set above the limits of custom or even of justice. As the weak need the enclosure of custom, we are all directed toward the sphere of justice around us if we are not to end up in the jungle of arbitrariness and tyranny. Excess, which prefers extremes, loses the way and goal from view and lures others, bodily and spiritually, into the confusion that benefits no one. One version of our text calls attention to the fact that excess can also appear in the shape of an elite consciousness and activity. To this should be added that there is an elite, that there are privileges conceded to it or claimed by it in the Christian community only when it reflects the image of the society surrounding it and denies the image of its Lord. Unfortunately, however, there is an elite and privileged Christianity in the sphere of the White Man wherever a nationalistic and economically dominant bourgeoisie rules the churches and, at best, tolerates outcasts alongside it. Taxes and alms do not suffer from this. But in every closed society genuine love is choked, and one of our greatest problems is how to open the communities in this country again for heaven and earth. Openness for the near and far assumes we no longer take ourselves so seriously, as if everything revolved around us, that we no longer reckon what is due us, and, naturally, that we absolutely do not take from others what is theirs or belittle it. None are open for heaven and earth who, mistrustful, fear being disadvantaged, aggressively defend themselves against being neglected, and bitterly keep score of injustice, in order at some later day to present it to God and humanity.

This, of course, is all too human. But it is plainly not a humanity that grows from the love positively described at the conclusion of our section. What incessantly stands the world on its head, and what even Christians so seldom credibly represent, is so simple—that is, profoundly to rejoice, thus from the heart and with all one's powers, not in injustice, but in truth made actual; not to howl with the wolves and bray with the asses, not to take pleasure in one's own advantage, and not to be silent when those alleged to be useless, and in any event who live in the shadows, are even further repressed among us, elsewhere on the earth around us. We would have to be much more detailed than the time allows. It is clear that imaginary persons left to themselves are not at issue here, but ourselves and others, insofar as we are linked to each other and share particular conditions. At issue is not humanity as isolated, apart from what we today abstractly call structures. Love does not become concrete when it ignores these structures, when it does not engage in a truth that is actualized. The truth that opposes injustice allows all God's creatures to lay claim to our respect, our help, our service for their temporal well-being and eternal salvation. In the name of Jesus, what are called human rights are superseded by those rights that God has toward God's creation, thus also demands for this, God's own creation, and intends to see realized on earth. It is dangerous when out of love persons put themselves at God's disposal, dangerous for these persons themselves, because their love inevitably comes into conflict with the dominant opinion, with the existing order, with all the established systems, the interests of the privileged and the might of tyrants. But this love is dangerous also because it awakens hearts and heads from sleep, is no longer content with alms where everywhere unnumbered sacrifices are offered to the greed for profit. It knows that God judges the old world and brings about a new world of righteousness to which Christians must give witness now. So it cries: Save the other and by it realize God's truth! This love is revolutionary, and it must be so because it originates in the resurrection of the dead at Easter and extends to the resurrection of the dead in all the world. The exuberance of the concluding verse is to be understood from this perspective: "It bears all things, believes all things, hopes all things, endures all things."

This "all things," repeated four times and set at the beginning for emphasis, is disturbing. It is easily heard. But who does what is said here? Who bows the shoulder under that burden and endures in every conflict? Whoever has dragged a wounded soldier on the stretcher out of enemy fire knows how heavy the burden of one single person is. And what is that compared to the horrible burdens of an earth struck down with suffering? Who has not collapsed when tortured by others, by circumstances, or by one's own flesh or heart? Where is conquest over that conflict? Even the Bible corroborates what everyone experiences in a long life: "Cursed are those who trust in mere mortals and make mere flesh their strength" [Jer. 17:5]. How can one still trust and hope in all this? We must inquire in this way for the sake of honesty, and in order not to be intoxicated by rhetoric, as occurs only too easily and often. But when we do so, we learn that, throughout the entire chapter, love is spoken of as a power. Encountered by it, we do not have it in our power but are, conversely, its servants, perhaps also apprentices of its truth. So we are personally not at all what is claimed by it—namely, that which abides. We continually emphasized that we are on the way, have not reached the goal, but are under a promise and command. We may also say that we follow the One who abides, and that we reach out to him; we have whatever we have only as disciples have their master. This means that the power of love, spoken of so personally here, is what we experience and receive from Christ, from his energy into which we are set as his disciples, so as to hand it on on earth. His image is mirrored in our life, the life of his servants. His image denotes that humanity which is always all for the other, and thus it brings the open heaven down to what is closed on earth; it brings what abides down to what is transitory.

With this said, we are at the last section of our chapter. Christianity as well shares temporally the fate of a world that is passing away, in which everything must fall away, however permanent it seemed to be. What we do can in the best instance be a witness and sign of what is to come. Even the miracles and gifts of God we have experienced may only be understood as provisions for the journey, having the mark of the fragmentary. Revelation leads us before the face of the One who abides. It makes clear to us, first of all, that we are still among those who wait, who must hold out with what is fragmentary, ourselves mere signs of grace within what is provisional. Signs always serve others. We are not destined to be profiled as a work of art. The meaning of our daily work is that we remain on the way and do not stop. Properly understood, we live in the moment, as lovers do, intensively and radically, ever in departure and breaking off. Those with possessions look anxiously to what is happening to them and, under their burden, continually fall behind. We stretch out of the ruins of the past and the fragments of our growth and aging toward what is ahead, and we take along whoever is ready for it. Over those who have withdrawn into the ghetto, longings and illusions and anxieties are suspended. Only that one comes into the open who resolves to journey with Abraham into an unknown future, with Moses into the wilderness, with Jesus to the place of the skull. Only there do Christian freedom and resurrection from the dead exist. The apostle admonishes us to outgrow what is childish. The mature learn that everything has its time. They go comforted, patiently and wakefully on the way prescribed, no longer belonging to themselves, and thus not ignoring what is thrown at their feet; above all, they are not concerned for their own advantage and success. They do not need to be victorious. They are content to know that their Lord called them to service with all that they are and have, and he seeks only faithfulness from them. Failures, disappointments, fatigue, not least dying, are calculated in from the outset. The raptures of the glossolalic do not last. The proposals of the theologians are criticized or rejected by their students. What prophets in their time proclaimed as God's will may already be out of date in the next generation. But for this reason, faith and hope do not allow us to give up.

A final parable speaks of the inhabitants of a cave who see in a mirror what occurs outside, but in the darkness see it only shadow-like. So also the wanderers must live with broken insights and take comfort from the promise.

Not for our sake, but because we have a Lord and go his way, clarity lightens from the end into our time, and so lightens the day when we will know as we are now already known, will know face-to-face, no longer puzzling and merely directed to fragments of what remains. Faith and hope are in apparent contradiction. Today we have the eternal only in the provisional, the heavenly only on earth, the perfect in fragments thankfully to be used. But in love the meaning of such contradiction is clear: whoever perseveres in the discipleship and mission of the One who left his Father's glory to move in with the Father's children lives truly in heaven, not just in the end time. Our eternity is not like that of the philosophers, that we survive the battle; rather, in love we share in the work of grace. Love is divine being and doing. God, as Jesus shows us, does not give it in isolation. God is Immanuel, thus God for us. God did not create us for isolation, to which sin can only lead. God called us so that we would be there for God, and that must be reflected in existence for others and for a world that belongs to God. As has been beautifully put, Christian existence is "pro-existence," as our God is "pro-existent." What abides is present, where God and God's creatures are together with each other, in loving relation. But oddly enough, this occurs only when both go out from themselves, on the way toward the other, when they become earthly. In conclusion, let us put it in a paradox: we must throw our hearts into the temporal and open to the other in order to arrive at what remains and to be with God. Amen.

⊹ 8 ⊹

The Appeal to Reason (1977)

For if I pray in a tongue, my spirit prays but my mind is unproductive. What should I do then? I will pray with the spirit, but I will pray with the mind also; I will sing praise with the spirit, but I will sing praise with the mind also. Otherwise, if you say a blessing with the spirit, how can anyone in the position of an outsider say the "Amen" to your thanksgiving, since the outsider does not know what you are saying? For you may give thanks well enough, but the other person is not built up. I thank God that I speak in tongues more than all of you; nevertheless, in church I would rather speak five words with my mind, in order to instruct others also, than ten thousand words in a tongue.

Brothers and sisters, do not be children in your thinking; rather, be infants in evil, but in thinking be adults. . . . Let two or three prophets speak, and let the others weigh what is said. If a revelation is made to someone else sitting nearby, let the first person be silent. For you can all prophesy one by one, so that all may learn and all be encouraged. And the spirits of prophets are subject to the prophets, for God is a God not of disorder but of peace.

1 Corinthians 14:14–20, 29–33

I n more detail than anywhere else, this chapter refers to worship in a Pauline community. There are troubling reasons for this as for the entire letter. Corinth is experiencing the inbreaking of the divine Spirit within earthly conditions. Like a storm the Spirit seizes the Christian assembly, effecting miraculous events and ecstasies (of which speaking in tongues during prayer

A Bible study held at the German evangelical *Kirchentag* in Berlin. First published in *Deutscher Evangelischer Kirchentag, Berlin 1977: Dokumente* (Stuttgart: Kreuz-Verlag, 1977), 115–25.

and preaching are particularly conspicuous, understood to be the language of the angels), and by it the community is set at the doorstep of heaven. It is understandable that such a condition should confuse the hearts and heads of those involved and all but destroy the order of the gathering. While at worship services known to us as devout and quiet, painfully endured rules of behavior are at times more reminiscent of a burial than of the host of the redeemed; in Corinth each in their own way makes known their feelings without bothering about the fellowship. The assembly demonstrates the freedom of the blest, at least on festival days and at the Lord's Supper, as an anticipation of the future world. It may be that influences of the Hellenistic mysteries are also at work, mysteries with which Christians, in the midst of the harbor city, easily came into contact prior to their baptism. Paul is horrified at the situation in the congregation. Gross moral offenses, thoughtlessness toward the weak (leading to the violation of consciences), and highly dubious factions are all the reverse side of an enthusiasm that imagines it is removed from temporal norms. The apostle forcefully exercises his authority to restore somewhat feasible order. Our chapter indicates that, in a style highly reminiscent of a decree, he gives instructions later converted to canon law. Of particular importance to him is that the Christian worship service has and maintains a clear task. In it the congregation is to be built up. This does not mean, as we are, of course, inclined to assume, that pious feelings should be tended and religious experiences handed on. Rather, what we call edification is put off. The slogans by which Paul in our verses describes the task of the worship all read: teach, learn, be admonished. They indicate what he understands by edification: the gospel is to be made intelligible, interpreted, appropriated, and preserved with a view to the present. In worship God's good news is to be heard and learned precisely for our own time. Everything is put aside that hinders this and makes it impossible. Everything must be corrected that does not clearly point to this goal. Thus, when in its basic features our text outlines something like a Christian order of worship, this order as a whole as well as in detail is conceived as service to the gospel. If this remains uncontested and unmistakable, room is given various gifts and activities, even that of speaking in tongues. But it is easy to see that this last admission is difficult for the apostle.

Paul declares that he himself can speak glossolalically, and that he can even outdo the Corinthians with it. He also practices it in his private prayer. But he explicitly asserts that, in the assembly of the congregation, five intelligible words are of more worth to him than ten thousand in tongue-speaking. The reason for this is given in uncommon detail. There are Christians who are unable to link any sense with the stammering of the enraptured. When, at the *agapē* meal, the thanksgiving is spoken over the bread and wine by a glossolalic, they do not know when to say "amen." They must be given consideration though the congregation gives highest value to the ecstatic ability. This applies no less to those who, as is actually to be translated, sit at the place of the unbaptized. In mind are gentiles applying for baptism or invited by friends to be present at the Christian worship, as must have often occurred in the practice of mission. Paul is aware that to these guests speaking in tongues must appear as childish bawling. By it they are more frightened away from than brought near to the gospel. This absolutely must not happen. So, once more, the Corinthians are admonished to put off childish ways and to be grown up. We may remain childlike in refraining from evil, but not where the insight and understanding of the good news are involved. Surprisingly, the apostle does not absolutely forbid tongue speaking in worship so as to allow it only for private prayer and song. If he were to do so, the congregation probably would not follow him. In any event, he clearly sets limits to his agreement: ecstatics may only speak when interpreters are present and can interpret their stammering.

On the other hand, Paul assigns highest significance to prophecy. We saw earlier that by *prophecy* is meant proclamation that carries the gospel into the present situation, thus actualizes it for what hearers are present. We have occasion to listen very carefully here, and to draw consequences for our situation. It was not without profound understanding that the Reformation spoke of the living voice of the gospel, and actually set it in opposition to the printed word of the Bible. Christianity cannot dispense with the tradition of Holy Scripture and the confessions of its fathers, by which the prophetic message is to be tested. But we are not to live at second hand, as from the canned goods of the past. God is present today. God's Spirit moves about not only in the time of the first disciples. But we can prevent the Spirit's immediate access to us, and have often done so when forced through the sluices of tradition recognized in the church. In our text, the prophets who are contrasted with those speaking in tongues have this in common with them: they represent the living voice of the gospel, the present will of God, the power of the Spirit now revealing itself in the congregation. The prophets are to hold fast what was said to previous generations, but they are to expound it in such a fashion that the worshiping assemblies experience and understand what it means today in terms of promise and comfort, as well as of admonition and warning. The Christian community is always in danger of taking flight from its own difficulties into the transfigured past and associating with those who have overcome, instead of practicing solidarity with those who suffer conflict in our time. It is so easy to make of the gospel a fairy tale, to make of the "thus saith the Lord" a "once upon a time." Such artistry is enthusiastically practiced everywhere around us, and it cannot be denied that it can warm the heart of the listeners, give rise to their enthusiasm or thoughtfulness, laughing or crying. But the gospel is no fairy tale, by the magic of which we become unfaithful to the hour struck for me, for us, by which we emerge from the dust of the toil of our way into the gardens dedicated to the dead. Since Easter the question is, "Why do you look for the living among the dead?" [Luke 24:5]. Unnumbered Christians have never yet arrived at their own present time, have recast the truth into a pious legend, edify themselves without God's Word and work bearing fruit. The apostle reproaches the speakers in tongues for their lack of fruit. They move in caves in which the word is no longer heard: "Bear one another's burdens" [Gal. 6:2]. Every burden has already fallen from their shoulders. This is the state of the blest, of which we may occasionally be reminded but to which we do not yet belong, as the prophets reminded us. In worship, praise of the coming kingdom is noisily heard from our ranks, just as the children sang hosanna to the Christ striding toward Golgotha. Still, we remain under the sign of the cross. Thus, in all it does and receives, the assembly on Sunday prepares for everyday mundane worship of the coming week, which must bear fruit. The prophet names the promise and mission of the disciples of Jesus today and points to that earth that awaits us because it needs us, even when it persecutes us or wants to lure us to apostasy.

Now, if we look at our text as a whole, we can say in summary that Paul, while encountering his congregation as a prophet, shares and values the ecstatic gift. He tells the congregation what it needs more than ecstasies and speaking in tongues. He also tells the same to us, who perhaps reach out for ecstatic experiences in the wake of the Corinthians. With our religious feelings we are all in danger of breaking out of our mundane life on earth into a higher and safer world, and by it becoming seed without fruit, disciples without a mission, a church without promise. In its assemblies as in its worship on earth, Christianity has more need of reason than of pious experiences and heavenly raptures. We must often repeat this word, utter this sentence, and as much as possible even spell it out, because it ought to arouse some attention. Who would arrive at it if our text did not address us with it? Is it surprising that in our congregations, our chapter, as many others in the Bible, has remained unknown, and actually gives theologians relatively little concern? Of course, it is always noted that instructions are given here for worship, and that enthusiastic utterances are strictly limited. But the range of our text is scarcely set forth so that we would have to encounter it as something unexpected and be shocked by it. We ask seriously, Is the Bible really heard when we do not continually learn something new from its pages and are no longer shocked by it? Can it contain God's Word when this does not occur? So it happens that where God actually speaks to us, we reluctantly think and say, "This cannot, may not, be." Who would ultimately disagree that we indifferently read past texts that are incomprehensible to us? This, surely, might have been more largely the case with our verses than elsewhere. Nowhere in the New Testament has the right, value, and necessity of reason been more emphatically defended. We are inclined to speak of a canticle, and should consider that what is obviously required by worship should apply to everyday life. So also, a process of unlearning would be due, particularly in our German congregations. We are not exaggerating when we maintain that, in general, those congregations have invested more value, hope, and trust in the miraculous, in religious emotions, and in set traditions than in the reason of a Christian. We need to consider the reasons for this.

No doubt, the theology of the professionals is implicated in this. In the past, it often felt more obligated to the academic sphere of research than to Christianity, though the latter need not have been excluded. Conversely, the findings of professional theologians have seldom had an effect on the worship of Protestantism, though they considerably impaired the community's ability to think as well as its connection with the intellectual currents of the modern age. Even the service of biblical theology was for the most part not accepted. In fact, it was so often unknown that it was suspected of wanting to manipulate the evangelical message. This reproach is not to be rejected out of hand. Ultimately, representatives of the theological guild are also human and are, no less than others, vulnerable to the temptations of their art. As has always been the case, there are pastors who do not lead their flock with the shepherd's staff but with the scepter of unlimited rule. There are and always have been the so-called laity who know how to win the reputation for a particular holiness or who drag sturdy followers behind them and integrate the community politically or economically within their interests. There are and have always been economic, national, liberal, sectarian groups that recruit their supporters on church property.

Piety has never yet protected itself from the fact that the Bible, the gospel, and Christianity can be manipulated and corrupted. Everyone who is truly innocent is invited to stone the sinners. But who is innocent here? Who never had at least a bit of desire to shape God and God's will, even others, according to our own insights and desires? Who never had the desire to retouch Christ's image on the basis of our own and to make others, even in their faith, to say nothing of their way of life, dependent on us? We cannot ignore the fact that Germans have had a penchant for schoolmastery, often for *Führer*-ism of all stripes, for the mischief of stereotypes following from it, and with Christians joining in unconcerned. In any event, self-security and arrogance in the academic sphere are only a reflection of that from which church circles are not exempt. Repentance is needed and useful on all sides. For this reason, theology also cannot simply oppose the community. No Christian can avoid becoming a theologian when ready and able to give an account of his or her faith. Of course, there is good theology and poor theology, exciting and boring, a theology with the experience of a life, or of many generations, behind it and another that betrays merely an empty head and a hardened heart. Both are in the university as well as in the edification hour. The reality is always more complicated than propagandists and fanatics will admit, and original sin is more extensive than even those pious folks calling themselves orthodox will admit. With a bit of good will and the insight that we all live from forgiveness, the momentary conflict over theology in German Protestantism would be thoroughly decontaminated and actually made fruitful for the *oecumene*.

Still, it is not enough to consider the crippling of reason in our ranks solely from the perspective of the present. It has deep roots in the past. More severely than in the rest of Western Christianity, in German churches the shock of the French Revolution has had an abiding effect for almost two hundred years and, just as in politics, urges us toward romanticism and reaction. Despite Wichern,[1] Löhe, Blumhardt,[2] and many others, the social struggles of the previous century have not been taken seriously in any radical way by our middle class as a challenge to the Christian conscience. The efforts put forth need no more to be concealed or minimized than, for example, the social legislation of Bismarck. Conversely, it cannot be denied that, here as there, anxiety in the face of a possible revolution is greater than respect for human dignity, greater than shock over the suffering of the proletariat. In the previous century, the problems of public life were for the most part addressed only from the perspective of their national and anti-revolutionary effects; this resulted in and was revealed by the rise of National Socialism, which would otherwise never have gained power among our people. The churches, for their part, have transmitted such effects almost without limit to the congregations and the homes of their members. On the widest front, though probably no longer admitted, the result has been divinely and humanly to sanction the protection and development of the existing situation. This is taking its revenge up to our own time.

The mentality of the German affluent society after the Second World War has grown from this inheritance, and therefore can be widely shared, even by

1. Johann Hinrich Wichern (1808–81), theologian, social pedagogue, founder of the Inner Mission of the Evangelical Church.
2. Christoph Blumhardt (1842–1919), Lutheran theologian, one of the founders of Christian socialism in Germany and Switzerland.

Christian circles that do not simply bow before the idols of mammon and success. Above all, we must see that the conflict of that period is being repeated today on a global scale. In place of the proletarian suffering I was given to see and trace in my youth, in sight of the pits and steel works of the Ruhr, today, at least in parts of the Third and Fourth Worlds, a hell on earth has emerged. Again, there are national and anti-revolutionary effects that do not allow us to believe the reports of eyewitnesses and the media; that strengthen us in our blindness and self-interest; and that, in church circles, have actually driven to a declaration of war against the ecumenical movement as an accomplice of revolutionaries. The fact that idiocy and blindness are actually characteristic signs of original sin renders much intelligible, but it is no excuse. We may be allowed to ask whether the Father of Jesus Christ is being disposed of on the quiet and replaced by a god of the philosophers and a pagan ideology, for which what is at issue is not the salvation and life of its poorest creatures but calm and order among all the underlings.

Naturally, what I am saying will be decried far and wide as political argument, while no offense is taken at the fact that, with little exception, our grandfathers proclaimed the union of throne and altar as the basis for religion and morality—thus powerfully spreading that syncretism complained of today. Even in the church, justice, for the most part, takes its place on the right. Perhaps someone will simply state that these recollections do not belong in a Bible study and are harmful to the edification of the congregation. Then there would be ignored what the apostle made sure of, that instruction and learning are, on principle, taken into the congregation; and for this very reason, he calls for reason. We have also experienced what Jeremiah 31:29 unforgettably formulates: "The parents have eaten sour grapes, and the children's teeth are set on edge." Our own history, the condition of our congregations, their currents and needs, are incomprehensible when we no longer, as in the books of Moses, reflect on the history of the ancestors. This will, of course, be done for the sake of God's mercy and not for the honor of humanity. It is necessary not only to unearth patience and loyalty but, no less, to be aware of increasing guilt. Reason means to be able to hear. Critical thinking is concerned with reality. The apostle fetches the enthusiasts back to earth, where burdens await them that are not magically eliminated by ecstatic experiences. If we shy away from the reality in our everyday life and in the past of our ancestors, here as there, truth and sins are buried. There is then no building up, as Paul demands, but only edification, which makes of humans saints or heretics. From this follows everything that characterized the Corinthian enthusiasts: no longer an awareness that forgiveness pardons, but a robbing of sinners' protective cloak and setting them naked before their judge. A god is imagined who looks at his people through his fingers. Our attitude toward the tortured world and its unjust structures does not appear so important when only orthodoxy is to be observed and pious experiences undergone. Where the Spirit who raptures to heaven is experienced, Lazarus may crawl unseen before the gates, capitalism is allowed to make the poor poorer, and the cross of the Nazarene remains a touching story but not the place where God and human truth are recognized and appear in the earthly service of grace. Renewed and radicalized Christian reason begins at Golgotha.

May we go so far when aware of responsibility for such statements? For this reason also our text deserves careful study: because the apostle goes even further in it. From him stems the admonition "Do not quench the Spirit" [1 Thess. 5:19]. But despite his criticism of an enthusiastic congregation, this does not hinder him from decreeing with a virtually incomprehensible rashness concerning the time when the divine Spirit has to be silent in the worship assembly, and how often he may speak. Paul not merely forbids public speaking in tongues when no interpreter is present. He likewise forbids more than two or three prophets from speaking. The hearers are not to be overtaxed but to retain energy for reflection and, as is clear from the text, in a way totally contrary to our custom, time for discussion. Nor does the officeholder have a monopoly on the expression of opinion. Learning best occurs when one discusses with the other. The prophets, moreover, may not all speak at once, but have to do so properly in series, so as not to create mutual disturbance and lead the congregation astray. If someone is suddenly, irresistibly seized by the Spirit, the previous speaker must yield their place. The apostle dismisses the objection of his Hellenistic environment, that one may draw no limits to the freedom of the Spirit. He cold-bloodedly and authoritatively asserts that the spirits of the prophets are subject to the prophets, and can therefore be held under control.

These instructions culminate in the command to critically test all prophetic speech. Unfortunately, it is unclear whether this is to be done by the congregation as a whole, which is moved by the Spirit, or by individuals among the members especially apt for it. What is decisive is that the testing does not stop. Where the Spirit is on the scene there is always false prophecy as well. We have not forgotten that not very long ago tyrants were actually recommended to the community, and the gospel was set in the shadows of blood, soil, and race. Today the current runs in the opposite direction. We are encapsulated from the world as in a ghetto—concerned with apocalyptic visions of the world's end rather than with contributing to its life, with making it more humane— sending faith on its way with the maxim "No experiments!" That the result is marching in step, that the vocabulary of the language is never, ever changed, that repeating what is generally known empowers the convinced and frightens the others, is not disturbing. That the Creator does not cease to experiment with the earth, that the Father of the crucified Jesus unceasingly takes risks when he takes us into his service, is not considered. We can also betray the Holy Spirit in such fashion that we allow the Spirit's storm to become the stale air of old cathedrals and the Spirit's fire the warming flame of a stove in the parlor—just as a hundred years ago we were concentrating again on the theme "God and the soul" and, in express contradiction of the *oecumene*, registering our own neglect of the world. Here we are to test and discuss whether this is the true will of God, and the renewed reason of the Christian is needed for the task. Its measure is the discipleship of that Nazarene who descended into the hell of earth and who, as the returning One, holds before us this word: "Just as you did it to one of the least of these who are members of my family, you did it to me" [Matt. 25:40]. The gospel enlists our reason in its service because we must be stewards of our Lord on earth. This is said most beautifully in Philippians 1:9–11: "This is my prayer, that your love may overflow more and more with knowledge and full insight to help you to determine what is best, so that in the day of Christ you may be pure and blameless, having produced the harvest of righteousness that comes through Jesus Christ for the glory and praise of God." These words deserve serious reflection. Related to everyday life, they take up what our text requires for the Sunday festival. The entire horizon of space to which the call to reason resounds is made clear so that we know: here is your place, your promise, your task. In the disciples of Jesus, the eternal kingdom will thus become actual on earth.

Christians are and remain those who grow. Wherever one knows one is already at the goal, we who are still in discipleship are superfluous. The on-lookers may linger and enjoy. The believers follow the Word, which points them to the unknown future of their Lord. Reason does not let them lose their Lord from their sight, or his Word from their ears, for otherwise we are left to ourselves and surrendered to the earthly. To grow means to be on the way instead of ending in enthusiasm. But on the way one connects insights and experiences. After what has been said, it is no longer necessary to assert how our longings and expectations contrast so greatly with the apostolic promise. What do we really learn in the course of a Christian life in addition to everything we otherwise receive? Is it just emotions that lift us beyond everyday life, or have we gained experience with which we can prove ourselves in everyday life, live more meaningfully, and die more comfortably? Surely, we scarcely err in the judgment that today young people look most for experience from the Christian community. They ask whether in life and death we have found mere fate and accident or promise and grace, and thus can say "Yes" to both.

Are they disappointed in us just as in the host of propagandists because we offer them pious speeches, elaborate systems, and all kinds of human religiosity, but no credible, acceptable, basic experience? We owe those weary with slogans and ideologies an accounting as to whether over our life and death these words may and should stand: "This man was with Jesus of Nazareth" [Matt. 26:71].

Theologians and ideologies move to and fro; it is here that the decision is made and the confession that we have to give God and the other. But if this is so and we have resolved to follow the Nazarene, to remain forever with him, then fruits of righteousness are due. That we receive salvation solely by faith and without works of the law may never be obscured. But likewise, it may not and shall never be forgotten that, as messengers of divine justice, we have to encounter an earth sinking in unrighteousness and to bring forth fruits of this righteousness. It is not done with our praying and singing on festival days, or in the closet, and even less with our proclaiming the end without living the truth that "God opposes the proud, but gives grace to the humble" [James 4:6; 1 Pet. 5:5], that God does not sanction what exists, and that with the new heaven God also intends a new earth. I am not certain it is wise to speak of revolution here, but I am certain that in view of an affluent society concerned only for security and increasing what exists, every other word cannot clearly enough set forth God's justice and intent. Fruits of righteousness mean at least that Christianity resolutely comes to the side of the victims of our affluence and, with word and deed, turns away from the fleshpots of Egypt. The best to which we are called is clearly not what suits us best but that on the day of Christ we can say: "Your brothers and sisters, Lord, were mine. Under the cross where you were cursed, I have learned to be in solidarity with those whom the earth condemns. I have gained knowledge and experience, no longer shaken by demagogues and fanatics. We must separate ourselves from the wolves and asses of this world for the sake of being something to the praise of your glory. But this is possible only in love."

This has returned us to the point at which we began: on earth, faith can only be in love, and love without the use of reason remains blind and dumb. Salvation that is not expressed in the well-being of those nearest and farthest is illusion and superstition. Salvation does not end with the pious who are sated and living in good fortune, but it aims at God's kingdom; and, for this reason, it must be given worldwide from one to the other. If we do not remain in the chain of those who give, we become robbers to whom the kingdom is closed. Characteristic of the New Testament is the word about loving the enemy. Here all barriers are cleared, and we are never at the end. In every moment we are again at the beginning. Just as this is one insight that is gained with love and by which love becomes rich, so there is a second insight: that through love the nearest or most distant truly becomes our partner. But even this is Christ's work in us, and thus the aim is Christ's rule in our time and on earth. We must now look back toward the first commandment, which in a certain way describes the center and content of the entire Bible: "I am the LORD your God." It is from this that faith lives. "You shall have no other gods before me" [Exod. 20:3; Deut. 5:7]. This is the truth and power of Christian love. Finally, this love stands and falls with eliminating the demons. In the midst of the darkness it sees God's world and nourishes it in anticipation of that day when the freedom of the children of God is no longer suppressed by human tyrants and anonymous power. Service to it means more than giving alms, which by itself is a despising of the creature. It is the freedom of all who fall among robbers and, likewise, the freedom of those who resist the idols and demons unto blood. There is reason, not merely emotion, in such action.

Where the Father of Jesus Christ takes us into his possession, the realm of possession ends. There would be much to say about this. But it is enough now to hear the last word of our text: "For God is a God not of disorder but of peace." Christian reason speaks to combat wild enthusiasm. But what is meant is not the order of a society that has led its flock to arid land or been concerned with teaching rebels to fear. The issue for the apostle is that peace return. In addition, there must be clarity in the jungle of feelings and illusions, so that people no longer violate God's creation in the name of their dreams, setting up their order in arrogance or in a panic-stricken anxiety, which is despotism. The peace of God arrives where demons retreat and possession is healed, where the Holy Spirit works reason and love. Amen.

⊹ 9 ⊹

Guests of the Crucified (1979)

L et us look first of all at those congregational gatherings reported, for example, in 1 Corinthians 11:17–24. They take place every evening and are connected with a celebration of the Lord's Supper. A common meal opens worship. In addition, every member of the congregation has brought along something of his or her means, and care is taken that all those in need can at least satisfy their hunger here. Fellowship thus surrounds those gathered and is expressed particularly toward the poor, sick, slaves, widows, and orphans. For this reason the celebration is called *agapē*, love feast. At that time, the Lord's Supper was obviously not yet an appendage to the preaching service. And it was not conducted merely occasionally but belonged inseparably to the Christian assembly. Finally, it was not limited to a bit of bread and a sip of wine but formed the most important part of a regular mealtime. As heart and soul were quickened, the body also got its due, and that in a festival in which the individuals grew together into a fellowship of the body of Christ.

Remarkably, in 11:25, Paul says that the cup had been handed around "after supper." This could mean that the distribution of the bread took place sometime at the beginning, but the handing on of the drink at the conclusion of the love feast. In this case the Lord's Supper would be, as it were, the frame of worship together with the proclamation of the prophets, instruction

A lecture given for the "Panel on the Eucharist" at the German evangelical *Kirchentag* in Nuremberg. First published in *Deutscher Evangelischer Kirchentag, Nürnberg, 1979: Dokumente* (Stuttgart: Kreuz-Verlag, 1979), 352–61. A variation of it given in 1981 at the DDR *Kirchentag* in Görlitz was, of course, not published.

in Scripture, common prayer, and praise. Then, at least in the Pauline area of mission, the early Christian community came together daily at the table of Jesus. And its members, in sight of the present Lord, were guests of the Crucified and witnesses of the Risen One. By way of earthly satiation they anticipated the festival of the kingdom of God and jubilantly felt themselves to be representatives of the heavenly community.

We must keep this in mind as vividly as possible in order to comprehend what first seems incomprehensible to us. The apostle comes to speak of the Lord's Supper only because it is misused in Corinth. Clearly, in early Christianity it did not occur so stiffly and at times even eerily as is common with us. The Corinthian community was in essence composed of the lowest stratum of the population of the harbor city. Many could only come to worship when their employers dismissed them after the day's labor, or when they could slip away from the family of a large household. That they were then often late is clear. But there were well-to-do members of the congregation who were more likely in charge of their time and became impatient when they had to wait too long for the others, who were not even certain the others would come at all. They had brought along food and drink and, because they were hungry, already began with the meal. The mood rose in amiability, the more they feasted. For them, too, satiation was not merely the issue. They felt they were guests of the coming heavenly rule, but remained truly human, and in no way behaved as representatives of a middle-class society with a fixed moral code and ideal moral views. Some would no doubt rather avoid than observe order and laws in everyday life. They hungered and thirsted for freedom from oppression by patrons and slaveholders no less than for bodily food. They wanted to forget earthly toil and finally, with the angels, be allowed to praise the victorious righteousness of God. Whoever has once been seized by rebellious impatience cannot ignorantly look on when the outcasts of society break out of the usual conventions to demonstrate their citizenship in heaven, when in excess of enthusiasm they become drunk and leave those who are delayed only remnants of the meal destined for all. Naturally, this cannot be approved. But it puts us before the question Paul gives the Corinthians to consider: When does one become a worthy guest of Jesus's table? The answer to this is to be given from different aspects.

It would no doubt be helpful if we could speak only of the Lord's Supper. All other paraphrases are too indefinite and can lead to misunderstandings. So it is not an error when we most often say "Lord's Supper" [*Abendmahl*]. Early Christian usage and the words of institution justify this description.

Still, it is left to our discretion as to what views we connect with it, and the danger is that our personal expectations, needs, and experiences at any one time decide the issue. This was the case with the Corinthians. They celebrated the inbreaking freedom of the kingdom of God, and in ecstasy over it they forgot their earthly path and their poorer fellows. With us, perhaps, remorse dominates over our guilt and our many vain attempts at beginning a new life, at getting right with God, with our parents, marriage partners, children and neighbors, but also with ourselves. Who would exclude both types from the celebration that altogether allows room for salvation as well as for remorse, and that intends to impart freedom as well as forgiveness? But ought it to be the main thing? In that case, does not the shadow of our sinful or pious humanity, of our longings and desperations, fall on the one who says to us, "My body, my blood for you"? What is decisive is that he and he alone stands in the midst, that he and he alone is heard and received. Everyone can see today what results when we ourselves are most important to us. Fewer and fewer guests are found at the table of Jesus, and those who come do so less and less. Going to the Lord's Supper becomes the mark of pious groups, which, naturally, cannot replace the entire congregation but feel they are the true community and only too easily and often fall away into sectarian presumption. Where the entire community no longer clearly and regularly follows the invitation of its Lord, celebration of the meal easily becomes a cult affair, where the last of the faithful find refuge, a wall of separation in the midst of Christianity and a barricade against that world that God intends to bring home. Then, as at Golgotha, the Christ is abandoned by his disciples. To look to him, to hear him, to receive him, and to allow him to work in us is decisive. He draws all we otherwise need behind him.

The Lord's Supper means to be called before his face, and that is the most simple, most comprehensive, and most beautiful description of the disciples, which not even a heavenly host can exceed: We stand before the face of Jesus. But does this statement suffice? Some may think this is too simple. Can and ought we get clear of the theological conflicts that for centuries have been connected with the words of institution of the Lord's Supper and that still separate confessions from one another, as if they applied only to specialists? The professionals would be amazed and horrified to learn that, together with their theological debates, they are for the most part no longer understood or supported by the so-called laity. The gulf between them and their own congregations is at times wider than that between theirs and other confessions. This is no proof that dogmatics deserves to be dubbed superfluous and that practice should always have priority. There is no life and no discipleship that could manage to dispose of thinking—of distinguishing between true and false and stating precisely what the faith of their heart really is. Conversely, we may not leave life and discipleship to the schoolmasters and, where possible, to the judges of heresy, who would fanatically imprint their image, perhaps also their imagination, on us and pin the same uniforms on the congregation. We can refuse food to the hungry by attempting through analyses and tests to determine their nourishment value. Incontestably, there are theologians and church leaders for whom, in a world torn apart, confessional separation is more important than the fellowship of the Crucified. What is reverently and questionably called a "sacrament" is only too often exaggerated so that the Lord who gives it to us appears in the background. From the words "My body, my blood for you," every child hears that we are not to swear an oath to a religious party or ideology, to church traditions or the speculations of our forefathers. To allow oneself to be raptured into mystical depths and metaphysical heights is not to everyone's taste, and certainly not to everyone's salvation. At the table of Jesus none of us are spared taking from the words of institution, in quite childlike fashion, the truth that our Lord will come to us, move in with us, will give himself to us to be our own, in order then to lay claim to our heart and life. Can we expect, believe, or know anything more? Is this not enough for everyone and a heavenly joy already experienced on earth, that our Lord gives himself to us and in his meal sets us for time and eternity before his face?

-|--|--|-

The first key word read, "the Lord's Supper." As the second there follows, "Guests of the Crucified." With the words "My body, my blood for you," the One who gives himself to us to be our own does not do so for no reason. After Easter he acts toward us in such a way that he points us to his cross. He will never do otherwise. Even on the last day his enemies will recognize him by his wounds, because these distinguish him from all the idols and lords of the earth. Who Jesus truly is must be experienced from Golgotha. Here, as nowhere else, what is at issue with the true God and the true Man becomes clear. The Christ must go into death—more yet, into the hell of hate, contempt, and scorn—to help us. Can any affirm this without most deeply losing illusions about themselves and this world of ours? Whoever has stood beneath the stake of the Crucified knows that salvation does not grow from our own reason or strength. But at the same time, one is aware of a God who throws off his glory and takes on the apron of a slave in order to be like those who have forsaken him, who rebel and entrench themselves against him, who in their service to idols are crazy for power and lust. Golgotha is the place where the depth of human lostness and the depth of a self-denying mercy intertwine. Here, for this reason, each finds oneself and one's Lord in one's own peculiar way. All who hate and scorn along with others here will from now on set justice and order and the status quo over humanity. All who look on indifferently will make their own interests the measure of life. All who learn the truth about themselves here and, with Jesus, learn to cry "My God, my God" [Matt. 27:46; Mark 15:34; Ps. 22:1], will have Golgotha in view their whole way and by it will define their relation to the nearest and farthest, to principalities and powers, to society's rules of the game and the political necessities of our time. Golgotha was and remains a place of blessing as well as of curse, at which the spirits in Christianity still divide without all taking notice of it. For the true and the false church, otherwise scarcely to be divided, necessarily divide when it is necessary to say yes to Jesus's cross, to allow the Crucified to be Lord.

There are religious movements aplenty. Many are profounder and mightier and more fascinating than Christianity; thus Christian communities will forever cast an eye to right and left, will strike compromises, take out loans, and betray Golgotha. But the truth of the gospel connects the lordship of God on earth to Jesus's passion. In its shadows alone the godless experience salvation. To be guests of the Crucified is not an experience merely for pious hours between thick church walls and within the circle of the devout like-minded. To be guests of the Crucified spells the pilgrimage of the disciples and also their goal. This is what Paul has to hold to against the Corinthian enthusiasts. There is no objection to seeing heaven open over oneself, to seeing the Holy Spirit fall on the community and be at work in it. But the issue is whether the opened heaven still allows the image of the Crucified or only the fulfillment of our dreams to be seen, whether the Spirit remains the power that gives us the Nazarene as Lord, or whether it alienates us from everyday life on earth and allows us to forget the battle prescribed for us. The Corinthians evidently did not feel they were guests of the Crucified when they celebrated the Lord's Supper. Those who before their conversion may in part have belonged to mystery cults saw Christ in the manner of a pagan redeemer—as a leader of souls out of the constraint of the stars, and out of demonic threat, toward heavenly freedom and immortality. That certainly suggested itself. Just as they, he had lived as a proletarian, and like unnumbered rebellious slaves, he had been crucified by the Romans as a terrorist. All the more fascinating was the effect of the good news—that this One, damned on earth, had broken through death and fate and wanted to draw his believers after him where suffering, weeping, and tears disappeared. The Lord's Supper in Corinth became a mystery celebration in which one rehearsed one's way through deepest humiliation; allowed oneself to be called into the glory of the Conqueror; and, by union with him, partook of heavenly nature.

Nineteen hundred years have passed since. For that reason, has the way in which the Corinthians celebrated the Lord's Supper nothing to do with us? Do we not see the cross chiefly as an intermediate stage on the pilgrimage toward consummation, see Jesus as a model of the fact that in suffering is tested what is to be made worthy of salvation, see the place at his table as a site of relaxation for the weary, of religious elevation beyond our mundane life, of sight into an eternal home? None of this should be proscribed as forbidden. But if the Lord's Supper offers us nothing else, then for us too it is still a mystery celebration in which God and pious souls are found together and the earth is left behind. But that is the crucial point. At the Lord's Supper may we exclude the earth, so to speak, and anticipate heaven in such fashion as though we already belonged to the host of the perfected? The question is very polemically put, but for all that still necessary: Today, at least in our Western churches, is not reveille too often blown where more marching would be required? In our worship services do we bother too much about our own and very often imagined needs, without having resisted unto blood, not seeing that whole continents have become playgrounds of demons? How can we celebrate the Lord's Supper when in the midst of an affluent society we continually adapt ourselves to the reigning conditions, are no longer aware of idols, to say nothing of naming them by name and daring to offer them defiance? The fact that the Corinthian community longed for heavenly freedom from the misery of the slums is understandable. It is right, and it is Jesus's intent, that even today the weary, solitary, incurably sick, those shattered on earth, be comforted with the invitation, "Come to me, all you that are weary and are carrying heavy burdens" [Matt. 11:28]. But the majority of our visitors to worship find themselves in another situation: their everyday life is determined by a society that dances around the golden calf, relies on the police for the protection of its possessions and its privileges, relies on NATO against the communist danger, and hopes that the dear God will allow them to live and die as peacefully as possible without the worst trouble. On Sunday, and at the table of Jesus, do the guests of the Crucified still desire this, and are they allowed to justify it in everyday life, praying for their divine protection and urging their Lord that after this time he crown them with a little place in Abraham's bosom? A *Kirchentag* that does not trust itself to put this question audibly and bluntly does not deserve its name.

Paul dared to ask the same thing of his proletarian congregation in Corinth. He must have shocked them most deeply when he shouted to those who boasted of their heavenly nature: "Unworthy!" This is the third key word for us to consider. We have come into a dangerous thicket, in which innumerable Christians have always gotten entangled and which so frightens others that they would rather go without the Lord's Supper altogether. For this reason, before we even enter into the matter itself, we must first of all do a bit of "demythologizing." These days we call something unworthy if it offends propriety or injures our moral ideas. As a result, millions have continually asked whether they could fulfill the external and internal conditions that appear suitable at the table of the Lord, or that suit current convention. Whoever is older remembers that his parents and surely grandparents went to the celebratory meal in black clothing or frock coat and top hat, then like a penitent procession circled around the altar. The organ played muffled, and pains were taken not merely to look conscious of guilt but also, from one's deepest heart, to be conscious of it. The more all this succeeded, the more worthy was the celebration and the participants. We have no right to look down on a custom practiced for hundreds of years. In this way, devout people honored their Lord and witnessed to their recognition of him as their judge. If we have ever stood in a church filled to the last pew by such guests at Jesus's table, we will of course no longer encounter human piety without reverence. Still, devout piety is not evangelical without further ado. There is an unmistakable contradiction in the fact that the community of Jesus devotes so much thought and concern to its worthiness and then goes to the Lord's Supper with trembling, while their Master fetched his guests from the fences and hedges, from among Samaritans, heathens, tax collectors, and whores, and called them to joy instead of to fear. What in his time was valued among Jews such as Pharisees and scribes as particularly worthy was only weakly represented in his host of disciples. At his table, the so-called good society was for a long time more the exception than the rule. How did it happen that the questionable types at least visibly appeared less and less often at worship, and the Christian community, almost universally, at least in our congregations, now represents the respectable bourgeoisie?

We must bore in even deeper. Certainly, from time to time we all need to reflect on ourselves and, as it were, take stock of our acting and allowing. Those who never critically examine their own lives and totally hold off the day of judgment for themselves alone might more and more forget their humanity and accuse others of guilt and mistakes all the more. Conversely, even with the strictest self-examination we scarcely arrive at the depths of our heart where defiance, despair, and the desire to deceive oneself and others are mixed. But the only ones who can appear before the eternal judge are those who beforehand have opened their arms to God as the Father of the lost son. Clearly, we and previous generations have misunderstood the invitation to the table of Jesus if we do not consider that Christ seeks the fallen, the weak, and the guilty and gathers around him only what is unworthy before God. Wiping dust away and removing dirty spots does not alter the nature of the old man. Where he who could be called the most despised and unworthy becomes our Brother, we will follow him into his humiliation, must expose ourselves without limit to his light, and must stake our salvation on his mercy alone. It is always only those who as such do not deserve it who sit at Jesus's table.

With Paul, then, to be unworthy means something other than what it means to us. The word is taken up by him from the language of commerce, where it means that the two trays of the scale are not in balance. "Not adequate" would be the precise meaning. So the apostle is not referring to the internal state of members of the congregation, but rather to their behavior at the love feast. Those persons do not behave adequately—that is, they behave contrary to the Lord and his cross—who, at Jesus's table, do not wait for their fellows, who, where possible, feed them with leftovers or let them go hungry, while they themselves feel raptured to heaven and noisily announce their salvation. There is only one single crime at the Lord's Supper worthy of death—that is, a fellowship denied. This is betrayal of the One who left the place at the right hand of God to rescue the unfortunate from contempt and abandonment and make them members of his lordship. For their sake, he enters the power of death and hell. Therefore, that person is and remains a heathen who does not give the nearest and farthest a share in grace and all its gifts but lets them, like Lazarus, lie before the door and at best feeds them with alms. At Jesus's table, one can praise, pray, be devout, and yet be a betrayer like Judas (who, after all, celebrated the Lord's Supper). Fellowship is also a mark of proper worship, and every disciple lives in superstition who leaves the neighbor uncared for and unloved in the earthly inferno. That one is, as Paul says, guilty of the body and blood of Jesus, in one's own way creating Golgotha. We may have been one with the angels and on earth have anticipated the kingdom of God. The judge of the last day will, nonetheless, ask us: Where was your brother Abel?

Now to draw a few consequences from what has been said. Protestants, at least, should refrain from the insane and incorrect way of speaking of the mystical feast that would suit only a mystery celebration. If we were able to learn something at all from 1 Corinthians 11, it is that what was involved at Jesus's table was not merely the union of souls with their heavenly Lord. But if we do want to speak of the meaning of the celebration in this way, it must at least have been clear to us that, just as in baptism, the Lord's Supper unites us with the heavenly Lord through being incorporated into his earthly body. Just this is stated in 1 Corinthians 10:16–17 and 12:12–13, thus the sections that frame our text. But precisely this is what follows from our text. The word "soul" is totally lacking, but the bodily is constantly emphasized. One eats and drinks heartily and noisily; the institution speaks of body and blood, and does so to establish bodily solidarity. For the apostle, at least in our verses, everything turns on the fact that the meal creates and preserves community and is rightly celebrated only when the community is present for it. This should not be understood legalistically. These days, our church districts have become so large that we may perfectly well be encouraged to hold the Lord's Supper in families, houses, and so-called basic communities, as incidentally occurred in early Christianity. But what remains irrevocable is that in such situations not only the like-minded come together. Where we distance ourselves inwardly and outwardly from those who as disciples believe, think, and act in other ways than we do, sects arise. Then Christ's earthly body is no longer built up, but he himself becomes head of a church party, his rule a domain in which schoolmasters and inquisitors have the last word, the pious are once more nicely together and can no longer be disturbed by the others. A Christian community wears no religious uniforms. Rather, though this sounds paradoxical, it lives in the constant state of mutual disturbance. Otherwise, it did not arise at Golgotha; its Lord did not make it more human, but doctrinaire and illusionary.

If this is actually the situation, then in our time every Lord's Supper can only be celebrated in remorse and protest. For no one can deny that everywhere in Christianity what is precisely occurring is what Paul labels as dishonoring the body and blood of Jesus, and it threatens with temporal and eternal judgment. In fact, everywhere and without letting up, Christ's invitation to come to his table and before his face is revoked by Christians, theologians, church leaders, and confessions; and refusal of fellowship at the Lord's Supper is practiced and defended. For such there is no justification or excuse. Here, God's name is profaned, God's kingdom hindered, God's will changed into its opposite, and all talk of the unity of the church unmasked as pious prattle. We will not be united. We want unity only when others are subject to our ideology. The so-called laity are gradually taking note of this. For this reason they distance themselves more and more from the table of Jesus or, against the command of their confession and spiritual counselors, come furtively to ecumenical worship. It is a protest against the reigning theologies and those who have power in the church. The Lord's Supper is ecumenical or no longer the Lord's Supper, but a sectarian celebration, because the Crucified calls to his table all for whom he died. The dogmatics were only written later. When even

Judas was not excluded, and when baptism is generally recognized as valid, it is not the one who celebrates with alien brethren who commits sacrilege, but the one who refuses fellowship with them. Before the churches call others to repentance, they ought to do penance. For those who do not tolerate guests of the Crucified no longer tolerate the Crucified in their midst. Such are no longer members of the body of Christ on earth; rather, they represent closed societies and religious fellowships of interests.

In conclusion, this is to be put more pointedly. I have intentionally spoken of a closed society. In the churches of the White Man at any rate, this best describes our normal celebratory meals, and this is precisely what the early Christian worship services with their love feasts were not. Even candidates for baptism and even unbelievers could share in them; and no doubt many from the slums of the harbor city were also there, who only wanted to satisfy their hunger at the table of Jesus. Where guests of the Crucified gather, it always occurs as a fundamentally open community. If that is not the case, the body of Christ cannot grow on earth as, according to the Risen One's missionary command, it should. To put it sharply: where Christians come together, the happy home life must be broken through. Then there are no longer those who are fortified in it against the evil world in order to satisfy their private needs for edification, for comfort and placidity in the sight of their private god, but then also others, on the outside, who have no baptismal certificate, who do not pay church tax, who are promised help neither by God nor by humans yet need the good Samaritan to come over to them. The Lord's Supper is the festival not only of those most profoundly unworthy but also of the needy, the yearning, the trashed, the despairing, and damned of this earth. It is the reflection of Golgotha in our present time. No one is a guest of the Crucified who cannot throw off the loaned or imagined cloak of his piety to be near and be a neighbor to the naked, freezing, and despised outside the church doors. Where we truly celebrate the Lord's Supper, the word of Psalm 23 is fulfilled: "You prepare a table before me in the presence of my enemies."

Let us not forget that the Corinthians celebrated the Lord's Supper in view of the imminent end of the world and were an open community also for the reason that they celebrated it as before the face of the Crucified, thus also in protest against and resistance to the demonic powers and forces of this earth. One cannot be a guest of the Crucified without challenging his enemies and declaring war against all tyrants. Where in the Lord's Supper the earthly body of Christ is built up, a new world emerges; something of the promise that our God is an enemy of the proud comes true. He creates another earth and another heaven than we dreamed of—that is, one in which the lowly, violated, and lost finally come home and to the Father. Flotsam from the east and west gathered in the Corinthian community: harbor laborers, slaves, small manual laborers, women of dubious repute, widows, a few well-to-do, earlier adherents of a synagogue or of a mystery religion. Nothing united them but the one Lord. But this Lord gave them a place at his table, satisfied them bodily and spiritually. He gave them prophets and speakers in tongues who proclaimed the breaking in of a new time, worked healings, and exorcized the evil spirits among them. He filled them with his presence so that just as at Pentecost they were as if drunk from it. Just as earthly barricades are falling here, just as social distinctions and contrasts in everyday life can no longer be maintained for long, so these worship services have worldwide significance. The presence of Christ possesses a power that continually bursts existing relationships, breaks through the boundaries of classes, peoples, races, economic systems, and cultural traditions, makes the open community a signal of freedom for all those oppressed by principalities and powers.

In Corinth there was awareness that Christ's appearance "in the presence of the enemies" occurs as it had earlier occurred at his birth and at Golgotha, that his disciples are called into the conflict between him and the adversaries of his lordship. As the guests of the Crucified take a seat at Jesus's table—allowing themselves to be fed and given drink by him, to be filled with his Spirit—they also take their departure from the tables of Egypt, in which all care for themselves, live at the cost of the nearest and most distant, and give homage to the idols of this earth. We cannot celebrate at two festivals at the same time, and at the same time serve two masters, cannot pray at the same time to the Crucified and to the tyrants of this world, cannot sacrifice his undivided power to the affluent society and behind church walls acknowledge God as Lord and judge of all God's creatures. We must remain in the fellowship of the community founded at Golgotha. Faith too has its price, and love is not content with less than our life. On earth the guests of the Crucified, for the sake of this Lord and the freedom he has brought, must appear as rebels against the principalities and powers of this world. It is so because the cross of Golgotha does not fit earthly dispositions. It speaks of the One who, even in the midst of the inferno, serves the lost—and who makes it a law of his kingdom that we follow him there and prepare a seat at Jesus's table for the others.

Can we not choose a symbol for this? Perhaps, given the circumstances obtaining with us, it is not possible regularly to connect our congregational assembly with the celebration of the Lord's Supper. Perhaps we can allow the love feast, as the Corinthians held it, to be revived in smaller circles or on special occasions as, for example, on a *Kirchentag*. But would it not be possible and meaningful, now and again at least, to begin our worship service immediately with the celebration of the Lord's Supper, so that all take note that they are unconditionally invited by the Crucified as guests—to practice at Jesus's table, in a world everywhere closed off, the fellowship of a community open to the earth and heaven, celebrating freedom in the face of its Lord and his enemies? For we are witnesses to the fact that the Christ no longer leaves us alone and has established his kingdom among us. His meal is the place at which we, his guests, celebrate the Crucified's bursting through the rule of the principalities and powers of this world; his meal makes his disciples conquerors.

Presence of Mind (1969)

Presence of mind [*Geistesgegenwart*] is one of the most beautiful German words and one of the rarest German virtues, probably formed from astonishment that the unexpected occasionally happens. It far exceeds that dimension of quick-wittedness growing from reason and wit, and it is not simply the reversal of what the Anglo-Saxons call absentmindedness. That the Spirit [*Geist*] is present [*gegenwärtig*] always presupposes Pentecost, even in a secularized world and language. It must occur on earth and through human beings, breaking through the unreasonable and giving to the rational more than the stamp of the merely expedient—that is, of what is necessary. In Christianity there is too much talk of the Holy Spirit. It is not unreasonable to demand that Christianity should give evidence of the Spirit and the Spirit's power, or at least that it should express itself in a presence of mind. Otherwise we justly lose credit.

There is no doubt that disaster looms over German Protestantism. We have treacherously yielded to the idea that we came out of the Third Reich and the war battered yet still deeply intact. We deceived ourselves (as we mostly forget today) such that, in the unimaginable distresses of the first postwar years—when we improvised, restored, strengthened institutions, and gave charitably—we forgot one final self-examination, or, better said, repentance. That was and is understandable, but disastrous. Perhaps we could not do otherwise, because in twelve years, or however long its hours lasted, we could not hurdle centuries, already physically overwhelmed. Be that as it may, it is

---

A meditation first published in *Evangelische Kommentare* (March 1969): 138–44.

time for us to stop being deceived—by talking about reconstruction, public goodwill, and all the inner or ecumenical bustle—and to face reality.

Included in this reality is the fact that among us a youth is growing up that can barely see historically, or is no longer at all aware of the two decisive experiences of our own past: the rise of dialectical theology and the church struggle. It is not merely change in generations that separates us from this youth and allows us overnight to be numbered among the aged. This youth knows it must enter a world that no longer will stand under the sign of the Christian West. But it sees us captive to that period in which, since the French Revolution, the bourgeoisie had fallen prey to nationalism and, since industrialization, systematically carried out the subjugation of the whole earth, oppressing all the weak, metaphysically supported by the power, business, and privileges of Christianity precisely when charitable, pastoral, and missionary brutality had been mitigated and egoistic interests concealed. Has the youth been wrong to see us this way?

It is futile to wander into the distance. The West German situation, since the war, is clear enough for every reasonable person, though readiness to give space to critical insight is continually on the decrease. We have not done well to recover so rapidly, thanks to the monstrous exertion of all and of every individual, likewise to the extraordinary foreign aid and the suddenly changing world-political constellation. In a decade of success we have not considered that we would have to pay with more than our work and subscribe to enforceable changes in the future. In the decade following, what was gained was cemented, and its fruit enjoyed. Patriarchal figures radiated confidence. The enormous economic and social progress appeared to justify it, and problems that emerged were relegated to the shadows. In general we were scarcely conscious that a proletariat no longer existed among us, that the middle class and the farming community more and more rapidly dissolved, melted down into a meritocracy, and that everywhere managers came to power. The parties divested themselves of the antiquated ideological garments in which they show themselves to their voters, mostly on festival days. Instead, by virtue of their actual function they became the megaphone and equalizer of interest groups. Those who did not belong to them resisted them as nonconformist and, with their own kind, formed a numerically uninteresting minority of opposition to the ruling trend and knew less and less whom they should vote for. They reacted by reading *Der Spiegel*, perhaps *Die Zeit* or the *Frankfurter Rundschau*. Naturally, a group of intellectuals was particularly affected by it and could be dismissed as "pip-squeaks" since they did not appropriately represent the so-called educated class. Nor was there generally any awareness that despite all the mutual assurances there was no striving for reconciliation with the East. The reunification of Germany was shifted *ad kalendas Grae-cas*.[1] The unification of West Europe was not achieved. Our allies were most content with our status quo, understandably wanting to see their investments amortized, with the result that the federalism to be defended by all means therefore took on Biedermeier-like shapes under what is at best a second-class leadership, all of which can no longer be remedied by any kind of reform except at the cost of the military budget.

Prelude to a Barbaric Future?

These by-no-means-complete, but only salient, entries on our debit account are often named and constantly obfuscated. We would unavoidably have to settle with them because they are on the books and other European lands are not much better at it. After the lifting of the financial crisis by touting the ever-growing social product, one could, with small steps, be content with further patchwork if in the meantime the North-South conflict had not erupted; if America had not discredited itself and the Western world through the war in Vietnam and the racial problem; if the Czech tragedy had not revealed Russia's desire to remain, if no longer the leading power of communism as such, at least of the Eastern Bloc, and to continue smoldering the fires in the Near East. The balance of political power, indicative more of interrupted war than of a desire for peace, has inexorably shifted. The following generation will have a more endangered life than we. Our experiences over the past fifty years were perhaps only the relatively harmless prelude to a barbaric future in which the issue for each and every one is pure survival.

It is to the undeniable credit of a radical wing of the academic youth that they instinctively grasped these horizons and, in more rousing fashion than that of all the experts, carried them into the hypnotized amnesia of our population. From the first moment they were feared as an infection, and attempt was made to rein them in with a health cordon. Their attempts at solidarity with stronger groups have remained touchingly naïve and shatteringly fruit-less, thus have become more and more desperate and unfortunately more grotesque. Without question, the present isolation is also self-inflicted. Yet against every irate objection it must be stated that the escalation of revolts did not begin with this youth.

Local events at the Free University of Berlin, an institution certainly no longer worthy of the name, have enabled academic and magisterial authorities

---

1. *Ad kalendas Graecas*, meaning "to the Greek calends," or never.

to express stupidity, arrogance, and harshness in a quite one-sided game, urged on by an inflammatory press. In the process it became clear in a flash that behind its mask of complacency and pomp of affluence, all of West Germany has for twenty years been living in panic-stricken anxiety over unrest. Presence of mind would have prescribed composure, humor, and generous compromises rather than the club of the police. Following the proven or perhaps still unproven model of great politics, nervousness and lack of civil courage began with deterrence. Then the spark spread to other universities.[2]

There, too, the result was the same satyr play. Since the conflict could not reach beyond the universities, they became the source of the blaze, but now to a spectacular extent. We see much that is distorted in the light of the fire, but we still see better than in the twilight, in which the owl of Minerva takes its flight. Here, if not exactly a proletariat, there were rightly dissatisfied masses without sufficient space and without individual care, with education not related to the present but mired in an outdated system and a lost universality. Critical analysis cannot possibly call this accidental and isolate it as such. The university example illustrates the mental state of our people.

We are unable to cope with the twentieth century, the true character of which is really only becoming clear to us today. And we are prepared for the approaching twenty-first only from the side of the natural sciences and technology. The façade of the reconstruction, which is not in the least criticized, conceals the spirit of the events determining our generation. It consists in the fact that through an abysmal breach in our history and in the midst of the shrinking of the globe and the advance into outer space, we have regained our connection with the nineteenth century. By this I am not referring to a consciousness that critically acknowledges or deals with its own past. In general, such a consciousness is not even alive in the humanities, to say nothing of the population in general—the politicians, citizens, workers, or the youth in particular. What I mean is the pull of mostly unshakable traditions, methods, and forces in which we who are older grew up. Those representatives of a generation once called "skeptical"—who, in the meantime, have advanced to the highest echelons of leadership—have, probably with thorough consistency, developed into opportunists of power who preserve the problematic

2. In the late 1960s, the Free University of Berlin was an important site for the emerging German student movement, also known as the 68er-Bewegung, an influential protest movement that took root in West Germany. Drawing inspiration from third-world decolonization movements and the Black Power movement in the US, the student movement challenged West Germany's alignment with the capitalist West and shone a light on the persistence of authoritarianism and the failure of the earlier generation to deal with its Nazi past. The protests soon spread across the universities of West Germany and were met with heavy police repression.

inheritance less with new ideas than with the help of cybernetics. All who prefer security to risk are willing to be guided by these opportunists. But where we avoid the great risks, we do not shape the future but end up in the past, the unpleasant features of which are covered by "bread and circuses." Though the mind may be given nourishment for a while, the spirit withers away. The collapse after two world wars has given the death blow to the idealistic faith of our fathers and reduced liberalism as a form of life to the recognition of a pluralistic and morally laissez-faire society. The classical idea of humanity becomes the special possession of modern mystery associations. An intellectual and ideological vacuum is spreading out in all sectors. A society that is so inwardly disintegrating can actually be held together with bonds to the nineteenth century. In that event, the key words read: economic expansion, social balance, a minimum of national feeling, political order, and authority of the specialists and functionaries in all institutions.

Confrontation of the Bourgeoisie and *Bürgerschreck*[3]

Again, in the face of the frequent hysteria, we have to praise the academic youth: in its intelligent representatives and so-called progressive groups it was, of course, not the first to see through these conditions, but ensured that alarms were set off about the general outrage that could not be ignored. To say that sociology became fashionable, or merely a misused playground, trivializes the problems. But with some goodwill it is understandable. In any case, here we had a lot of catching up to do. And the fact that a Marxism—strangely alienated from Asia and coupled with psychoanalysis—forms the basis of a movement "articulating" itself in Chinese-party jargon shows that these youth too are no match for scientific and technical progress. This kind of Marxism also takes the models of its theory and behavior from the nineteenth century. Thus emerges the specter of the old confrontation between the bourgeoisie and the *Bürgerschreck*, which is sometimes romantically relaxed through various happenings. If one does not want to be judged by the extremists and idiots on the Right, it is unfair to judge the other party only from the extremists and idiots on the Left. In general, people in West Germany have not yet so clearly separated themselves from the eggshells of a brown past that they should be

3. This word has been left untranslated because there is no clear equivalent in English. Here the word refers to social, cultural, and political activities and activists associated with the German student movement (e.g., anarchists, communists, punk rockers, and the provocations of the artistic avant-garde). In short, the word refers to that part of German society associated with young people who intentionally and expressively seek to shock and provoke the cultural and political conservatism of bourgeois culture.

morally outraged by the red *couleur*. The judgments of the political judiciary against former mass murderers are widely disproportionate in comparison with those against young revolutionaries, who by no means have remained unpunished. The different standards that are applied here do not support the incessantly proclaimed state under the rule of law [*Rechtsstaat*] and the impartiality of the judges.

The easiest way to punish the young revolutionaries is to deny, with formal arguments, the political mandate to student bodies. And in our democracy we also choose from worse dilemmas than the parliamentarians would afterward admit. We in the minorities very often feel violated without anyone's taking notice. "The depoliticization of the university" is a cheap slogan of those who fear the actual realities of their own politics or who, for the sake of their personal peace, incorporate science into private life, although they leave their own sexuality out of it. Naturally, one can handle individual groups more easily, especially if one plays them off against each other. But to the extent the voice of the minority resounds and is registered, it is undemocratic to forbid chosen representatives of a given community to speak politically. Different decisions may be legal and still substantially illegitimate. The discontented and suffering have a right to share in speaking and responsibility. Otherwise they are driven into anarchy. As the debate in parliament over the restless youth indicates, politicians should not really be so naïve, if their wisdom and common sense are not to be subject to considerable doubt. To respond to *Lieschen Müller*[4] and "Klein Erna"[5] and give support to the petit bourgeois [*Spießbürger*] is politically stupid when it comes to the future of a people and its most important educational institutions. Still, even the prime minister, minister, and party leader of the pied pipers do not feel ashamed in this affair. In any case, this is the impression that remains even after appreciating well-intentioned efforts.

I have personally come to know the old German university in its most ideal shape—as the arena of conflict between teachers and students on behalf of the truth; as the release for independent and critical thinking; and, consequently, as education for responsible freedom. And for more than twenty years, as ordinarius,[6] I have attempted to preserve it, always to actualize it afresh and to hand it on. The structural errors and great or minor human weaknesses were also present forty-five years ago, and certainly no less was the material distress of the student. I have nevertheless studied and taught with pleasure; nowhere, except in a couple of elite English universities, have I seen better,

4. *Lieschen Müller*, a 1951 West German musical comedy film.
5. Klein Erna, the butt of Little Erna jokes popular in Hamburg.
6. "Ordinarius" = full professor.

and I grieve with my whole heart over the loss of what has left its mark on me for my life and research. The fact that numerically small groups were able to change this into a field of rubble within two years is only understandable if one regards them as executors of an internal decay. At its core is the sudden massification of our universities and the inability of their organs and the organs of the state to structure these masses in a timely and radical way. The privy councilor ideology [*Die Geheimratsideologie*] of a "Marburg Manifesto"[7] did not grasp this at all and, like other parts of our nation, dreamed about a lost past, and therefore cooperates in the reactionary self-assertion in a really impressive way. I would like to dream along with them, but I cannot deny the reality and leave an already seriously betrayed youth in the lurch. I would rather separate myself from my own generation.

And the Church?

What does all this have to do with the church? Paul would answer: Very much in every way! For four hundred years German Protestantism has been strongly intertwined in national affairs. That its institutions to a great extent understand themselves as apolitical, and today repeatedly call for the depoliticizing of their essential forms of appearance, does not alter that fact. The human is a political being. No community can avoid this fact, especially when it is a "public right." Of course, in the last four decades, we have arduously had to adapt to democratic conditions, and not at all with sweeping success. The social pluriformity, which must not be confused with divisions of class structure, is at bottom no longer contested without too much practical knowledge about how to begin with it. The advantages of the welfare state are accepted. But in the end, the older generation, at least, continues to be oriented toward the idea of the authoritarian state. It is self-evident to anyone half-informed that the theories and practices of political democracy cannot simply be transferred to the church. Still, something considerable could be learned from that area that would make us more agile and open to our time. After all, we do not merely teach the universal priesthood of all believers. We also practice church leadership through synods without having to assert their relevance and greatest possible functioning capacity. Early Christianity and the New Testament do not at all commit us to a hierarchical-episcopal order and to

7. In April 1968 the "Marburg Manifesto" was signed by 1,618 university professors of West Germany reacting to the activities of the German student movement. The document voiced strong opposition to university reform and compared the situation in the German university to the Chinese cultural revolution.

the primacy of the office in the congregation or in the church as a whole—the beginnings of which are surely already evident in the early church; although they are, to a great extent, still intersected there by other organizational forms. For example, the Pauline doctrine of the charisms develops a totally different model for establishing the church and its service. However, in the last hundred years, anxiety in the face of enthusiasm [*Schwärmertum*] and the romantic reaction to the French Revolution have always hindered us from venturing with any consequence in this direction, or from succeeding beyond creating concessions.

Obedience to the powers that be is deeply implanted in us. A conscience bound not to the *libertas christiana* but to obligation sanctioned this obedience (as long as the obedience did not result in religious conflict and, consequently and inadmissibly, broaden the obligation). The authority of the church office reflected this obedience, and it was no accident that it could be combined with the summit-episcopacy of the prince. The theology of orders anchored it metaphysically: a series of steps led from heaven to earth and back, on which, along with the angels, Christians also climbed—or, rather, proved subservient. If, in addition to all this, it has been forgotten that Jesus had already characterized Christian obedience, in his debate with Pharisaism, not as blindness but as a mode of seeing (as love must also be), then one will proclaim, with Dorothee Sölle,[8] imagination [*Phantasie*] as an alternative to blind obedience. This affects that reality from which we come and in which, to a large extent, we stand. Nevertheless, it ignores the matter we have to represent. Christian obedience may not be formalized. It takes its orientation, measure, and promise only and permanently as a relation to that Lord who bears the unmistakable features of the Man of Nazareth and whose work is the humanizing of humanity. For this reason, we can never categorically fix or limit him to a particular activity. To join the Nazarene and to be human through his Spirit is a lifelong adventure that no system or casuistry can regulate. In him we are constantly called to presence of mind, to reason, to the uttermost use of the imagination [*Phantasie*] and to many risks, including death in discipleship.

On the way from Galilee to Golgotha, things seldom went in orderly fashion. Surprises were constantly strung together. Those who are no longer surprised

8. Dorothee Sölle (1929–2013) was a student and close friend of Käsemann and a German liberation theologian who taught, among other places, at Union Theological Seminary in New York City. Here Käsemann is most likely referring to her *Phantasie und Gehorsam: Überlegungen zu einer künftigen christlichen Ethik* (Stuttgart: Kreuz-Verlag, 1968), translated and reprinted in English as *Creative Obedience*, trans. Lawrence W. Denef (Eugene, OR: Wipf & Stock, 2007).

by anything, because they always know everything in advance, and whom the atoning death so satisfy that they are no longer caught in the adventure of the Nazarene, are spiritually dead—even if they pray without ceasing, sing, and have the thickest dogmatics in their heads. They do not know the power of the resurrection, even when they see heaven open above them and yearn for the heavenly Jerusalem. That we no longer hope in the resurrection, or that it evaporates into a belief in the immortality of the soul, has something to do with the fact that Christians have become such respectable citizens. Resurrection of the dead has no place in the realm of bourgeois order or in the sometime and somewhere behind it. Those who are willing to take risks in their living and dying are to be trusted (not merely the bravest among the obedient). For those willing to take risks live from the first commandment and encounter, day by day, the idols that must be resisted. They cannot be servants of human beings and will necessarily always be uncomfortable companions. Naturally, spines may reveal the hedgehog, but not necessarily the Christian. Conversely, suppleness and velvet paws will more likely reveal the cat or the tiger than the Christian. A sociology concerned with the Christian may yield unusually interesting critical information about visitors to worship, those who pay the church tax, and organizations and institutions. Concerning the disciple following Jesus, sociology will have nothing at all to say, because for the disciple there are no social laws or previously determined rules of the game. With the disciple—to take up Ernst Bloch[9]—the *homo absconditus* [hidden human being] is revealed, not so invisibly as to be surrounded by no turmoil or to be incorporated without difficulty into the natural history of the *homo sapiens*. If the disciple's place is to be fixed with relative appropriateness, it is to be included among those whom the Master has marked as hungering and thirsting after righteousness.

Not Ideology, but Discipleship

This is a very dangerous place, hard along the boundaries of the revolutionaries, and therefore less taken up by Christianity than it should be. Conservatives are not absolutely excluded. Romans 13 is also in the New Testament, and in it are actually rules for the community such as are also contained in the Pastoral Letters: catalogues of virtues and vices from Jewish and pagan

9. Ernst Bloch (1885–1977), German Marxist philosopher who fled from Nazi Germany to Switzerland (1933) and then went to the US, where he wrote the first two volumes of his major work, *Das Prinzip Hoffnung*. Returning to Leipzig in 1948, he drew the disapproval of Communist Party officials, who forbade him to publish and, in 1957, condemned his works. In 1961 he defected to West Germany and taught at Tübingen University.

tradition. Still, the conservatives must be true to their Lord, not (as they mostly are) to their own old Adam. One may be as reactionary as the rock in the surf, provided one is breaking the surf together with the Lord. There is no fixed pattern for the Christian because Christianity is not ideology but discipleship. Here everything can be found that would otherwise run side by side indifferently or diverge in hostility. Not even theology unites so deeply, as surely as the argument over what is decisive must be carried on in it, because we cannot be oriented without reflection. Yet there are many confessions, as was ever the case. We will achieve unity only in the solidarity of those who differ, if we want to live truly ecumenically. As long as it is clear who our Lord is, and that we strive to follow in earnest, there is a place for everyone beside us, and there is fellowship even in the midst of harshest debate or the most diverse habits of life. This applies not merely in terms of toleration toward what is unavoidably human. Rather, it has something to do with the lordship of the Crucified Nazarene who died for all and lives for all. He went and he goes straight through the camps of this earth without allowing himself to be caught by anyone. He always gathers his disciples from the most remarkable places, actually from the hedges where vagrants make their camp. His kingdom is a gathering and reconciling of the rebellious and irreconcilable.

The presence of mind of Christianity today will before anything else consist of its being reminded of this, thus of preparing for departure from the ties of bourgeois society. This cannot happen overnight, since, institutionally, at least, we are greatly entangled and cannot simply shrug off responsibility for this society like a worn-out garment. Moreover, the way into the future will for a long time lead through deserts, so that we cannot prepare for it thoroughly enough. Conversely, we have no time to lose, must view everything in terms of the needed departure. We ourselves should hear and tell everyone who is willing that the hour has struck for us. There is not the least doubt that after the collapse of the German university in its traditional shape, the churches will form the next battleground and are already such. At least with our organizations, but probably with all that we have and are, we are belatedly moving toward that zero at which our nation stood twenty-five years ago, and from which, possibly only superficially but not intellectually, it has distanced itself. Naturally, we are not called to play the role of soothsayer. But we are not allowed to close our eyes to the reality. Naturally, we may not politicize the churches and their subdivisions to the extent that they are sworn to specific parties or to the extraparliamentary opposition. On the other hand, we live in an everyday life in which the provocation to genuine democracy must be brought home to everyone due to world conflicts. Christian hallowing of this everyday life is to be conceived as an exercise of freedom, may no longer

be paralyzed as the slogan of "depoliticizing" reflects. Even political significance and effects are reflected when, in a totally inappropriate inwardness, the
managers of existing power are allowed to play on their field undisturbed so
that, thanks to our passivity, they win their auxiliary troops from our ranks,
more or less as a matter of course.

Socially and politically, the churches should not allow themselves to be classified among the interest groups, however advantageous. They have a social
duty to oppose the continually growing dominance of these groups by serving
on behalf of the minorities they have harmed, and at least creating room for
open conversation. Nor may they allow themselves or their individual members to be manipulated, be it from the Right or the Left, and above all not by
great coalitions. We have been politically misused long enough beneath the
slogan of "depoliticizing." The Gestapo used that slogan effectively when
it left heaven to the Christians and sparrows but took what was earthly to
be their domain. Against this the Barmen Declaration, clearly futile over
the course of time, made protest. The lordship of Christ does not end in
the sphere of an individual ethics; it has been affecting political and social
structures for nineteen hundred years. It may no longer be the kingdom of
an inwardness that takes flight from power into a habit of mind. Our service
commits us to all our possibilities. Otherwise we, along with the unfaithful
servant in Jesus's parable, bury the talent given us. The servant's limit is only
his own lust for power, not that of others. He will recognize expertise and
not want to admit where this expertise is missing. He will avoid especially
solemn statements, the result of which can only be that we have nothing to
say or that we avoid conflict. If there is any trumpeting at all, then it must be
done not with flutes and shawms but with those horns and trumpets which,
if necessary, according to 1 Corinthians 14:8, open a campaign. We also
quench the Spirit by tiptoeing, and we render ourselves laughable when, high
on the horse like the giants in Spitteler's[10] *Olympian Spring*, we demonstrate
against the mighty but, because the horses' hooves are tied with straw, avoid
unpleasant noise.

More Fear, Less Fear

Original sin—which manifests itself in stupidity, injustice, and complacency
—is not eradicated on earth, according to our faith. But this does not forbid
us from denouncing it, opposing it with all our might, and limiting it where

10. Carl Friedrich Georg Spitteler (1845–1924), Swiss poet, was awarded the Nobel Prize for
Literature in 1919, in appreciation of his epic *Olympian Spring*.

possible. We should not surrender politicians, industrialists, bureaucrats, and professors to it, especially when attempting to rescue students from it. That those attacked will describe it as an impermissible political misuse of Christianity cannot be held against them. The Romans crucified the Nazarene on precisely these grounds. We should have more fear of the Lord who judges us and less of earthly authorities. Our task leads into the world just as surely as it may begin in the closet and behind church walls. The Lord intends a new creation, not merely those hospitals in which the final service of love is done to the dying. Soon enough, perhaps, our voice will have to be silenced. Until then we have to use it in and out of season, to announce salvation to individuals as well as to exorcize the demons, which, understandably, are unhappy over allowing themselves to be driven out. The churches are not mystery societies. Their Lord entered the world of profanity in order not to leave the toiling, burdened, oppressed, and rejected alone there—and to block the way of the proud, of tyrants, and of illusionists. Christian presence of mind will always be vital by way of this remembrance, while church boredom grows from lack of discipleship. As long as we are not yet in heaven, we have something to do on earth, since faith without action is window dressing. We can do very much less than revolutionaries require of us—but more than we think is possible or than is good, perhaps, for us and others. The Spirit helps us in our weakness not merely in prayer but also in the courage to act. Historical criticism does not rob us of the expectation of miracles—which, instead of falling from heaven, need humans as their instruments. At issue is not what is extravagant but what is thrown at our feet in the midst of murderers, Pharisees, and Levites, just as with the good Samaritan. We need only open our eyes to do what is necessary. In the New Testament, good order is not tied to the law and the police but to the conscience and the respective needs as the only thing necessary.

Fundamentally, this always means solidarity with those in need. Prudence recommends looking away and continuing on the way to Jericho. Simplicity risks caring for the attacked and perishing in doing it. What sermon is credible that does not urge this simplicity? Lazarus lies before our very door. He asks whether we are looking out or are too busied with ourselves, perhaps even theologically and ecclesiologically. The call to Adam, "Where are you?" [Gen. 3:9] is taken up by the other, "Where is your brother Abel?" [Gen. 4:9]. We can answer both only at the same time. Where this occurs in the right way, it is said of the Samaritan (against the denying Peter), "This man was with Jesus of Nazareth" [Matt. 26:71; Luke 22:56, 59]. Can a Christian or a Christian community seriously assume that the resurrection of the dead would be of the least use to them if such an utterance were not the last word over their service?

But if this is the situation today, the Spirit who once drove Paul this way and that through Asia toward Europe points us back from our old and sated Europe toward Asia and Africa and into the Third World, without the need for visions in a dream. The cry "Help us!" can be overheard by all who do not close their ears. If Christianity were characterized by presence of mind, it would have the power to force the Western world to do its duty. With its members spiritually revolting in ecumenical unity, it could be the pacesetter of peace and rationality and could pragmatically outplay the profiteers. In doing so, it would announce that it no longer understands the everywhere rebellious youth merely as a *Bürgerschreck* but that it shares their concerns and, conversely, no longer abandons them to the ideologies. These youth also need solidarity to free them from isolation and from captivity to current events, to set them before meaningful tasks. They have sprung from narrow national defiles and eye distant banks because they justly loathe the managers of a European middle-class politics and will no longer allow themselves to be blinded by the affluence of a society cranking up its own lust for pleasure higher and higher.

The youth make it easy for us to indict them. In the churches too, voices that react, in concern and indignation, to their wild carryings-on are on the rise. Privately and officially, pamphlets are handed out with partly blasphemous, elsewhere childish slogans. Church leaders feel moved to take positions that make for sharp separation. The confessional movement "No Other Gospel" triumphs: Did it not give a warning for years, without getting a suitable hearing among the institutions? All this is understandable when one is personally caught in the whirlpool and compares the current attacks on Christianity with those still ringing in the ear from one's youth. We will not give the least concession to friend-enemy thinking, on whatever side it spreads. We will not allow all the racket to be taken for an articulation of the truth, will not recognize the dullest, unsalable goods of rationalism to be the final theological achievements, even when they are broadcast on television and sold under professorial assistance. Sociological criticism in the church is meaningful, but with each one who wants to be a Christian, sociological restricting of the gospel will bite into granite and, in any case, rapidly collapse from within from an inner poverty. Still, we should make various things clear before we sound the trumpet for the united counterattack.

First of all, it is necessary to consider quite cold-bloodedly that for over twenty years we have lived in the windbreak, an abnormal situation for the community of Jesus. The one for whom this has not been unpleasant has in any case not possessed the least sense for the unavoidably approaching storm, and just as our entire nation has rested on imagined laurels without feeling the thorns. In a certain respect, it is desirable to be a theologian today, since faith and superstition are encountering each other once more as befits a respectable theology. In any case, we are out of the zone of silent indifference. What we have to say and where the shoes pinch is under the magnifier again. The so-called world has this right. We can only welcome it for its own sake when the theological offspring strips us naked before entering a position that more than ever wants to see traditional convictions congruent with the whole person in clarity and resolve. This cannot happen early or thoroughly enough. It trains us in the art of discussion with humor and passion, in which German Protestantism displays an enormous deficit.

Second, we should consider that this youth has presumably appeared with a lighter backpack than we who were stuffed full with dogmatics and historical research. At certain times it is more important to be able to represent a few things precisely and tirelessly than to represent the academic type that repeats a style of education gotten out of hand. Life and death at times depend on one's being movable. Our churches are more in need of mobility than of armor. If too much wisdom has been swallowed before the exam, experience indicates that later on digestive disturbances inhibit the joyfulness of inner growth. Third, we should give the following generation room to break with their forebears, as we likewise did as disciples of dialectical theology, of the rediscovery of the Reformation, and of existentialism. Our efforts have clearly not been so outstanding that we would have achieved the great breakthrough. It has more or less led merely to resistance.

Now, I regard opposing this resistance, and opposing *à tout prix* the experiments of those who are younger, to be impractical. For theologians as for all others, one's own experiences are more useful than all the pedagogical and disciplinary measures. If one has often enough butted one's head against the wall, one most often draws the necessary consequences. And slow ripening benefits not only wine. If the professors of theology would for a while be set in the situation of the missionaries in the bush among the headhunters, they would learn a lot from it. That the emphasis of the disciplines of church history, systematics, and New Testament in our days passes over to practical theology appears to me to be long overdue (as little as I think of neglecting my own field). Fourth, it needs asserting that church education was to a great extent useless, given that young people so easily drown in the deluge of the university and that in theology they must once more be thrown the rudimentary sentences of [Luther's] Small Catechism as a life preserver. Whoever takes a high-and-mighty attitude today has perhaps, before first beating their breast, not sufficiently considered the lack of effect in average preaching and instruction. Whoever is learning that, in worship and in religious instruction, their children are becoming irritated with Christianity may judge the youth more mercifully and the alleged servants of the Word more bluntly, especially when one belongs to their number.

Rationalization of the Church's Big Business

Whatever the situation, the undeniable crisis should in no case lead us to strive, as in politics, for a great coalition of all who prefer apologetics and the defensive to robust debate. Today, at every place, at every time, and in every way, we must take our place with the critics one by one. They may form basic groups. We must meet them not as functionaries of an organization but as disciples of the Nazarene. This detoxifies the atmosphere, forces us to objectivity as well as to humanity, releases us from shortness of breath, and allows the initiative very rapidly to pass to oneself. Wild creatures become quite well mannered and even attentive when the Lord appears in the place of institutions. The church's presence of mind is always expressed in the fact that it leaves the field to him when traditions and organizations have become questionable. Here we may not in the least give way; here there must be constant dispute despite the risks. The primacy of Christology ahead of anthropology and ecclesiology, to say nothing of sociology, is not merely theologically decisive. It must be practiced and taken account of in our behavior.

Then, too, deeply penetrating church reforms will be necessary if possible, however much frustration and pain they will bring and however patiently we must proceed with them. It is absolutely out of the question that our "big business," like our economic activities, should and would have to be subject to a "rationalization." We must keep in mind the fact that every ineffectiveness costs power, money, and people, which should be urgently invested elsewhere. More yet, every ineffectiveness drains us of trust, courage, and offspring. This would have to be dealt with in more detail. But hints may allay the suspicion that real imagination is lacking. What appears to me to be unconditionally required—in the cities, first of all—is the abolition of the parish district. The pastoral office in its present shape is overtaxed. In any case, congregations can no longer be adequately entrusted with soul care and the diaconate, to say nothing of house calls—though they are vitally important given the diminishing of contact within the church. Under such circumstances the parish is illusionary. Church centers, in which widely diverse teams of theologians and so-called laity collaborate and share the tasks according to the capacities available, or hand on to voluntary assistants for specific emergencies, are better suited to the conditions. Poorly attended worship services miss their purpose. Whoever shies away from a somewhat longer church path should leave it entirely alone. The sermon should at least be dutifully prepared by the pastors in common. At regular intervals there should be arrangement for a sermon to be read, or for an address at worship held by a layperson qualified by calling, and with a discussion to follow, in which perspectives and problems of concrete everyday life, of life at work, of the diaconate, the *oecumene*, and of theology should be discussed. What is traditionally called edification should be promoted in private circles and besides information tended to in Bible studies.

In conjunction with this, the study of theology is decidedly to be reformed. It too no longer fulfills its purpose of guaranteeing the "pure doctrine" in the best possible way. It taxes the intelligence of at least a third of the students, cramps them personally and alienates them from the future world in which they will live. Actually, another third of academically trained theologians would totally suffice to engage in common preparation of the sermon and church instruction and to cultivate urgently needed contact with intellectuals and specialists of all types. In this way we would unburden the universities. Work in the faculties could be intensified, the standard considerably raised. The individual would more intimately gather with teachers and fellow students. A seminary-diaconal education of the remaining theologians by the churches would not need to lead to a *Clerus minor*[11] if, from the outset, special tasks were undertaken in terms of the modern world of work and society and later allowed for no difference in salary.

The goal is not to lower education—which is in no way necessarily connected with this proposal—but to end an illusionary uniformity of the educational path that corresponds neither to a pluriform and continually specializing society, to individual talent or inclination, nor to the requirements of a community service structured on teamwork. If it succeeded, this tendency would clearly gain more and more pastors or full-time workers, a situation that should have been taken care of in another, if at all possible, non-diaconal calling. The minority of academic theologians, single-mindedly prepared, would probably raise the general level in a fruitful way. If at all possible, education should include a year spent in another confession, on the mission field, or in developing lands, in theological-pastoral refresher courses within intervals of three to five years to be made obligatory.

Protestantism is moving toward the most difficult crisis of its history. We are not spared great risks, and we can sense great opportunities. We need presence of mind as never before.

---

11. The Latin term *Clerus minor* in this case is a reference to lay ministers.

⊹ 11 ⊹

Love, Which Rejoices in the Truth
(1972)

C hristian existence is concerned with connecting truth and love. The history of the churches proves how difficult this is. Throughout that history attempt has again and again been made to reduce the two to a single one: earlier the opinion dominated that whoever supported truth also served love along with it, since for human beings nothing is more important than truth connected with eternity. The more one became conscious of one's own historicity and was detached from metaphysical thinking, the more the reverse slogan prevailed: since you love your neighbor even from the greatest distance, you prove the power of the truth known to you. Both views can be correct, since in fact truth and love belong inseparably together in our life. For good reason, Paul writes in 1 Corinthians 13:6 that "love rejoices in the truth." But precisely by doing so he separates the two. My first thesis is that we do not really know or have either truth or love if we separate the two or if we simply identify the one with the other. In either instance the result is an unsalutary confusion.

It should be stated quite openly that for the most part Christianity was inclined to deny love for the sake of truth, as conversely to allow its faith to be absorbed by love. Its mission and its debate with the so-called heretics

A lecture given in Los Angeles at the International Congress of Learned Societies in the Field of Religion. First published in *Religion and the Humanizing of Man*, ed. James M. Robinson (Missoula, MT: Gateway Printing, 1973), 55–65, and in *Evangelische Theologie* 33 (December 1973): 447–57.

irrefutably record the intolerance with which millions were violated, tortured, and murdered, with the result that the truth portrayed in such fashion had to appear as a horrible delusion. Seen from that perspective, the Enlightenment periods are really luminous. In those periods the person was accepted without a conversion being required. For the sake of past but not forgotten guilt, all who proclaim and practice the gospel of humanity deserve our sympathy, or at least our respect, even when they do it in the name of a theology of the death of God. Extreme solutions of this type reveal how incredible the Christianity of all churches has become. As long as we are merely enraged over this we are obviously not able and willing realistically to take note of the inhumanity of our world. Consciously or unconsciously we still assume a hierarchy of values that the White Man created. But then our eyes and unfortunately also our reason become dulled to the needs of those who have become and are daily the objects of the exploitation and tyranny of this hierarchy of values.

It should be clear that I am not in the least prepared—for the sake of some kind of faith, confession, theology, or institution—to minimize the universal human duty to love everyone. But this gives me the right to remind us of a problem that since Augustine must be treated in dogmatics, a problem that tore religious communities apart and still today has the power to distinguish the spirits. It stands under the watchword of *fides caritate formata* [faith formed by love] and harks back to the Pauline statement in Galatians 5:6 about faith active in love. Naturally, no objection is to be raised to this if, according to the word of the apostle, this formula simply states that without love faith is meaningless and imaginary. Still, the meaning of the key Latin term is that faith is only the disposition of love, and conversely love is not only the fulfillment of the law but also the actual intention and reality of faith. Faith, then, has its reality only from love, thus becomes its point of departure and path of march. Put theologically, this means giving to sanctification priority over justification. Not by accident Reformation Protestantism defended itself most violently against this view and clothed its resistance in the antithetically intended formula of the *fides verbo formata* [faith formed by the Word]. Here, faith has its nature and continuance solely from the hearing of the divine Word. Love then appears as the result and protection of such hearing. It is the thankful answer to the evangelical message actively to be made known in the concrete relationships of our everyday life. To many who are no longer acquainted with the church's dogmatic tradition, this problematic will appear as confusing, the repetition of controverted theological formula as antiquated. But as a science, theology cannot dispense with recalling a contested tradition, if its intention is to gain orientation and mediate security in the jungle of diverse traditions. Christian faith must allow itself to be asked whether it still has its own object to represent or whether it is useful only to an old and new morality as handyman for the dependent. Perhaps, because of the lethargy of our hearts, the unreason of our heads, the lack of instinct in our wills, there must continually be stated what we should already know. Faith need not be ashamed of auxiliary service. But theology is superfluous when our impulses can be led away from sound human reasoning by a general ideology or a particular social pedagogy. In its function the claim of truth can never be altered to a program of action, even when it occurs under the theme of love.

Thus my second thesis reads: as soon as we enter the sphere of concretion, what love really means and how it should be manifest is not at all settled from the outset. As a rule, the given situation spoils the prettiest concepts, so that we are handed over either to a schematic convention and its casuistry or to personal discretion. But if we have recognized something to be currently needed, we do not yet escape the ambivalence of the correct insight, of goodwill, of the deed to be done. In all of love it is a matter of relations. But relations have the fatal characteristic that they can be manipulated, misused, or refused by the partner. More strongly than by our intention love is defined by the fact that it must be accepted. At least the disciple of the Crucified has no illusions about how seldom even genuine love arrives at its goal. Psychoanalysis may actually deny the possibility of ever acting unselfishly. In any event we all know the phenomenon of misguided, despairing, falsely interpreted love. This does not end in the personal sphere. Revolutions show that the proclamation of universal human love can lead to bloody terror. In everyday life it is often unmasked as a beautiful dream, shattered as soon as there is someone who is unsympathetic toward us or with whom we must live longer. The many books written on this theme at least make clear that the situation is not so simple and obvious as is usually maintained. Love is variously shaped and ambiguous, often a pseudonym of our egoism and our blindness. It cannot do without a definition by what we call truth. Paul praises it as the highest charism and then in clarifying adds: "It . . . rejoices in the truth."

This sounds like a devotional sentence and of course has been understood as such. The theologians should not settle for this. They are called to reflection and must allow themselves no anxiety that others view their distinctions as hairsplitting. Whoever ignores experience by making speculative or pragmatic leaps, held fast in dogmatic tradition, lands, together with what they wish, in a reality that is always complicated. We are, of course, oriented to love, and marriages awaken the impression as if it were the simplest matter in the whole world. But comedy and tragedy make clear the embarrassment and aberrations that, in everyday life, continually render what is most necessary and patently obvious the most difficult and often the most unreasonable. Here, as nowhere else, the humanity of human beings is at stake and must not be left to theories and experiments. We do not have humanity as a fixed possession. Whoever does not deceive oneself is at best on the way. Inhumanity and beastliness dominate our relationships and thus ourselves more forcibly than truth and love, which, not by accident, are described by the New Testament as eschatological blessings of salvation. When Ernst Bloch opposes to the Christian assertion of the *Deus absconditus* [the hidden God] his utopia of the *homo absconditus* [the hidden human being], he offers merely an atheistic alternative. Theologically, the two belong together. We are not yet what we shall be, according to 1 John 3:2. And according to Romans, together with the unredeemed creation, we wait for the revelation of the glorious freedom of the children of God [8:21, 23]. It is one of the greatest errors of traditional anthropology that we define what is human by the category of being rather than of becoming. We do so even when we speak of development. But in doing so we miss what is fragmentary, the dissonances and the discontinuities of our life. The disturbances are felt to be abnormal. But there is not enough room for the unexpected where one imagines one knows what is normal. In the age of the computer we certainly do not get by without statistics and programmers. But the specifically human will always maintain its place in the area of the unpredictable whether we deplore it or feel that it is good luck. We are never free of the theoretical and practical dilemma of uniting truth and love instead of separating them, or of leveling their dialectic, or, according to situations and opportunity, of giving precedence to the one or the other. The dilemma reveals the deepest crisis of a humanity ever threatened and to be won ever anew.

My third thesis serves to solve the dilemma just noted. We must, in any case in Christian theology, define the relation of truth and love from the horizon of freedom. I know that this last concept also, when taken by itself, is no less problematic than the other two. It gains fixed contours only in relation to them—that is, by marking the place where their possible conflicts intersect. According to the popular view, theologians must move in the sphere of harmony, not of conflict, and even in their proclamation of freedom keep strictly to it. My firm opposition to this is that in such an instance they cannot at all bring the message of freedom. There is freedom only in the concrete, thus in the area of tensions. Whoever may find pleasure and pain in abstractions, theologians, however, by virtue of their calling, have to do with conflicts. They preserve their humanity by not avoiding conflicts in any way. Otherwise they should not have the word *freedom* on their lips.

To clarify this a bit, I will return to the passage in Galatians 5:6 already cited, which speaks of faith active in love. No one will by any means be able to call the context "lovely." The entire epistle is an embittered polemic against aggressive Judaism in favor of the freedom of a gentile Christian community. The conflict with Peter, prince of the apostles, used as an example, is positioned in Galatians 2:14 under the keyword "truth of the gospel." It is made totally clear to the Galatian Christians that this truth stands and falls with the freedom given them from the Mosaic law. Concessions such as Peter made at Antioch, evidently under strong personal pressure and with the best intentions, betray the gospel, even when intended to prevent an irreparable breach. They fall under the solemnly uttered curse in 1:8–9, which applies even to angels. Paul is thus aware of an absolute limit to the love so effusively praised in 1 Corinthians 13. This limit is set in exactly the same way against the Corinthian enthusiasts who boast of their Christian freedom and practice it in a radical way. If the neighbor's conscience is harmed, or the edification of the community hindered, such freedom is nothing but arbitrariness. The apostle thus finds himself in a double front, against nomists as well as enthusiasts. The truth may not be infringed on for the sake of love; love may not be infringed on for the sake of truth. That is, if the two are not to be lost. Coherent with this assertion is the apostle's unique relationship to the other practical problems in his congregations. He in no way rejects compromises. Quite the contrary, they are continually advised. In 1 Corinthians 9:19ff., he describes in moving words his readiness for service to all, and he expressly includes Jews under the law. Jewish Christians may remain true to their tradition undisturbed, while its acceptance is denied gentile Christians.

Conversely, for Paul the eating of flesh dedicated to pagan gods seems personally altogether harmless. Nevertheless, the enthusiasts who appeal to such insights are strictly admonished to desist from it in the presence of scrupulous members of the congregation. Whether Paul himself is a resolute ascetic or not, he allows for marital intercourse, and even divorce when desired by the non-Christian partner. In Romans 14, he relativizes existing taboos, but he opposes the emancipatory tendencies of Christian women and slaves in 1 Corinthians. And in 1 Corinthians 15:29, he at least does not scold the superstition of those who allow themselves to be baptized as magical proxy for their dead relatives. We could almost say that he thoroughly agrees with the strong in the matter, but he in fact appears on the side of the weak. Is this not opportunism and self-contradiction in flagrant form? How can one radically affirm truth to the point of cursing the one who deviates, and at the same time continually call for consideration and love toward the overscrupulous? Are not conflicts settled here in a totally arbitrary way and casuistically fogged? Since this problematic is nowhere more clear in the New Testament than in Paul, we will discuss our theme by way of his example. Does not his statement that love rejoices in the truth remain a beautiful illusion—worse yet, an edifying phrase—when it becomes concrete and complicated, thus when realities encounter us?

These questions need to be put in order to explain why I am throwing the concept of freedom into the debate. Without it we go around in circles and do not get free of the conflict of truth and love in the Christian life. Of course, it must first of all be repeated that in Galatians 2:14, as well as in the entire epistle, Paul identifies the "truth of the gospel" with freedom. It is precisely this that he reinforces by taking up the keyword of the enthusiasts in 1 Corinthians 3:21: "All things are yours." This is interpreted very pointedly and with cosmic breadth: "Whether Paul or Apollos or Cephas or the world or life or death or the present or the future—all belong to you, and you belong to Christ" [1 Cor. 3:22–23]. Accordingly, for the apostle, freedom is not mere togetherness in the lordship of Christ but its earthly form of appearance. It is a life that is confident, unbiasedly accepting and using everything and, conversely, most deeply held by nothing but Christ. Freedom is this alone— and always in the area of conflicts, threats, and anxieties and endangered by arrogance. In this situation the Corinthians find themselves with their groups in conflict with each other. Surely, the gospel could also be described by righteousness, redemption, peace, joy, sonship, sanctification, and much else. Yet they are without exception signatures that do not characterize Christian *humanitas* sufficiently sharply according to its nature as being in conflict.

There is freedom only in resistance to the principalities and powers dominating the earth, which Paul sees summarized in the trio of law, sin, and death and to which he allows our fleshly existence to be subject. With theories one cannot do anything about them. They can only be overcome in praxis. Therefore, all theological concepts are meaningful only as signposts and as the horizon of a particular praxis; otherwise they are totally worthless, at most the building blocks of a Christian ideology. But if law, sin, and death are entangling the whole world, then they mark the status quo in which we always find ourselves. Then Christian freedom must always denote exodus from the usual and apparently obvious. Even when this freedom outwardly corresponds to tradition and convention, it will retain the element of the surprising that elicits the remark "See there, a human being!" But it will far more frequently call forth the irritation normally connected with an exodus from usual views and ways of behaving. Role expectations are burst by it. It is never certain that the freed Christian is dedicated to a permanent camp, a ruling opinion, specific principles and norms as a party supporter. If Christians do this for a limited time, their solidarity will remain critical, and it will often be expressed as opposition and protest against the majority. Unique individuals avoiding manipulation, they must desist from the current trend, and the society around them will often be uncomfortable.

Consequently, this is to be put more pointedly. When law, sin, and death in actual fact most deeply manifest the earthly status quo, beget reaction and revolution, beget the meritocracy with its exploitation and its conformism, every status quo of bourgeois or Marxist society is always put in question by the freedom of the Christian stigmatized by the call to exodus. Unfortunately, for the most part, church history witnesses to this only insofar as it is the history of heresy. In general, Christianity has been imprisoned as a conservative tradition, able to be regarded as a power for preserving the state, thus not by accident for subsidizing it. For this reason, revolutions were almost always connected with an attack on church institutions—and, in fact, on the gospel itself. To be fair, we should of course concede that the situation is the same with human history. In it as well, humanity has without exception been more disavowed than attested. Whoever on the basis of such experience does not invariably despair of humanity should not judge and damn the gospel simply on the basis of history. The human being cannot be defined a priori as an *animal rationale* when not philosophical theory but historical reality is in view. For this very reason the historical disgrace of Christianity is no ultimate proof against the truth of the gospel. It only makes clear that Christian freedom cannot be ruined or secured by institutions. Such a freedom reaches only so far as the message of the gospel is followed by an ever-new openness to reversal and new departure. In this reversal and departure, however, it has always occurred that gods and demons are overthrown; the social status quo and the political status quo no longer remain taboo, and they begin to totter. The frank response to every possible risk should be that in our present world Christian freedom must more than ever be conceived on the basis of this promise and task. The trumpet must be blown for attack instead of for defense. The individual is only helped when one engages in battle and resists the powers of the world. Today, care for human beings is care for the earth.

With this statement I have reached the other side of my problematic. The truth of the gospel is manifest in the freedom of a Christian over against the ruling powers, opinions, groups, and social conventions. But how is it with love? Will it not necessarily deny freedom by accommodation, concessions, and compromises? Based on the requirement of love, have not the churches forever seen Christian duty in a mediating balance or in a strict neutrality between contending parties? Have they not been engaged in merely making statements, and in fact paid homage to opportunism? Did not Paul fall prey to self-contradiction by relativizing proper insights in concrete situations? Do we not unavoidably fall into theological schizophrenia when we seek to connect truth and love? Whoever does not inquire in such radical fashion stirs up foam and is unable to think at all.

I refer once more to 1 Corinthians 3:21ff. There, in grandiose fashion, the freedom of the Christian is based on one's belonging to the *Regnum Christi* [reign of Christ] and making this known on earth. What is all-important here is the sudden change: "All belong to you, and you belong to Christ" [3:22–23]. Freedom is thus described *sub contrario* [under the opposite] as being under a lordship. Romans 6:12ff. sharpens this by speaking of freedom as a way of obedience and in fact of slavery. We must take this as the key to our problem, and in no case may we employ it idealistically. Obedience is not a variation of Christian freedom; rather, the latter is the concretion of obedience. Neither may we make the truth of the gospel into a system of individual truths derived from a generic term, and to be casuistically developed. The truth of the gospel—according to 1 Corinthians 15:1ff., for example—is nothing less than the risen Christ, who, contrasted with other redeemers by the marks of the Crucified, creates for himself on earth a community that follows after him. We have him only when he has us, and thus becomes our Lord. Obedient faith is the only proper relation to him. When there is reference to salvation, peace, justification, reconciliation, grace, joy, and sanctification, it describes the experience of the disciple. But what is constitutive for the disciple is that one must continually listen to the voice of his Lord and in such fashion continue the earthly way of the Exalted One.

As this Lord gives himself in the fullness of his gifts, conversely he lays claim to us precisely by being and remaining our Lord with an exclusivity nothing can relativize. In the New Testament the first commandment—"I am the LORD your God. . . . You shall have no other gods before me" [Exod. 20:2–3; Deut. 5:6–7]—is taken up in Christology. Only when we allow Christ and none beside him to be and remain our Lord do we gain freedom from the powers of the world that continually seize hold of us in our flesh. Then, we necessarily come into continual conflict with these powers and their forces, are thus called to testing, and also to an exodus from their power and whatever earthly status quo there might be. In so doing we show that we belong to the kingdom of the Risen One and also suffer the fate of the Crucified, the woes of the new birth toward the humanity of the children of God.

Where God is at work in Christ, just as at the first creation, God is at work to bring about those who are and want to be nothing else than genuine human beings. As the earthly realization of his lordship, his freedom frees us most deeply from caring about ourselves (which plunges us into despair and pride) and thus opens us for the neighbor and the earth. Those who no longer need to care for themselves have time and power and interest for others and cannot retain freedom for themselves; they must hand it on. Precisely this denotes Christian love: to create space for the neighbor and the earth as the space of an open life. Again, this reveals participation in the kingdom of the Risen One as participation in the sufferings of the Crucified. The breakthrough toward a common humanity occurs by way of the same promise, the same danger, the same pains as one's own birth toward the man or woman of God. Love is the freedom of the children of God turned to others and all, the truth of the gospel in the mode of participation and communication. There is no conflict between truth and love, as certainly as there is misunderstanding and falsification of the two, and as certainly as both are to be preserved only in the context of continual conflicts. Both are one because Christ in his relation to us is their content. Both are different insofar as the Lord who gives himself gives us freedom, not merely as his intended gift for us but also as a task of preserving, since a liberated humanity can only be expressed in common humanity.

We have not yet answered the last question, whether in the concrete situation what was theologically explained in its unity and diversity does not continually scandalize or get completely muddled. Before us, then, is the rigorous dogmatism that separated confessions and damned heretics as well as that love which would do no one harm and relativizes truth. To be a disciple of Jesus is never a settled reality. The temptations of the flesh and the force of the powers threatening us cannot be denied. Humanity and common humanity on earth retain the mark of the provisional, and their consummation is still to come. But above all, it is necessary to listen and to live knowing that the Lord never gives himself to his disciples once for all and is always ahead of them. We do not have him in our power when we name ourselves after him. What is decisive is to what extent he in constantly new ways takes us into his power, to what extent the gospel continually seizes hold of us, shapes us according to his image and frees for his service. It indicates both the promise and the limits of being a Christian. In it truth and love affect each other. Put theologically: the primacy of Christology is not only dogmatically but practically the central point of our life. This means that there cannot and must not be any concessions and compromises whatsoever when we must give an account of the Lord who defines us and the freedom he has given us as the earthly realization of his lordship. Here ends that other duty, here begins the unavoidable conflict with the world and with a false Christianity, and here freedom leads to offense and the cross. The Christian may sacrifice everything except the Lord and the freedom that is the mark of Christ's lordship on earth. Otherwise the Christian lapses into idol worship, is no longer identifiable as a Christian, and must betray the gospel of truth.

But if this is preserved, then everything else is allowed and is possible. In the end, the one whom the Lord has bound can no longer be bound by principles, norms, conventions, and social structures and thus also no longer by dogmatic theories, church, and confessional forms of community. To the extent these things have value, they exercise the function of incentives for reflection and experimentation, no more and no less. Without reflection and experiment there is no life. Each one has their own particular status, their own capabilities and weaknesses. Each lives from traditions and institutions handed on, is directed toward cooperation and acting on someone's behalf. Without fellowship faith is crippled, and in the course of time it changes its impact with the changing situation. Because human existence and the earth are at stake, the Christian can either adapt to or oppose antiquities. But the Christian cannot become uniform because one must serve, and will not become uniform because one must bring freedom. Love respects human differences because it is realistically oriented to the concrete and abhors rigid conformism, because it is engaged for the sake of humanity as well as of the individual creature. Its Lord alone is its limit. He dealt with all where they were, and yet he continually broke through the existing taboos for the sake of individual life. As long as his freedom to remain our Lord is not infringed, we can sacrifice our own human freedom, and in fact must do so.

In conclusion, this may be intensified in the statement that today more than ever faith must develop reason and imagination [*Phantasie*]. All the churches, along with our world, are in one of the profoundest crises of their history. It cannot be denied that they all are urgently in need of reforms and exodus from earlier ruts. But their needs are overshadowed by the crisis of reason, which everywhere shows itself to be inferior and to a great extent helpless against the mechanisms, apparatuses, and forces of the economy, technology, and social and political conditions. To come to its aid with the utmost energy, with all the wealth of imagination on the part of love, even affirming the most extreme means, is the commandment of the hour as well as of faith that acknowledges Christ as the salvation of the earth. The battle against stupidity is more strenuous and apparently more hopeless than that against evident evil, because it is carried on in the undergrounds of society and awakens the outrage of the majorities. Without reason and imagination [*Phantasie*], the earth sinks into chaos, humanity is lost, and brutality will always demand new victims. For the sake of the Crucified, the churches and their members cannot remain neutral here but must uncover injustice wherever it occurs and cooperate in its removal. In just this way today, love rejoices in the truth.

✝ 12 ✝

The Proclamation of the Cross of Christ in a Time of Self-Deception (1974)

As Paul states in 1 Corinthians 1:18ff., the message of the cross of Christ is scandalous. Whoever can imagine the figure of the One hanging on the gallows must find it hideous. Whoever tries to wrest from such a death a last shred of meaningfulness, as is usually the habit with one's own dying, is helpless. Already in antiquity it appeared perverse to connect a message of salvation with it, and in every period pious folks will feel it to be a blasphemy when divine revelation is maintained at precisely this point. Approximately two thousand years have inured us to these offenses. Obviously, we more or less grow accustomed to everything. Today's film production brings it home to those who no longer learn of the horrors of war. But it is something else whether we get to see horror and shamefulness without being able to change anything by it, or whether we connect the salvation of the world with the murder on Golgotha. The theme of self-deception is directly involved when we ask why it is we no longer always and immediately ever think of the darkness over Christ's cross where it is spoken of. Why are we so inexplicably inured to the scandal of its Christian interpretation? No doubt, the church is first of all responsible for it. It has its perilous effect in our speaking mostly of the cross instead of the Crucified, thus replacing the person of Jesus with a symbol that subtly more and more loses its vividness and its weight and facilitates thoughtlessness. Heroicized or trivialized, the cross that no longer depicts the Man of Sorrows in the concrete can be made an emblem of graves and churches, a piece of jewelry for women, clergy, and the military. Then its reflection is such that the Crucified becomes a heroic silent sufferer, an object of tender sympathy and finally of kitsch or pious business acumen. But need one be disturbed here? What was just referred to may appear harmless as long as it is not a symptom of a flight from the reality of the Crucified. But just this is to be feared, and it is often proven to be the case, that we remove from his image the hideousness of the Grünewald passion in order to get ourselves out of the danger zone of the scandalous and to render him harmless. He and we become not only unbelievable but strangely untrue when we visualize him otherwise than he encountered us in reality and once for all.

According to Luther's Small Catechism, no one can come to Jesus and believe in him as Lord without the work of the Holy Spirit. If this statement is true, the demonic shows itself in the attempt—always ascertainable in church history—to domesticate the Nazarene in a new way; to put an end to Golgotha due to its sinister character, so acutely sensed by pagans; and to divert our message of salvation from the underlying scandal. Everything is falsified where the single scene fades that shows us the One judged as godless and convicted as a political insurgent before the gates of the Holy City, in an earthly no-man's-land. But whoever is firmly fixed within tabooed limits and ideological encampments must also haul the Christ to wherever one wants him, make him a partisan of a doctrine, a representative of a convention, the projection of one's fantasy. If he no longer sets us before his face—that is, in the field of his death by crucifixion—we set him in our shadow, and thereby end in demonic deception, and remain in debt to the earth for the truth about him.

In any event, what pertains to this truth is that on Golgotha two men are hanging alongside him who have been sentenced as zealots, thus as political criminals with religious motives. I emphasize this aspect, though it is not the most important for me, because with us at present the political task of the Christian community is hotly debated, and I would like to express my agreement with the church memorandum dedicated to this theme. In the no-man's-land in which the Nazarene dies we unavoidably have to do with politics, whether or not we want to. It is correct that in the church struggle against the Nazis we almost universally restricted access to this insight and lived with the illusion of being able and obliged to limit our resistance to the churchly realm. But it is just as correct to say that neither our opponents nor the alleged neutral observers attributed such an intention to us. According to them there was only political resistance or none at all. Such an alternative is in fact meaningful only where we must decide between humanity and inhumanity. In this situation a Christian statement or a church statement is always and necessarily a political factor. Whoever denies this seeks and finds at this point a third possibility for Christians and the church, makes of the gospel a call to private piety. Further, such a person does not consider that even silence toward existing situations and the uncritical recognition of traditional convention have political consequences. Our Protestant Christianity is still most intimately attached to a bourgeoisie, which for centuries regarded inwardness as the place for religion but toward the outside heralded nationalism and justified it by the fourth commandment. Especially for pietism—which, despite its origins, became the vanguard of a conservative bourgeoisie—since the French Revolution, the alteration of traditional order, to say nothing of every interference with inherited property and moral convention, had a sulfuric smell. One was still ready to risk for this faith. Usually, however, one rather risked civil courage in the economic sphere than in political conflicts, where experts were allowed to act and restless youth to react. On the other hand, I do not claim that Jesus pursued political concerns and urged his disciples to do so. Still, the legend of the Bethlehem massacre of the children indicates that, from the beginning, he was politically suspect and that he died before the gates of the Holy City as one thrust out by the "good" and ruling society.

Church or theological authority cannot overlook or obscure the fact that the first commandment has consequences that are unavoidably political. God—who claims the world as God's creation and wants to be served in our everyday lives—at most leaves children, the sick, and the aged in peace and quiet. But he commands us to care not merely for the soul but also for the body, for the welfare and salvation of our neighbor. We therefore cannot look on when the neighbor's conditions on earth are life destroying, and it is not enough merely to respond to it with alms. We ourselves are needed totally when the other suffers and is cast out. What this means in a shrinking world is clear, since now, by virtue of increasing information, we see our neighbors with ever greater clarity, as far as in South Africa and South America, in India as well as in the Eastern Bloc. They put the question whether we will give to the Creator what the Creator is due—that is, what is human in us as in others—or whether we will betray the Lord of the earth with what is human in us and others, and where possible, with the pretense that we should not meddle in God's affairs. Certainly, such an alternative does not end outside the political sphere. Along with Golgotha, "Caesar or Christ?" is one of the great themes of our history and a continual question posed to Jesus's disciples. Are we prepared to enter into the discipleship of our Lord before the gates of Jerusalem, of Babylon, and—if it should come to that for us!—of capitalist society? Perhaps we are spared from doing this in the most radical way, for which there are remarkable examples in the history of the church. In any case, our hearts are not allowed the neutrality of the observer. If the heart is truly made restless by the question of the divine rule in the world and of our neighbor's welfare, it will forever behave in a politically restless way. Positioned by the Crucified, rest cannot possibly be the citizen's first duty.[1]

We must proceed further. As the title above the cross indicates, Jesus also died as a political insurgent and, as such, became like those hanged alongside him (though he was not a zealot). To this extent, he represents not only entanglement in the contradiction of earthly powers but also a God who can be scorned as a failure. At the side of the Crucified, along with the faith of his disciples, the superstition of his despisers takes root. We are at an alternative: either we are witnesses of the One whom the dying Christ calls his Father or we claim to be masters of our own fate and in every possible way assert ourselves against a supposedly defeated God. Sharply put, we maintain that we have to do with the reality of a world that lives most profoundly in resistance to the God of the crucified Jesus and that, for the believer, is thus substantially (despite all the advances of civilization) a world that again and again, and increasingly, reveals that it is a jungle. From Golgotha the brutality of a world that is selfish and tears itself apart is even more obvious than cynics state. As early as the second century, Christians were accused of atheism because they de-deified the world. This indictment has its indisputable right. Golgotha and Olympus cannot tolerate each other. The first commandment is opposed to all mythology. It is comical that Christian groups still defend themselves against Bultmann's requirement to demythologize, as if they personally had to deal with Beelzebub. This is what happens when one no longer knows that the Crucified in fact and necessarily "demythologized" the world and those in it long before conflict over the Bible.

Historical criticism of the Bible should at last no longer be treated as a menace or as a reason for the weakness and lack of courage of a Christianity become bourgeois. The propagandists of anxiety and church division moving about in the country stultify themselves and their hearers as long as they do not indicate the positive significance of all individual criticism of the Bible, which is not a book fallen from heaven. Criticism keeps heart and reason awake to see that the God of Golgotha demythologizes not merely religious books and pious views but the world and those in it—setting them out of deception and into the truth about themselves. Hebrews 10:31 says "it is a

---

1. This is most likely a reference to a German saying from the early nineteenth century, which maintained that peace and order are the citizen's first obligation.

fearful thing to fall into the hands of the living God." This requires a halt to those who yearn for the fleshpots of Egypt, who use religious opiates as a sleeping and sedative drug so as not to have to surrender a deceptive picture of world reality. Instead of wandering through the wilderness they tarry again at holy places, at domains of order, at islands of the saints, or at least of the unconcerned. But the Nazarene blocks us from such a way back. Unlike the people of Qumran, he did not establish cloisters near the Dead Sea, but sent his disciples like sheep among the wolves. His promise did not guarantee us a tranquil life, not even bare survival, but rather those biblical experiences: "You prepare a table before me in the presence of my enemies" [Ps. 23:5]; "If I make my bed in Sheol, you are there" [Ps. 139:8].

It seems as if I exaggerate, though these days we are careful to protect ourselves from strong language, so as not to disturb objectivity with rhetoric. But must we not seriously reflect on whether the Nazi period and the horror of the concentration camps, rather than being an exception and, as it were, an accident in our history, actually initiated an epoch of worldwide barbarism to which we are more and more exposed? The links to a tradition handed on to us shrink from day to day. What we called education in my youth, as an inherited legacy as well as a goal, seems irrevocably lost, though a flood of information to an incalculable degree overwhelms us and, in doing so, manipulates and dulls us. Bloodthirsty placards at demonstrations or universities testify to a coarsening in the confrontation of all with all. The shrieking for more democracy, in itself thoroughly reasonable, for the most part serves group interests or slides over into anarchy. Everywhere society is disintegrating, in soul more severely than outwardly. Polarization under the aegis of friend-enemy thinking clearly determines even church relationships. Those who are not integrated into the workforce remain, despite all social efforts, more and more at a distance. If a German proletariat still scarcely exists, then it will grow anew from the families of migrant workers. Bank raids, the taking of hostages, and other types of terror naturally cause sensation. But what is characteristic is the will to achieve power and, protected against unpopularity, to retain it, by virtue of which, in a dance around the golden calf, almost everything is allowed. It is not my concern to compile this for the sake of a Capuchinade.[2] Rather, it seems to me that the horrors and destructive tendencies (of such a sort as have never before been seen in all the world) testify to the fact that both the White Man's control over his own home and his power over those outside are breaking down. His technology, bureaucracy, and economic forms of exploitation

2. "Capuchinade": a harangue according to alleged Capuchin monk style.

can only partially halt or hide it; and, on the other hand, they allow it to rapidly accelerate.

The demythologizing of the world as a jungle in which there is struggle for power, pleasure, and survival cannot take place without our accounting for our own behavior in view of such a reality. This leads again to the theme of our political responsibility, for which reason I deliberately did not speak of it earlier. To put it just as provocatively: if the world is not demythologized so it can be seen in its real condition, this corresponds with a mythological picture of the human, who in fact largely gave rise to it. It is regarded as antiquated and very narrow-minded to affirm original sin. In fact, the term really is dubious to the extent early Christianity connected it with biology and sexuality. Still, the global entanglement of humanity by evil must be spoken of in a way that is entirely unambiguous so that it cannot be ignored today. At this point, the churches have not the least occasion to exercise respectable and cautious restraint. Nor should they shrink from being most embarrassed at confessing a dogma that is binding for them. If demythologizing should result in making cuts here and (in the wake of the so-called second Enlightenment) return again to the conviction of the human being as basically good but corrupted or endangered by conditions, then in this form and intention demythologizing can, of course, only be seen in antithesis to the gospel. I am speaking of demythologized humanity in express contradiction to such a superstition, which distorts Christian political responsibility.

It is advisable to start now personally with us—and again, where we are politically challenged. It is one of the sinister capacities of human beings that our will is stronger than our reason and, equally beset by desires and anxieties, may even prevent us from seeing and hearing. In the church struggle we had to learn to our total bewilderment that normally we do not inwardly perceive what lies open before us and can be heard by anyone, if it does not suit our imagination. We can hide and blind ourselves to injustice, shamefulness, and misery. This is happening everywhere in the world today to a degree no less than it once did under the Nazis. And, just as then, it is always happening among Christians. Here it is appropriate to call people to conversion (not least those who seem to have taken a lease on the term). First of all, the Man of the cross is victorious only by breaking through the illusions with which we screen ourselves from the reality of the world. He fetches us from the pious circle of fog that so often lies in the shadows of our church towers, in comradeship with those of like mind, in the so-tidily-fenced-off field of operation of our morality and convention—from this fog so thick that one can smell it and cut it with a knife.

Along with hearts, the Nazarene also opens eyes, ears, and reason for earthly realities. He frees from that atrophy of soul that sees the other only in one's companion, that tolerates the brutal struggle for power when one finds it legally difficult to manage. This atrophy also seizes the ecumenical movement when it so bravely accuses those who no longer accept without resistance exploitation by a "law" forced on them by oppressors. Is the church diaconate exhausted, say, in service to the lonely and to those physically or psychically in need of help? Does our message of religious pedagogy only apply to individuals or pious groups? Where this has become the sign of life that characterizes us, Golgotha need not have occurred. In Christ's day there was diaconate and religious instruction aplenty in Israel. In such a context he would have remained one among many and never become a scandal. The signature that marked him was that in the name of God—who intends that all God's creatures be helped—he joined sinners, tax collectors, and zealots. He thus broke through pious community, through the taboos of conventional morality and hallowed tradition. It drove him into a deadly conflict with ecclesiastical and political authority. Diaconate in the conventional sense is necessary without any limitation. But the question is whether Christianity of all confessions and varieties does not unremittingly betray its Lord and desert to the camp of his enemies when, in a primarily theological way, it navel gazes and diaconally looks after only those whose backbone has been broken, so that they can be forcibly integrated into good society. Have we totally forgotten that the Nazis recommended this very thing to us, then wanted to leave us in peace?

It appears to me to be a monstrous perversion when the gospel and confession are invoked and misused in order to be removed from the world of the abused and enslaved, to abandon them to their rulers, undisturbed by the horror of the victims, to seek after personal earthly and heavenly bliss. But we blaspheme the name of the Father of Jesus and separate God from God's creatures when we do not accept with the good Samaritan, without looking right and left, those who have fallen among the robbers. I do not want to belong to the hypocrites—the Pharisees and Levites—and make help dependent on the proper behavior of those who are assaulted, that they nicely and silently endure violence and solemnly promise a future of defenseless passivity. The tyrants may set the rules of the game for the struggle in the jungle—which are not to be kept by them, of course, but are surely to be kept by those who are to be eliminated. But a Christianity that defends such rules of the game or even remains silent about them works hand in hand with the bloodsuckers, deserves no respect, maneuvers itself out of bounds, and should not complain about it. Those who want to watch their backs, who refuse to dirty their hands, and who cowardly seek to guard themselves from trouble cannot be their brothers' keepers, cannot advocate for what is human, cannot be servants of the Crucified. That is clear and simple to pronounce today.

Demythologization of humanity means repentance for the Christian. But at the same time, it is an attack on an unabated Enlightenment pathos that demands reverence with slogans such as "maturity," "autonomy," and "emancipation." If one eliminates the side altars in one's own place of worship, do not then offer up incense before idols in the open-air arena. Such a militant expression could be misinterpreted as if, as has so often happened, faith should be played off against reason and the dignity of humanity should be infringed upon. Precisely the opposite is the case. Perhaps the Christian faith has only seldom before had so much reason to be enlisted on behalf of (and to be most intimately connected with) reason—for the sake of conscience and to contribute to a common humanity or, as I prefer to say, to the humanization of humanity. I have formulated this militantly because, despite all the Enlightenment pathos, reason seems continually to get lost more severely and extensively, while a faith truly defined by the Crucified Nazarene could become a reliable and helpful comrade for it. This faith protects from possession. In saying this, I am going beyond the statement that the human being is more strongly ruled by its will, and the desires and anxieties leading it, than by an unbiased mode of thinking that is open to critical judgments, to purposeful living, and on occasion also to a change of mind. In view of the world we daily experience, it might in fact be too rational to describe ourselves as the prey of our interests and the object of alien manipulation. The phenomenon of possession, however one may explain it scientifically, was already in Hitler's time hauntingly real, and since then it has currently become global. Its characteristic is that a living person becomes detached from all other relationships for the sake of a particular function—that is, ceases to be responsive to anything besides a single utopia or existential fear and can only experience difference in community in terms of the same addiction and a uniformed dependence. In place of growth there emerges a standstill that, fixed on one role, always allows the same disc to be replayed, altering the human being into an automaton. I spare myself examples of this because politics, economic life, and science abundantly indicate the impaired relation between the generations. On the other hand, theological analysis is important.

Just as possession is the anthropological reflection of a world thrown back into the jungle, so it most clearly reflects what we traditionally call original sin. Thus it becomes clear to what extent the Crucified is able to heal it. Golgotha shows what is involved in breaking the first commandment, whether in impious arrogance or panicky despair, in personal guilt as under oppressive fate. In an almost childlike way, Luther defined the promise of the Christian life: "We should fear, love, and trust in God above all things."[3] In doing so he also set forth the mystery of the Nazarene in that "above all things." For this allows us to name him the Son of God and to become aware of his distinctiveness. Of course, we all know about overwhelming fear and, at least in particular sectors of life, about blind trust and the longing for a saving love, which we for the most part practice only brokenly or selfishly, in the process signaling our disappointment learned in the frequent change of partners. The One who strides toward the cross lives the first commandment: because he loves the Father and honors him as Creator, he also does not rank those with whom he has to do on the scale of values of the prevailing powers and conditions. He sets them "above all things"—even above that which we have and do not have, and above what we may or may not be able to do. He thus rescues us from the jungle in which it is necessary to achieve, and he teaches us to reckon with God, who has mercy on those in need. But where this happens reason also gets space, power, and servants. Where God becomes human, we likewise may and must become human, and can actually become so. Unjustifiably, only what is unpleasant is frequently excavated from church history, something we in no way want to conceal. Whoever has to proclaim the gospel as revelation of help for the needy does not need to make of it a history of the superman [Übermensch].

Conversely, the host of those who have seen the burning bush and were stigmatized in the discipleship of their Lord should not be underestimated. There is the cloud of witnesses of which Hebrews 11 very graphically speaks, and by no means in whispers, as if it were a secret undertaking. There is that motley community of saints, eluding every template, continually falling in the desert, and again and again miraculously raised up, of which the Protestant must also be aware. As long as, in Jesus, this community hears the Father say "I am the Lord your God" in its midst, that "over all things" will be audible as answer to it. It must defy the superstition that runs after other gods, thus after the ideologies we created, the secret or open seducers and despots, the yearnings and anxieties of our own fickle heart. The One to whom we really belong is ultimately decided by whose voice we hear. Everything human depends on the One to whom we belong; thus it depends, in the critical situation, on the One whom we hear in such a way that he has the last word. That we allow the Crucified to speak the last word to us defines our humanity, our relation to earthly and transcendent powers. It is the one reality by which we want to see everything else measured.

What has been said may once more be exemplified by the keyword "representation." Representation resists a pious leveling that would render the

3. Martin Luther, Small Catechism, on the first commandment.

Christian community uniform in thinking, acting, suffering, and confessing, that would shape it after dead or living patriarchs, deliver it to the trend of a group, to the compulsion of a convention or confession. Just as no one is allowed to form God according to their image, so no one may attempt this with another (whether the nearest or the farthest, and especially not with our children). Otherwise with the last venture one practices the first—that is, idol worship—because one has no more power over the creature than over the Creator. Just this separates our God from the idols, as we can clearly see in Jesus's behavior. He accepted everyone in their peculiarity, and of course along with their merits as well as weaknesses. He made use of all for his service, each in their own way. In this way life does not become poorer, grayer, more boring. Rather, it becomes richer, more exciting, more adventurous in fact than ideologies are able to make it. Jesus allows for none of our many stereotypes and protects each of his disciples from violation by godless or pious narrow-mindedness. It scarcely needs to be said that this does not denote an easing of our situation as Christians. It is easier to swim with the stream. Many bitter experiences and errors are there for us to learn when, instead of following the crowd, we must seek out our own way since discipleship is no exercise program.

Conversely, only in this way do we become capable of representation. For the individual and the community are not opposites; rather, when not perverted, they mutually complement each other. Just as genuine community, in order to be vital, needs the many talents and ways of behaving, so the individual must also be unique and in need of supplementing so as to be able to be integrated as well as to serve. The Nazarene likewise separates us from the tyranny of the masses as well as from elitist arrogance. He makes us human and considerate just as he himself is. Since the expulsion from paradise, this is an arduous and painful way. We must be willing to take on burdens, allow ourselves to be misjudged and injured, even to suffer and to die as an outcast, as occurred to him. Conversely, when we come humanly to our fellow humans, something lightens, reminiscent of creation not yet fallen, and anticipates fulfillment. To be there in the desert and jungle of the world for the Lord and his own sets us at the place where possession ends and life awakens. The Crucified would not be the man of Golgotha if he brought us to an earth dreamed safe. But he makes us the raised victory sign of his glory by calling us to be his earthly representatives and, with the ardent expectation of the first Beatitude, he teaches us in love and imagination to uncover the buried talent (a possibility reserved for us). The biblical miracle stories are misunderstood when we do not also see them in the perspective of the cross. For the God of Jesus Christ does not appear in order to make us supermen, as the idols of the world promise. He reveals himself in the Nazarene in human fashion and effects humanity. For the believer, the signature of the Crucified alone is the measure of life and promise for the world.

As I began with an introductory remark, permit me to add a concluding remark. It may appear as if I had forgotten the second part of the theme handed me, according to which I was to give attention to the self-deceptions of our time. That is not correct. Perhaps it would have been useful to draw a comparison between our conditions and those of the year 1945, because the illusions and ideologies then gave us less to do, and despite all the horrors, wherever possible, something actually human occurred other than is the case with our affluence today. But the question is whether or not, apart from exceptional conditions, our self-deceptions change more than superficially and whether they always end in defiant and despondent hearts as well as an earth full of violence and misery. In any event, I did not want to speak behind the window. For I would prefer to think that in Christians' self-deceptions those of others are worsened, are multiplied rather than fade away. The devout also attempt to hitch God to their carts and, for this reason, have more need of a sight of the Crucified than the world around them. If we are conscious of our own illusions and dangers, we will certainly not overlook those of our contemporaries. Finally, let us not forget: the Savior of the world was the One who unmasked conceits—particularly those of the Pharisees and scribes—as idol worship, and thus had to die. Only when he may continue such work in his disciples, and we all together come under his judgment on our pious and godless self-deceptions, does he become Savior of the world.

✛ 13 ✛

Cross and Healing Activity (1974)

Three preliminary remarks: (1) I share the aversion of student rebels to monologue, and for this reason I will offer you less a proper lecture than an introduction to a conversation. (2) We continually learn that we are asked questions with which we do not rightly know how to begin. Exactly this has happened to me with the theme given me. Then, when we consider what the other who asks has in mind, we may possibly arrive at connections of which we were previously unaware. This is what has happened with the theme that was given to me. I still do not know whether what happened to me respecting the theme meets the expectation connected with it. Why this is so will be clear very shortly. (3) With a bit of competence I can only argue on the basis of my discipline if I want to avoid speculative statements. But when I view the theme on the basis of the New Testament, first of all, scarcely any lines of connection emerge. I will now make this clear in a few sections.

From a later period we are aware of the apotropaic significance of the sign of the cross, its use as a means of defense against demons. Victorious power inhabits it, as the legend of Constantine shows with special clarity: *In hoc signo vinces!* It is possible that as early as in oldest Jewish Christianity baptism

---

A contribution to the discussion at the Tenth Seminar for Christian Medical Service in Tübinger Tropenheim. First published in *Ärztlicher Dienst Weltweit*, ed. Wolfgang Erk and Martin Scheel (Stuttgart: Steinkopf, 1974), 200–208.

was performed as the expression "those who are sealed" in the Revelation
of John suggests: that is, the sign of the cross was made or written on the
forehead of the one to be baptized. The purpose was to place the baptized
under divine protection. From this perspective it would be conceivable that
use was found for the sign of the cross in the ritual of prayer over the sick
to effect healing, as mentioned in James 5. But this is pure supposition. This
exhausts everything the exegete can gather from the New Testament on the
theme "cross and saving action." You will understand that it has caused me
great embarrassment to have to speak of it.

-⊹-⊹-⊹-

My embarrassment becomes even greater when, as a historian, I am obliged
to point out that, in broad portions of the New Testament, and thus of early
Christianity, the two segments of the theme could only be seen in actual contrast. I must develop this somewhat more broadly. Two facts may form the
starting point:

1. There is not the least question that the healing narratives reported of
Jesus, as well as the miracle stories in general, are almost without exception legendary. To the figure of the great rabbi and prophet belonged answers to prayer and the ability to effect blessings and cursings, legitimized
by supernatural signs and wonders. In the Hellenistic world that deeply influenced Palestine intellectually, such in fact applied to the so-called divine
man—a category extending from the inspired philosopher through the all-
but-professional demon conjurer (who had also to heal the possessed) up to
the charlatan and swindler. We have a wealth of literary witnesses to divine
men and miracle workers, and, consequently, we can say with certainty that,
in the widest circles of early Christianity, Jesus was seen under this aspect
and that our Gospels describe him in this way, even when they connect it with
other messianic aspects. With some certainty, it can actually be proved that
individual miracle and healing narratives have been transferred to him from
the Jewish sphere—the narrative of the calming of the storm, for example, or
that of the herd of swine into which the exorcized demons were driven. I will
not pursue this further, but merely formulate the result: in the first century,
the Son of God could only be conceived of in an earthly way as a wonder-
worker, and the Christian community expressed and transmitted this faith
through a wealth of legends.

2. Of course, the community had historical permission to do so. For it is
likewise established beyond question that Jesus healed the possessed, was
himself conscious of this power, and in it saw a sign of his vocation and of the
end of the world breaking in with him. The healing of Peter's mother-in-law

is scarcely to be doubted historically. It is likewise established that to a great extent, in the Jewish Christian and later Hellenistic Christian communities, it belonged to the mark of an apostle that these first messengers of Jesus could drive out demons, heal the sick, and undergo ecstasies and that there was also an abundance of Christian exorcists whose successes in turn were interpreted as signs of the beginning inbreaking of the kingdom of God. We finally can go even a step further: early Christianity saw in Jesus the prototype of all the powers and charisms at work in it and allowed him to appear as the first prophet, teacher, apostle, and bishop—and thus also as the first exorcist and healer. And with the gospel story so described, the later Christian charismatics were legitimized by the model of Jesus. The legends are thus the deposit of actual experiences both from the story of Jesus and from the early Christian community. These legends are of such a sort that in them these experiences were coarsened and more and more exaggerated to allow the glory of Jesus and his disciples to appear ever greater. They are, finally, of such a sort that their problematic dawned early on, in at least certain Christian circles. In the world around them, the Christians were not the only ones who reported the miracles and healings of their master. There was a strong extra-Christian practice among exorcists and healers, so that the question concerning the criterion for deciding between the two had to be raised. It was customarily answered in such fashion that one saw the other party in the service of demons, just as Jesus was expressly accused by the Jews. Beyond this, at least among a few theologians, the insight had to emerge that Christian faith was not to be established by miracles and healings, even when they were obviously regarded as its accompanying phenomena. So far as I am able to see, only Paul, in 2 Corinthians 10–13, expressly criticized the community piety that required miracles.

What is the result of this brief historical survey? Far from recognizing its problematic, early Christianity as good as never touched on our theme. Not even this statement suffices. We must put it pointedly: early Christianity was scarcely able to see the thematic because it viewed the healing activity from the perspective of miracle, viewed the Spirit as the power of miracle, and connected this activity with the category of the divine man insofar as it described Jesus, his apostles, and their charismatics on the basis of this category that totally overshadowed the cross and the Crucified. In the end, the synthesis at which our theme aims appeared to early Christianity as an antithesis. The early faith did not ask: How can healing activity be justified and theologically differentiated on the basis of the Crucified? It could only ask, and in the Gospels of Mark and John actually did ask: To what extent did the One divinely sent, whose glory was manifest on earth in his miracles and healings, have to go the way to the cross? To such an aporia it answered: only by way of the cross did God lead to his exaltation. From now on the Exalted One is at work on earth through his apostles, charismatics, and the community, by virtue of the resurrection power that seizes hold of them—further, by miracles and healings that legitimize him and his own. With respect to our context, it has generally bracketed out the theme of the cross. Healing activity in and by the community has to do with the power of the resurrection, which is a proleptic allusion to the conquest of the earthly world and its distresses by the coming world—that is, by the resurrection of the dead.

This should not mean that this community assigned the cross no significance at all for believers, though that could happen, as the Corinthian enthusiasts indicate. Insofar as the community did not fall prey to such enthusiasm, it gave anthropological significance to the cross under the watchword of discipleship. The disciple must go the same way as his Lord on earth and thus will come under the shadow of the cross—that is, will have to endure suffering and persecution. The disciples are stigmatized by the Crucified and have their own crosses to bear, so that they, as it were, reflect and contemporize the earthly fate of their Lord. To the degree the idea is alive in Christianity from the very beginning, it is still loosely and unharmoniously alongside the other, that the power of the Spirit is at work in the community and through it works miracles. Perhaps we might at best say that the experience of the Spirit and the miracles worked by it comforts the afflicted community, giving it certainty of not being abandoned and power to bear the cross that belongs to discipleship. Put very pointedly, what was just described as an antithesis is now changed into a paradox: the host in the discipleship of the Crucified is at the same time the host held together by the power of the Risen One and offers to the world the drama that the outcast, persecuted, and suffering are not lying about and unfaithful. But here too the synthesis of our theme, the establishing of healing activity on the basis of the cross, is not yet arrived at. Nor is it arrived at from the other side—that is, that the disciple must become like the Lord, need not curse when cursed but must forgive, must live in the midst of the hate of the world around, must help where thrust into affliction.

For such behavior, the model of Jesus, but not the cross, is directly determinative. Nevertheless, there is an attempt here that can lead further. Jesus's example, thus also that of the Crucified, calls not merely to voluntary endurance but to action. Christians are not passive. They are on a mission, as was their Lord. They will thus accept brothers and enemies whether thanked for it or not. They cannot thoughtlessly pass by the stranger's distress. According to Matthew 25, the decisive question to the disciple at the last judgment will read: "What have you done or not done for my brother?" This brother is then described as the stranger who was not even recognized as the representative of the Lord, for which reason those who helped are amazed at their reward, and the rejected outraged at their punishment. Jesus draws his community into his vicarious service—a service that is to be, of course, both toward one another and toward the world. He intends that everyone be helped, and he makes us answerable for everyone who encounters us in distress. Insofar as we have the capacity for it, this obviously includes healing activity. But it must be underscored once more that all this is spoken of the exalted Lord, who will mete out judgment, but that there is yet no reflection on the cross as such. Something like a horizon opens up in which our theme can appear, but nothing more.

If I see correctly, everything said until now is surpassed only in Paul and, at best, a few of his pupils. There are reasons for this in the theology of the apostle, which I must at least briefly touch on. Paul broke with the Jewish law. This makes it possible for him to undertake the gentile mission by sacrificing the making of proselytes. His goal is to win the world for Christ. The breadth of this program is expressed in the fact that the entire Mediterranean area is grasped by it. But we should not forget that the world not only has the dimensions of historical breadth and depth but also the character of everyday life. Not just space and time but also areas of the profane are envisaged by the one who proclaims Christ's world rule, a rule related to human existence, to the sphere of corporeality with its possibilities for communication in the friendly and hostile sense. Whoever wants the world must will what is precisely corporeal and not be limited to what concerns the soul and spirit. Accordingly, corporeality is the world in the concrete. Because Paul strove for the rule of Christ over the whole world, he was not concerned with a primarily cultic worship of God but with worship in which we bring our bodies with all their capacities and possibilities for communication as an offering to God. For this reason, his mission put before him the task not only of winning souls and spirits but of wakening bodily obedience. Only then does it become clear that Christ is Lord of the world, that resurrection of the dead means completed lordship of Christ in a new world.

Another motif of Pauline theology to be mentioned here is this: that he no longer, as Christianity before and alongside him, allows the Spirit to remain a more or less impersonal, heavenly power that distributes miracles and ecstasies and finally produces resurrection energy. Because the enthusiasts understood the Spirit in this way, they felt that by possessing the Spirit they were already given a heavenly nature and removed from the earth with its obligations. A mystery community could arise in such a manner, but the lordship of Christ over and in the earth could not be realized, nor bodily obedience appear as the genuine nature of Christian worship of God. It was of fundamental theological significance that Paul connected the Spirit with Christology and, on that basis, understood the Spirit as the power that allows the exalted Lord to be present on earth. Now, bearers of the Spirit—and that means all Christians, since all received the Spirit through baptism—were no longer to be measured by whether they experienced illuminations, possessed the thrilling power of speech, or worked miracles. The decisive criterion of Christian, Spirit-led existence was now whether and to what extent Christ is present on the earth through his disciples. Due to the enthusiasts, this too must again be more precisely defined, because they saw the presence of Christ in the manifestation of his glory. Herein lies the necessity for the Pauline theology of the cross. The exalted Lord is the Crucified. If he is present on earth, it must become visible that he is exalted as the Crucified. The community that appeals to him does not receive its distinctiveness from ecstasies and miracles, as the Hellenistic mystery religions were required to show (as, for example, in the cult of the healing god Asclepius). The Christian community does not possess distinctiveness by participating in the glory of the exalted Lord but rather by carrying the cross after him on earth and thus allowing him to remain present on earth in his own distinctiveness as the Crucified. If we are no longer aware of the cross through the Christian community, we are not really aware of Christ as the One who is distinct from all other lords and gods, and the community is no longer fundamentally Christian, but a type of religious association. We may never skip over the Nazarene, even if we open all of heaven for him.

These theological reflections were necessary to make clear the point that now in fact the cross and healing activity can actually be brought together. Paul did not yet directly do so, or in particular reflect upon it. But he created the presuppositions for the fact that we can set this theme and discuss the problematic given with it. Now we must give several answers to our question, precisely because the apostle did not directly or thematically think through the complexity. The first thing to be stated is that Paul takes up those views we already noted under the keyword "discipleship." In this way he can bring an entire catalogue of sufferings endured in the service of his Lord. In the earlier-mentioned chapters of 2 Corinthians 10–13, he takes up his opponents'

question regarding the signs of an apostle, but he answers it paradoxically: if others see those signs in their marvelous experiences and practices, he refers to his service running with patience in toil and humiliation, though he could also boast of ecstasies and miracles. If he behaved otherwise, according to 2 Corinthians 13:4, he could not be a credible representative of his Lord. To the disciple belongs the sign of the cross—by which, according to Galatians 6, he has been in fact stigmatized in the body [v. 17].

Paul forces this view of the earlier community out of the sphere of practical experience into what is basic, as most clearly appears from 2 Corinthians 12:7ff. Sickness, of which we also usually hear, attacks him so that his existence is endangered by it. It is so severe that he traces it to the activity of Satan, describing it as a thorn in the flesh. Three times he prayed to the Lord for release from it, and in answer he heard the divine oracle: "My grace is sufficient for you, for power is made perfect in weakness" [v. 9]. This means that the God whom Jesus reveals is always the One who deals with useless material [2 Corinthians 3:4–6]; is always the One who, according to 2 Corinthians 4, entrusts God's work and the gospel to earthen vessels, to those dying on earth; in brief, this God is always the One who is Creator from out of nothing. Thus, from the very beginning of the world, God's activity is always justification of the godless and resurrection of the dead. Before this God one cannot and may not boast, neither about one's own wisdom nor one's own power nor one's own piety. The disciple must therefore not merely bear the cross. The disciple is useful in the service of Jesus only when this service is characterized by a continual being crucified together with [*Mitgekreuzigtwerden*], a continual experience of being afflicted, of being lowly and of belonging to the lowly.

With that said, three things mark the disciples of Jesus: (1) They remain in the purpose to which they were called only as long as they remain ready and able for service. All Christian authority can only be based on the practice of service, and it consequently has its limits. If others are no longer served, not merely church authority but also Christian existence itself ends. (2) To belong to the Crucified effects limitless patience and the staying power of love. What is meant is not a passivity of waiting, which has its hands in its lap until help comes. On the basis of the Greek term, *patience* means that one lifts shoulders to the burden laid on, thus is in position to resist inner conflict and distress. Christians do not have to be revolutionaries. They are, however, always rebels and nonconformists, not surrendering silently or idly to fate but enduring inner conflict and distress in every shape and struggling as witnesses to the freedom of the children of God. If God wills to be at work in the nothingness, grace allows us to recognize, first, how little we are of use for God's service; second, that all the world is imprisoned in nothingness; and third, that our service is precisely due to what is nothing, pitiful, beaten, oppressed, and dying. The long arm and the staying power of love are expressed precisely in the fact that we do not turn merely to what can be developed and is worthy of promotion. We are in resistance to death, the last enemy, and should make known in advance the resurrection of the dead by serving where, seen from below, there neither is nor can be final help, since everything living has lapsed into death. At issue is not merely putting death off or applying a religious opiate where there is agony. At issue is the need to come to grips with death itself, in whatever shape it appears. In the discipleship of the Crucified, and by those who must die and carry about them the symbol of death, there is announced and practiced in advance a resurrection of the dead in resistance to the fate of death.

With that said, we come to the last point: (3) The follower of the Crucified becomes a witness and forerunner of freedom. Whoever was made willing and able to die with Jesus loses fear of all the otherwise ruling powers, is finally bound to no human encampments, but can go out from and through them, lives from a radical reevaluating of the prevailing values. On the basis of the cross one sees everything differently than one sees oneself or appears to others. One becomes human as one renounces the dream of wanting to be more than human, and as one sees what is human both in what impresses and in the grimaces of what appears subhuman. Everywhere one sees the needy, those crying in arrogance and despair for the freedom of the children of God. On the basis of the cross one comes into solidarity with those who cry for freedom, becomes their servant, as Jesus was toward the pious and sinners, the strong and weak, the noble and despised. These are only masks behind which those in need of help hide themselves. This service cannot be uniform, because love knows no formula. It will change according to each situation. It can persist by our resistance to whatever is after preserving itself and achieving. It can raise up what is fallen. It can comfort where one must learn to bow under irrevocable fate. It can relearn where we need to unlearn what in all of life is at least as important as learning. Conversely, it will use what is available and not be content with what we know and have, but will seek new ways of improving help. It will not at all behave in an especially religious manner, but will persist in the mundane, where only what is human is encountered in its reality and where masks must fall so that creatures may reflect the image of their Creator in the Creator's world. To learn freedom, to prepare the way for freedom toward those who are not free and toward an enslaved world—this is the task, the calling, the possibility, the service of Christians who come from the cross.

This has furnished the presupposition of our theme, though it is not reflected on directly and in detail. In any event, Paul has numbered the service of healers and exorcists among the charisms. Today, the service of exorcists may be more necessary than that of healers. Perhaps it was ever so. The world is possessed, and only the meaningful service of healers may facilitate driving possession out. What our youth calls constraints and repressions suggests the phenomenon of possession, which, of course, can be hidden equally well in either ideologies or in revolutionary practice. Today we will deal differently with possession than conjurers once did. Pragmatic thinking, sober application of scientific insight, may now be in place. If this offers a horizon for meaningful healing activity—that is, does not merely occur for the sake of the individual—then, conversely, service for the individual has the meaning of pointing us to the concrete. That service must be so concrete that it does not forget that the human is a corporeal being and in that very corporeality is in need of help and liberation.

Now we are called to consider what, where, and how we must act. The gospel is not a formula but a calling that sets us, while thinking, in motion. Paul has only led us to the threshold where we have to start. He sets us in the service of the freedom made possible and reaching further on the basis of the cross, thus also in the service of the healing activity. He teaches us where the enemy is and where our limits are. He indicates the space where we must remain, and also demands that we break out of spaces that cordon people off. In his own way, he says what Jesus said: "Follow me!" In theory and practice, we are called to realize what this call makes possible, what it commands here and now, and with reference to the healing activity. Now the specialists may consider what they can do with it, and whatever they have to omit from it.

✝ 14 ✝

The Healing of the Possessed (1978)

In the Gospels the healing of the possessed is narrated as a mark of Jesus's activity. Before he comes to the passion narrative, Mark actually sets it at the center of his report. Healing of the possessed appears to him as a symbol of that service which drives the Servant of God into the sphere of earthly darkness, thus also into death, but at the same time as the symbol of that freedom which bursts the power of the demons and frees their prisoners. Today, both should very emphatically be stated, because in theology and in the church—at least those of the White Man—it is largely forgotten or taken up only hesitantly (with fingertips, as it were). For the most part, we no longer know how to deal with the demonic, and we are embarrassed when spoken to about it. Further, there is no doubt that the Enlightenment more intensely demythologized here than anywhere else. It has become unpopular or actually laughable to speak about the devil and the demons.

When there is occasional talk of it, when, where possible, incantations occur—perhaps far more than we know—we feel thrust back into earlier centuries and in certain instances have reason to recoil from shocking superstition. The monstrosities that until modern times were connected with obsessive belief in witches and the attempt to ban evil spirits cannot and must not be forgotten. They remind Christianity of the fact that it too was not at all immune from inhumanity. Under certain circumstances, those monstrosities keep a secret guilty feeling alive among us and thus contribute to repressing the theme of "possession" in contemporary theological discourse. But in all

---

A lecture delivered to the evangelical theological faculty at Greifswald. First published in *Reformatio* 28 (1979): 7–18.

seriousness, we must ask whether we are allowed to obscure central views of the New Testament in such fashion or—put figuratively—to shove them off on a false track when, in speaking of possession, we at best allow those views to stand in the corner as improper circumscriptions for psychic and mental disturbances meanwhile corrected by our science. This could not only unjustly trivialize biblical texts and historical traditions but also hinder necessary and truly illumining insights.

Naturally, I am not concerned with Christian-edifying apologetics that, sparingly applied and well considered, may be useful but in general only waste time and produce boredom. I would certainly not like to implicate myself when today—inside and outside the churches—an outdated ideology is often being warmed up and heralded once again as the deepest wisdom. Rather, as a theologian, I think that once more, and more clearly than until now, Christianity must state what original sin is. As an interpreter of the New Testament, I think this best occurs when we replace the dogmatic concept of original sin with the New Testament understanding of possession.

What is gained by this? In the place of one term that has become incomprehensible, does only another, and a more dubious one, appear?

To this I answer, first of all, that I hope in this way to be clearer, to take up an inherited Christian teaching that can be neither relinquished nor dealt with by accident in the catechism; but at the same time, I hope from the outset to exclude ancient misunderstandings. The term "original sin" unavoidably suggests the idea that what the Bible calls "sin" is transmitted through conception and birth and is most intimately connected with sexuality. Such a view is not to be justified on the basis of Scripture. It has led to dangerous theories and practices in Christianity.

In reality, where original sin is spoken of in a theologically appropriate way, the mysterious interweaving of guilt and fate in the life of all of us is in view. Each one is born into a world already ruled by the power of evil, for which reason it entangles each one personally in sin. Each one is of course guilty on their own, and thus individually attests to the destiny of the children of Adam. Still, sin cannot be reduced to the sphere of the individual event. Fate is expressed in the deed, and the deed points beyond itself to a common fate on this earth. Of course, we must be responsible for our actions, insofar as our heart and our anxieties and longings share in them. But we are not—as only superstition can imagine—ultimately our own masters; we are always heirs of our ancestors, children of our time, victims of our environment, the battleground of our own impulses.

Reason makes itself felt in a thoroughly critical and self-critical way. But it can seldom arrange for situations and must, for the most part, content itself with protest against them. Just like individuals, so also human societies carry in themselves the germ of sickness, strife, and self-destruction. Voluntarily or involuntarily rebellious, they infringe on the divine will, even on the creation from which they live. This is certainly no happy picture of humans and their world. It does not cohere—as I at once admit—with the ideas of the Enlightenment, which, since the times of the Greeks, then again since the Renaissance, have marked specifically Western culture. Conversely, today we should ask what we actually have to thank the Enlightenment for and where, misled by its slogans, we have been idealistically estranged from true humanity.

Fruitful intellectual movements always have a dangerous legacy. Often, if they are to retain their good sense, they must later be radicalized. The Enlightenment optimism respecting humanity's capabilities has been corroborated far beyond original expectation by modern science and technology. But at the same time, and again precisely by modern science and technology, trust in humanity itself has become questionable, a trust that in the French Revolution grotesquely allowed reason to be proclaimed as a goddess. We have made the world so subject to us that we move in its most distant spaces, use its hidden gifts and powers, to a great extent decode its innermost secrets. On the other hand, we plunder the treasures of the earth to such an extent that in the foreseeable future they must be all but exhausted, and for the sake of our desires we carelessly destroy our environment and especially the habitat of indigenous peoples.

As is chiefly apparent in the white race, human beings who plumb the universe in its breadth and depth, and with image and sound bring to us even what is most distant, at the dizzying height of their power also run into the limits of their humanity. More than all those preceding, our century is marked by brutality. One would probably more properly have to speak of beastliness.

From this perspective, does not speaking of the rational human and an ultimately (or at least, reasonably) ordered world have the effect of a conjuring up from out of our anxiety and hopelessness? Should not a radicalized Enlightenment finally call us to awaken from the dreams of a deceitful idealism and to see into the unvarnished face of reality? Especially to awaken from the intoxication of an affluent society that, conscious of its incontestable economic and social progress, falls over backward into unbridled lust? After us, the flood! But that can only be the slogan of those who care nothing for the lot of their children and grandchildren.

Personally, I will never get rid of the horror over a young generation—we already knew it then—dedicated to death, a generation that, in the hot summer nights of 1939, bawled out from the dancehalls (I heard it every night): "Everything blows over, it all goes away; to every September comes once more a May." Everything did blow over. May came, but over ruins and graves and abysses of despair. How, after thirty years, as is the case with us, can this be lost, no longer true? We have gone through conflagrations; we have literally climbed over mountains of corpses—a people that, without exaggeration, came out of hell. But the mass media daily make us witnesses of an earth that for the majority of its inhabitants has been a hell. If radical Enlightenment were not obliged to speak of it today, would not Christians at least have to be open to such voices and provide an answer?

In the last century we were involved in a dispute for and against a theology that calls itself historical-critical. At times the dispute is still carried on as an object of a final personal decision or a decision made by an entire church. Whoever really thinks in this fashion is, as so often in German history, marching behind the columns and is ignorant of the new front. The questions of historical criticism are not settled. But they now have weight only in the shadow of a biblical interpretation with which Scripture as its source gives illumination about our own reality and the nature of this world. Historical criticism also intended to contribute to this. It did so in view of the past, thus as it were in a mirror. Further, it is meaningful, but in our time no longer sufficient, and much too academic, when, occupied with it in the jungle of global conflicts, we do not see Adam and his earth in their true shape. In our time the gospel always intends to be newly discovered, not primarily or exclusively taken from the canned goods of tradition. Christ opens to us not only heaven but our heart as well; then he brings us into the openness of the world. Whoever closes one's eyes to our earth absolutely does not experience the open heaven. Fictions about humanity belong together with fictions about God.

Those who have illusions about themselves and the world around always learn only of an imaginary God. We do not share the eternal glory when we are unwilling to descend with the Nazarene into the earthly inferno. On this the spirits truly always divide. Only this is worthy of theological dispute. Those who, and in whatever shape, have had to do with the hell on earth around and in themselves, and from then on stand in a more radicalizing enlightenment, can no longer ignore the New Testament narratives of the healing of the possessed. It is not necessary, in the manner of ancient ideology, to see the devil and his evil spirits everywhere. But it would be no less dubious to leave to psychology and psychiatry—which I in no way would render unemployed—the task of the Bible expositor and reduce the reality of possession solely to diseases of mind and spirit. Precisely the strange features of the Gospel histories allow us to see this.

There, in the Gospels, the possessed are at home among the graves, separated from the community of life and bound by the ghosts of the dead. They defend themselves with all their might against Jesus because they do not want to be healed but to remain in night and solitariness. God's intervening and liberating hand is as unbearable to them as is the help of the community. They live as our terrorists in anticipation of their own death, under a closed heaven and in earthly isolation.

These narratives, which clearly set psychic illness in the foreground, must not be separated from others that trace bodily distresses to powers hostile to life and end in exorcism, thus with incantations. We know that the early Christian community knew of a regular profession of exorcists, as did Judaism before it. Despite all sorts of the most modernized theories, the question may be raised whether a meaningful theology should not be far more oriented to exorcism than to the technique of information—that is, to the distinguishing and dividing of spirits. Where Christian truth is at issue, lies and superstition must be diagnosed and driven out. Without question, this overtaxes the capabilities of opinion pollsters and the techniques of communicators. We must see, further, that the oldest community suspected that there were demonic powers even behind the powers of nature, since the latter imperil humankind, as in storms at sea. In just this way, this community believed that the passion of Jesus and their own persecution were caused by demonic evil. The Apocalypse of John actually proclaimed the Roman Empire a tool of the antichrist, to say nothing of those who as heretics or troublemakers made this community a playground of factions.

Taking this all together, it can no longer be maintained that in the New Testament possession is limited to individuals. With good reason confessional statements take up what in the Gospels is described in typically individual cases. In so doing, confessions give these individual stories a metaphysical depth and a cosmic breadth. They maintain that this world is in utter disarray. But this is expressed psychologically and pathologically, religiously, socially, and politically.

Paul has reflected on this situation more intensely than any other. As an ancient man, he himself naturally speaks of the devil and his evil spirits. But as a theologian, he is not content with speaking in an exemplary fashion. Rather, in systematic fashion, he characterizes the kingdom of darkness— which Christ the liberating one breaks into—as the triad of law, sin, and death. He regards these as powers that demonically enslave the individual as well as society, the entire world of humans. The state of affairs later to be described by the keyword "original sin" is categorically recognized and defined here as possession. The Gospel narratives define their context as the kingdom of the power of death. Hebrews 2:15 thus speaks most emphatically of us as creatures who through fear of death must be subject to slavery all our lives.

What would clarify our reality—worldwide, of course—better than this? Where are there persons, societies, nations, and continents not living in panic today? Whether panic over others or the future, over the loss of their posses- sions in the material, intellectual, and religious sphere or over the loss of their power, their place of work, their freedom, their nourishment for the next day: in anxiety over tyrants and exploiters and demons? We speak so pompously of "the improvement of the quality of life." We would be much more sober and clear if we asked instead how we get free from unconcealed or secret panic. In any event, that person takes a step forward who, rather than being driven from fear to lust and envy and intoxication, sees the power of death in its many shapes, who sees it staging its game with us, as in the medieval death dances. Such a person would also know that panic drives one to flight that can end in despair as well as in arrogance, that it begets loneliness, hate, and madness—"life at the wrong place." On the flight from death, there is no way out. Of course, we are capable of everything, and we would like to hold on to everything; but every day we learn that nothing holds us for long, everything must shatter into pieces, and in the end we always take flight to our own death. Anxiety now possesses heart and reason, and it removes everything called sense.

Within the sphere of death, the law too is mighty. What Paul meant by this statement would have to be more thoroughly analyzed than I can do here. But from our life experience we can see into the contexts it has in view. It is not by chance that we speak of the pressure to perform and of a meritocracy that, where we are concerned, had to result in a throwaway society, even for human beings. What is not young and strong and shrewd enough to work, and then to maintain the hard-won or undeserved inherited place, easily comes under the wheels, is used by others as a stirrup, or is shoved aside. The anxiety that, at least in old age, this could happen to us, or that an unforeseen fate could catch up with us one day, moves us to squeeze out of the moment all its possibilities, to eliminate possible competitors in every way and, as well as we can, to secure ourselves from future threats. Now we are going around in circles. Egoism always leaves less room for rest and reflection than for humanity. Paul maintains that there is actually something of this sort in the life of the devout and that even God's word as call to performance and self-assertion can be misunderstood.

This should be heard not only with regard to the individual but also with regard to church associations and whole churches. The one with open eyes will easily find corroboration for it and will be able to maintain that, only too frequently, the law has repressed the gospel. Even in worship we encounter those who want to work out and maintain their own salvation on earth and in eternity, who then hold up their religiosity or morality before God and the neighbor, expecting applause from both. Their pious feelings, experiences, and works should now be the criterion, even at the last judgment. The inevitable result of this is that God and the neighbor—formed after the image of our desires and performances—must admire our self-righteousness, so that all who are not established, who live in conflict with themselves and the world, are thrust aside, the promise of the Beatitudes is destroyed, and the community now collapses into factions of the more or less good and faithful. Here, too, the one who counts is the one who achieves.

This means an increase of possession and unholiness on earth. The reason is that our actions have consequences. None deny their own lord without at the same time endangering their earthly environment. Never and nowhere is there anyone established on their own, answerable only to themselves, and neutral. Even Feuerbach[1] must be radicalized today. Those who behave autonomously not only project their longings and anxieties onto heaven and thus make their own gods but also surrender the earth, torn from its true Lord, to ideological and totalitarian dependence. Where we set ourselves at the center, and thus turn our backs on the Nazarene, space once more emerges for all the demons from which we were delivered. Those who have eyes to see and ears to hear and a heart to suffer along with the imprisoned, tortured, subjected, and starving see, hear, and daily endure the reality of a world in which sin creates and increases possession.

Our Gospels tell us that the Servant of God becomes not only a human being among human beings but also our brother who, to help us, suffers with us. For too long we have allowed the Christian message to end in this way, as if common humanity were its goal and the sphere of the individual the locus of its history. Jesus, of course, calls himself a physician. Nevertheless, he who did not come to us for the sake of the healthy will help more than merely soul and mind. Just as he is concerned for the total person and thus for our corporeality, so with his word and work he intervenes in all the contexts of our life, and *for this reason* is crucified. Whoever will have only heaven at best counts as a fool. But where, by effecting change, God's kingdom lays hold of this earth, and where possession is unmasked as the mark of our condition, there all the powers enslaving the creation take up their defense. There, Pontius Pilate and Caiaphas, Pharisees and Sadducees, scribes and the masses become partners in the trial against the Nazarene.

---

1. Ludwig Feuerbach (1804–72), German philosopher and anthropologist, best known for his *The Essence of Christianity*, a critique of Christianity influencing later thinkers such as Marx and Engels.

This trial continues to the present day. All devotion to the Bible that declares every word of the Scripture sacrosanct but does not take sides in this trial is nothing but pious shadowboxing. Then it too serves to blind. Since Christianity was officially recognized and so-called national churches were allowed to be formed, the message of the gospel has been more and more methodically internalized and privatized. This seems paradoxical, but it is the real mark of our religious concern. Only where the gospel was spiritualized and privatized, fetched back from its attack on the obsessions of politics, economics, and culture, as medicine for the individual soul, did the organizations that administer the gospel more or less enjoy great freedom of movement. We can call it a fool's freedom. Naturally, it is not yet Christian when one imagines having a say everywhere by appeal to the Bible and confession, or when one can only criticize what exists and one neglects heart, feeling, and spirit in the intrapersonal area, thus neglects the diaconate and care of souls, all for the sake of more universal problems. Quite unequivocally, Christian responsibility must be so defined and delineated that only the human and humanity remain its task. This is the issue at all times and today more than earlier. Humanity is continually and everywhere threatened. We cannot speak seriously of the discipleship of Jesus where we are silent about the dehumanizing of the human, where such is even demanded.

The situation is similar to what was just maintained concerning the interplay between gospel and the church. To the degree we as consumers and producers, members of interest groups, victims of ever-encroaching bureaucracies, are monopolized by the modern meritocracy, by its compulsions, techniques, its national and supranational debates, humanity in and around us is lost. We no longer buy or produce what is needed, but what catches on in advertising. We scarcely still ask what is useful to us and others, but for the most part only what preserves our possession, satisfies our addiction to pleasure, and is useful as propaganda for our ideology. We live more and more in closed associations of the like-minded and cordon ourselves off from what could disturb us, divert us from our best-established plans, or actually compel us to limit our cost of living for the sake of service to the helpless and the disenfranchised.

Here the Nazarene becomes a troublemaker by associating himself with the victims of our universal competition for our own place in the sun, and he directs his criticism especially against the religious fellowship that plays the letters and law of its tradition off against the will of God and humanity. This Nazarene uncovers not only distress and guilt but also possession—that is, the lostness of the creation in the shadow of death and the power of darkness. Therefore, freedom is his work. It is worth leafing through our hymnals to search for the term and the subject it indicates. We will find it more seldom than other words that speak of redemption. We will even more seldom find that this word means more than personal liberation from all sorts of troubles. In general, Christianity has always stood on the side of order, of the existent, and of the authorities that would preserve both. Especially in Lutheranism, Christianity has continually appealed to Romans 13. Since the early period of the church, the enthusiastic and revolutionary views have been feared and battled. Thus, at least in the sphere of the White Man, an almost indissoluble pact has been struck with the bourgeoisie that, from time to time, allows the social high-water mark to be read at best from worship and religious behavior. We must emphatically deny that all this may be deemed necessary, perhaps even intended by God. Since the earliest centuries, there have been churches that have tied themselves to national, social, and cultural trends and that, for this reason, were regarded as being just as rebellious as we are regarded today—as in, for example, the circles of Black theology in the North, the liberation theology in South America, and the guerrilla movements in Africa and Asia, to say nothing of those who loyally try to work with Marxist movements. Whoever rejects from the outset as unchristian the *oecumene's* support of freedom fighters is, at least in church-historical perspective, nothing but a fool. Moreover, such a person uses arguments that were once lodged by opponents of the Reformation against Protestantism and its earlier forms. Such a one indicates an inability to distinguish between gospel and conservative practice and, as in Germany of the previous century, is more inclined to reaction than, say, to the cries of a proletariat exploited in body and soul. This one also reads the Bible one-sidedly.

Naturally, all are correct who state that Jesus was crucified among revolutionaries but was in no way himself a revolutionary. Still, in the interval, this debate has become so academic that one can only speak of pedantic school-mastery and literalism. And it should at least be considered how Jesus could at all succeed in the neighborhood of those guilty of high treason (zealots). If he had behaved toward the petite bourgeoisie of his time (that is, toward conservative, pious Judaism) as church majorities of the world around us behave toward the petite bourgeoisie of our time, he would have been spared the gallows. It appears that all the rebellious cries of the prophets, of the Baptist, of the seer John, even of the Epistle of James, are no longer read or retained in memory. Even devout people are accustomed to ban from heart and memory what does not suit their opinion. Traditionally, there is just as much silence as there is citation of the Bible. How can we forget that, according to the Bible's proclamation, God is an enemy of all the self-secure and sated, of all those clinging to their material or spiritual possessions, that he overthrows tyrants, exalts the lowly, and—thank God!—allows the nature of this world to pass away. If this were somewhere else than in the Bible, we would doubtless speak of revolutionary views and call the writers subversive. Is it holy and harmless because it is in the Bible?

All the revolutions of the White Man have appealed to the Bible. For one and a half millennia, even in the churches, reform and uprising have continually issued from it. Put crudely, the fattening of heart and head in the affluent society is making such progress that, for us and our world, it is vital to hear the rebellious voices from the Old and New Testaments instead of only the soporific melodies on justification from the law and on the order of the establishment. For our sake, the Servant of God descends into the earthly inferno and dies on Golgotha. And yet, where the gospel is denied, the Bible and Christian faith misused, the church's task and promise betrayed, there is no longer a visible and audible appearance for protest and resistance in the name of divine freedom.

This freedom is described in the Galatians epistle as the truth of the gospel. As such it breaks through the reserve of the privileged to arrive as a liberating power to the outcast, to those overcome by darkness. It is directed toward the resurrection of the dead. This would not be credible if it would not apply on earth to tyranny and stupidity, to all the various shapes of possession by which people are enslaved in body and soul, economically, socially, ideologically, and religiously. For us, resurrection of the dead must be a prologue if it is to be more than a pious sham existence that comforts those who have come off badly here and, robbed of all the usual possibilities for refuge, must cling to illusions. In the gospel the healing of the possessed is a prelude to the resurrection of the dead and, as it were, its earthly pledge.

In our century the reality of the world is evident to everyone who wants to see. No one can seriously deny possession when hundreds of billions are paid out for war preparations instead of for the elimination of misery in the underdeveloped earth and in whole continents. Possession is expressed in the panic that is hidden in the affluent society behind the lust for success, for pleasure, for more and more belongings, and which defends itself against any access to its prerogatives in order, at best, to share alms with the exploited and the starving.

There is also possession in the church when, forced to concede the *oecumene* in view of global mergers, the body of Christ is further split with preserving confessionally vested rights or with pious carping about the criteria of personal credibility—when conformism and accommodation are practiced in the face of the status quo and persons allow themselves to be infected by the anxieties of middle-class society.

Resurrection of the dead has in view the one who, out of guilt and fate, has become a slave to fear (thus also to presumption) but is then retrieved for a humanity freed for God and the neighbor. This very thing begins on earth when the Nazarene heals the possessed. With the command "Follow me," he conquers those who defend themselves against him and wish to remain inhuman. He opens eyes and ears earlier directed only to one's own anxieties and longings. He takes us by the hand to lead us out of the closed doors (behind which we have barricaded ourselves with the ghosts of our illusions) and into a free field, under God's heaven and in service to the earth.

Demons and demoniacs change their shape, each according to the times, situations, and people's imaginations. But healing of the possessed always follows when creatures no longer live and die for themselves but open their hearts to their Creator and their neighbor, when they return to the community of those addressed by the Beatitudes and allow themselves to be called to discipleship of the Nazarene in the unknown future of their Lord and to the adventure of a humanity ventured ever anew. God's future is unknown. Too often churches behave as if they knew God's future. Too often they are silent about humanity as meaning adventure and about us as God's experiment with the earth. But the open heaven and the open earth wait for those who hear this—and who hear it, of course, in the midst of a world full of graves, ghosts, and idols. For discipleship means to be open, for all the world just as for heaven, and the revelation of the glory of God begins on earth with humans becoming more human.

-⁀- 15 -⁀-

Meaning and Problematic of the 1981 *Kirchentag* Motto (1980)

Fear (Not)!

In 1 Corinthians 14:2ff. the apostle unambiguously demands the following of the Christian community, and I quote: "It is the same way with lifeless instruments that produce sound, such as the flute or the harp. If they do not give distinct notes, how will anyone know what is being played? And if the bugle gives an indistinct sound, who will get ready for battle? . . . If in a tongue you utter speech that is not intelligible, how will anyone know what is being said? For you will be speaking into the air. There are doubtless many different kinds of sounds in the world, and nothing is without sound" [vv. 7–10]. Speaking in this way, the apostle is concerned with genuine edification. But this is impossible when Christian speech is unclear, unintelligible, or left to arbitrary exposition by its hearers. One needs to know whether something was piped or harped, whether and where one must prepare for battle, or whether it is spoken into the wind. Whoever hands out mottoes is also answerable for their resonance and must consider it very precisely in advance.

The Problematic

What resonance will the slogan "Fear not" find with the West German citizen it invites to the 1981 Evangelical *Kirchentag* in Hamburg? No doubt, most will

A lecture given at the area synod of Hamburg and at the Evangelical Academy at Hamburg, September 25 and 26, 1980. First printed in the information book of the Association of Evangelical Teachers of Religion (Hamburg, 1981), 26–40.

be content with this motto and find their expectations confirmed to the extent they experience anything of the sort toward Christianity. "Fear not"—we can always hear this, and especially when we are doing well and have something to lose. "Fear not" could perfectly well be a box-office hit if it did not sound so edifying and biblical.

Secretly, and sometimes even openly, there is more panic among us than we admit. There are not only communists and terrorists and freaks but also economic decline and the shutting-down of workplaces, a flood of asylum seekers, threatening energy problems, war and war cries in the Near and Far East, in Africa and Latin America. There is a growing bureaucracy to which the security of state institutions seems more important than the freedom of the citizen anchored in basic law. There are factions making themselves mutually more and more incredible, and we all are subject to the stress of the compulsion to produce and consume, to the extent that the throwaway society does not already count the aged, pensioners, and disabled as waste. These mottoes may suffice if we do not closely examine private miseries such as sickness, accident, death, isolation, and alienation between married people, parents and children, neighbors, colleagues. Did committees and leaders of evangelical churches want to pose the slogan "Fear not" to all this? Christians would not need to be ashamed of it. Life that has taken comfort from the gospel goes comforted into everyday life on earth, into its cares and troubles, and courage cannot be separated from faith, though at present it cannot honestly be counted among the most prominent Christian virtues. Nevertheless, the motto must be inquired into once more. In the verses cited at the beginning, Paul criticizes speaking in tongues that poses as worked by the Spirit and professes to create edification. He thinks the Spirit is more hindered than communicated by it, and he would rather speak five words intelligibly for the instruction of the congregation than ten thousand in oracles. What is basic must of course be repeated and inculcated. But the preacher, just as he fears the devil, should fear the boredom that allows the hearer to say, after having heard the message, "This is just what I already knew and expected."

This echo indicates not only that we did not sufficiently strive to expect anything of the hearer but, more yet, that the Holy Spirit could not speak—that One who produces surprising miracles and shocking offenses but never boredom. We cannot press the Spirit into our service, but we can drown out the Spirit's voice with our manipulations. This happens when we make our own insights the norm for all others. It also happens when we conceal problems from the community, spare it dangerous decisions, and, with lullabies, break its habit of independent thinking. God's Spirit does not get his due where Christianity is domesticated, lodged in the emotional sphere, and adjusted to the desires of the world around it. *Kirchentage* can fall prey to manipulation in many ways. This is so particularly because official hierarchies have increasingly influenced the course of meetings that were initially founded by so-called laypeople and because the political polarization in our nation has, to a large extent, encroached upon the ecclesiastical landscape. The ideology of pragmatism, intent on balance, has for the longest time drawn the church bureaucracy into its vortex. What seems to it to be a need more and more regulates practice. Traditional ways of doing things are defended by core values that from a Christian standpoint are really problematic. The conformity of those who do not want their rest disturbed is promoted in the name of diaconal and pedagogical obligation. In this case, "Fear not" becomes an opiate for all who let God from heaven and all kinds of managers on earth care for their well-being but avoid personal responsibility toward global crises and would prefer to trust blindly.

A Political Interlude

On North Elbian soil, where the *Kirchentag* takes place, a timely theological debate is due over what may absolutely not be given us or expected of us as evangelical. Highly notable statements on state and church, made by the present chancellor[1] in a lecture delivered in 1974, and published in his book *Der Kurs heisst Frieden* [The course is called freedom] in 1979, correspond exactly to the question as well as to the local milieu.[2] The politician speaks as a member of the evangelical church when he calls for a commitment to democratic freedom. It is not by accident that, following his lecture, he can end by referring to the Bach motet *Fürchte Dich nicht* [Fear not] and actually see political responsibility substantiated by it.[3] We need not puzzle over the sense in which this is meant. The most important task of the church is that it communicate in a vital way the "knowledge and experience of the power over us and of the power over" our history, the experience of trust in God and (literal quotation) "also in his church."

In an openness much to be applauded, the chancellor confesses that he personally experienced humanity's need of a transcendent commitment during dictatorship and the horrors of war.[4] He thus would desire that the churches,

1. Helmut Heinrich Waldemar Schmidt (1918–2015), Social Democratic politician, chancellor of West Germany from 1974 to 1982.
2. Helmut Heinrich Waldemar Schmidt, *Der Kurs heisst Frieden* (Düsseldorf: Econ, 1979), 25–50.
3. Schmidt, *Der Kurs heisst Frieden*, 50.
4. Schmidt, *Der Kurs heisst Frieden*, 27.

as the moral power in our nation, give example and assistance on behalf of a conscientiously responsible activity[5] and of further education of the individual toward reverence for ultimate values.[6] He concedes that, in individual instances, political preaching and the political pastoral letter can be legitimate and actually necessary.[7] Yet he brusquely rejects the conscious and intentional dissemination of political ideologies in the guise of theology or in the cloak of the spiritual office, and in the same place he says with notable emphasis that individuals, the laity, we (literally) who "need the national church, who have need of soul care, ask not to be disturbed by controversial theologies and political preaching."[8] The speech obviously reached its height with this sentence. Now, in polemic, the spotlight falls on the understanding of "Fear not" at the lecture's conclusion. "Fear not" is threatened when controversial and political proclamation gains ground, for in that case the laity, thus the genuine church people, are disturbed—that is, the trust they need in the power over us and our history is shaken, as is also the transcendent commitment of the person and reverence for ultimate values. Clearly, the politician is making not merely a political but also a theological judgment, and very carelessly and in an absolutely untenable way. From the very beginning, all Christian theology was controversial, not because theologians are addicted to strife (which no one can deny) but because, in this world of ours, the gospel is controversial, because the message of the crucified Son of God and the God who humbles Godself can only be proclaimed and accepted as controversial. To make that immediately clear: the gospel of the God who humbles Godself and subjects Godself to crucifixion has always had a political dimension and, rightly understood, has always been a revolutionary message of freedom for all the humiliated and insulted, for those cheated of their worth, for the poor of the Beatitudes.

Nothing of this will be changed, though it cannot please an affluent society. The Third World stands before our doors where we do not want to see, hear, or reach it. It dies and flees before our doors, and to it the Nazarene says today: "Come to me, all you that are weary and are carrying heavy burdens" [Matt. 11:28]. But in saying this, he sides with a political party, though we would rather see him as neutral and prefer not to be disturbed by him. Christians who want to follow their Lord will, for better or for worse, have to meddle in the politicians' affairs, though these, over their worries about exports and workplaces, find 0.3 percent of the gross national product sufficient for the

5. Schmidt, *Der Kurs heisst Frieden*, 28.
6. Schmidt, *Der Kurs heisst Frieden*, 36.
7. Schmidt, *Der Kurs heisst Frieden*, 30.
8. Schmidt, *Der Kurs heisst Frieden*, 31.

Third World, with the investments of the multinationals into the bargain. Christians would be dumb dogs if they were silent toward press reports that in this year for the first time more than five hundred billion was spent for armament, and something like fifteen billion will go for the sale of weapons to the lands of the Third World, with their already eight hundred (some say "only" five hundred) million persons starving. When the armed forces and politicians regard such lunacy as unavoidable, it is a shame that all of Christianity does not begin to cry out and go on radical political strike. The simplest possible human understanding cannot be described as ideology—just as, conversely, that pragmatism which allows the screw of the arms race to be turned more and more to keep step with the opponent unquestionably does merit the name of ideology. This example shows that, like the famed sociologist Max Weber,[9] we absolutely no longer have to draw a basic distinction between an ethic of intention and an ethic of responsibility (thus the chancellor on page 44), according to which the politician must be aware of the net of impulses and effects, that is (I am literally quoting here) "of side effects, counter-efforts, counter-effects that must be right in front of our eyes, . . . while Christianity supplies the fundamental morality for it; it is precisely for this reason the national church is still indispensable in our society."[10] Obviously, views of a liberal idealism are taken up here, which for their part remind us once more of Lessing's[11] argument with the Hamburg senior pastor Goeze. In a world after Auschwitz and Stalingrad this no longer applies. Religious and moral intention that leaves the concrete decisions in public life to the experts and at best holds before them the mirror of traditional basic values, or that shouts "with God" at them before they enter daily into the arena prescribed for them, is nothing but a stimulant. We cannot and may not do without experts. But whoever is devoted to science knows that we can and may never rely completely on experts. In a democracy, everyone is jointly responsible; Christians cannot possibly have merely the function of prescribing energy pills for soul and conscience for the world around them, especially for those in power.

It will be clear now why this debate has taken place with the chancellor, for whose abilities I have the greatest respect. It seems to me that in his statements he represents wide circles and that his understanding of "Fear not" should in no way substantially determine the *Kirchentag*—even with episcopal blessing. This motto is not to be the advertisement for a universal trust in God. After

9. Max Weber (1864–1920), professor of economics at Freiburg and Heidelberg, sociologist, philosopher, jurist, and political economist, often cited as one of the founders of sociology.

10. Schmidt, *Der Kurs heisst Frieden*, 30.

11. Gotthold Ephraim Lessing (1729–81), German writer, philosopher, dramatist, publicist, and art critic, one of the most outstanding representatives of the Enlightenment era.

the earthquake at Lisbon, Voltaire in his *Candide* scoffed at it as absurd. Naturally, there are times when we make it through life with a few blue bruises.

For the most part, the situation is worse, to say absolutely nothing of the grave that awaits us. After the experiences of my generation—which passed through world wars, revolutions, dictatorship, and economic crises (if it survived at all)—it actually sounds blasphemous when this commercial is used for soul massage and calculated optimism. We have not gone out as the young man in the fairy tale in order to learn to fear.[12] Nevertheless, we have been painfully taught why only a few want to be reminded of the past. Not all have forgotten the many corpses on their path. Not all are spared the ghosts in their dreams, specters that have met them at every corner and with which, as once Jacob with his God, they have had to wrestle. One cannot shout "Fear not" at us without adding when, how, where, and why this should be possible, or of use. If all this is not added, only a naked, meaningless imperative remains. We may, of course, be ordered to hold our tongue or clench our teeth. Therefore, the command to not be afraid is just as senseless as the other, to love a specific person. Not even among Prussians will it do to ask, "Dogs, do you want to live forever?"[13] No heart has power over its anxieties, and no reason drives out demons that are not merely the deceptive delusions of our fantasy. Every person has the reason and the right to be afraid. We who in our life have gotten to know hell more than we liked do not allow ourselves to be fascinated or intimidated by a categorical imperative. We must be as realistic as the Bible.

A Theological Reflection

Hopefully, at the 1981 *Kirchentag*, people consider that, in the Bible, fear is an elementary part of the nature of humanity and our world and that it is mentioned in the Bible at least as often as the words "Fear not." Every event that ignores this fact is from the outset marked by the desire and need for at least a temporary anesthesia. Many cannot live without religious drugs, and many others interfere in God's and the physicians' affairs by handing out religious drugs to anaesthetize existing anxieties. Where anxieties are anaesthetized, love, which gives closeness and tenderness in body and soul, also dies—love, in

12. Käsemann refers here to the German folktale "The Story of the Youth Who Went Forth to Learn What Fear Was," collected by Jacob Grimm and Wilhelm Grimm ("the Brothers Grimm") in the early nineteenth century. The story is about a boy, the younger of two sons, who goes out of his father's house seeking to learn how to fear.

13. This appears to be a reference to the 1959 West German film *Hunde, wollt ihr ewig leben?*, about the Battle of Stalingrad (August 23, 1942–February 2, 1943).

which we can be sheltered and with which we can give shelter to others. Where anxieties are anaesthetized, the robots (the consumers) increase who entice producers just as producers entice their partners in consumption. Now one travels over the entire globe but spiritually does not get beyond the shadows of one's own church tower, party, illusions, and conventions. Then begin the last days of humanity, be it only for the White Man and his history. With eyes open, we can read the fiery writing on our walls: "You have been weighed on the scales and found wanting" [Dan. 5:27]. Anaesthetized anxiety leads to blindness that feels secure where most imperiled; one dances on volcanoes. As paradoxical as it sounds, humanity remains intact only as long as fear, and not only religious fear, is not battled by drugs, though this is happening everywhere and incessantly with the affluent middle class. In this context it must be stated that right through the whole Bible the command is repeated: "You shall fear your God: I am the LORD" [e.g., Lev. 19:14, 32]. Where this is begun—for example, in Leviticus 19:14 and 32—by it humane treatment is established toward the deaf, the blind, the aged. God is the Lord as Creator and Protector of humanity, and fear of God—as, for example in Exodus 14:31—is identified with faith in God. In Joshua 24:14ff., and elsewhere, fear is identified with a service that cannot be assigned to others. "The fear of the LORD," according to Psalm 111:10, "is the beginning of wisdom." We interpret it to read: it is such because it truly works what is human and sets one within a common humanity.

The devout, throughout the entire Bible called "those who fear God," are not removed from earthly creatureliness. Their characteristic (perhaps even basic) mood is fear. Even the believer comes up against the mystery of life, which ends in dying and before which we flee to the arms of tenderness and love. No one is lord of their own destiny; everyone at the very depths is a stranger to self and actually still in flight on the search for their true lord and their own identity. Humans differ from the rest of the creation only when they allow themselves to be found by their Creator and are given the place determined for them, as the call from Isaiah 43:1 describes: "Do not fear, for I have redeemed you; I have called you by name, you are mine."

The mystery of life around us does not simply cease, nor does defiance and the despondency of our hearts. Nevertheless, the fear of God gains the upper hand over our fear of the world and gives the last word to the One who also spoke the first word over us. This is most precisely formulated in Psalm 86:11: "Teach me your way, O LORD, that I may walk in your truth; give me an undivided heart to revere your name." Now let us note the remarkable play between the divine summons, "Fear not," and the suppliant's answer, "Give me an undivided heart to revere your name." Salvation emerges where our lives are no longer silent under an iron heaven, where they no longer cry out in anxiety—but where they become conversation. Whoever must grope through the darkness needs the helping word. Whoever is on the tiresome and perilous wandering through the alternation of growing and aging, joy and suffering, light and dark, love and friendship and solitariness and mistrust—whoever is, as it were, on the pilgrimage between heaven and hell—needs, from time to time, and on and on, to be summoned: "Fear not!" Now, we have established that this cannot at all be commanded. Is it suddenly no longer of value when both commands are in the Bible and are to be taken from it? Then is it only a mother's cheerful encouragement, suggesting to the injured child, "It doesn't hurt, does it"? Must we then, as for the most part surely happens, regard it as edifying prattle that of course does not change much but still encourages and, in any case, calms down?

It would really be laughable to put such a word in the mouth of a God who acts when God speaks and works what God promises. There is a third possibility, between the command to be obeyed and the edifying prattle used as an opiate, and that is the promise. Let us focus on this from the first commandment: "I am the LORD your God. . . . You shall have no other gods before me" [Exod. 20:2–3; Deut. 5:6–7]. This too is not easily said. Still, a miracle occurs when it is realized. It is only by way of a miracle that, as Luther's explanation formulates it, we "fear, love, and trust in God above all things."[14]

The often-invoked common sense will not consent to this. "Above all things" is what fanatics say, or perhaps those in love. Whoever is oriented to earthly realities will be for compromises. And if one wants to, should, or must include God in the calculation, one can still not ignore opponents, whether called gods or demons or ideologies. For "realists" the task is to find the balance between necessity and reality. But that is exactly what contradicts the first commandment and its alternative involving the "either-or" of God and the demons. We come out of the dilemma only when we recognize that on the basis of its introduction the first commandment is a promise. Whoever has heard "I am the LORD your God" no longer needs to submit to other gods and demons. But if one does, one has not really accepted God as the only Lord over oneself. Promise is the way into the open air when earthly reality and religious postulate are in conflict. Earthly reality says, "You may," but life depends on whether you do it. The biblical "Fear not" concretizes the first commandment and, like it, is to be heard as promise. It is not spoken because there is no reason to fear. Rather, it marks that moment when only fear still seems to correspond to reality. And it will not encourage taking a risk by which one goes head over heels into deep water, since the face of the rock gives no support. Therefore,

---

14. Martin Luther, Small Catechism, on the first commandment.

faith is, for the most part, more despondent than daring or heroic. When faith puts on a demonstration, it lives no longer from conversation with its Lord, no longer from the one true gospel that forms the center of the entire Scripture and there, again and again (as, for example, in Genesis 26:24ff. and in the first commandment), makes its "no other gods before me" and "above all things" possible by way of the promise: "I am with you." We must not blindly rush into adventure, whether seized by panic or arrogantly trusting in our own power and reason or, like a gambler, putting all our luck on the cards. We are sent, put on a path that we have to trace, without knowing the "when" and "where" and "how" of its end. Nothing is clear at the outset, only the word that sends us and also assumes responsibility for the sending. "Fear not" means you need not worry over what someone intends to do with you and what results from it, over how you yourself and whether you yourself will survive. You are led and are kept like a child by the Father's hand.

On the other hand, this does not happen as in the fairy tale where the child sits on the green grass and waits for what the wind of accident dumps in its lap. Christian existence is defined in Ephesians 1:14 to the effect that we can be something to the praise of God's glory. Fear of God is service in discipleship. The Lord remains with us as the One who bears the responsibility—totally and solely. Even in darkness and dying he surrounds us with his promise. But this promise does not leave us inactive. It sends us as its instruments into the kingdom of its love, for it is not limited by us. Rather, it intends to be borne further by us, because God says, not merely to the elect but to all God's creatures, "I am with you"; and throughout the whole earth God will be praised with Psalm 118:6: "With the LORD on my side I do not fear. What can mortals do to me?" Fear of God makes us jointly responsible for humanity throughout the whole earth.

This is precisely and matchlessly expressed by the German word *barm-herzig* [compassionate], which quite literally means the heart turned and held open to the poor—*barmherzig*. Because divine promise assumes all the needs of creation, it proclaims *Barmherzigkeit* [compassion], salvation for the poor who cannot help themselves by their own reason and strength. Because *Barmherzigkeit* has reached out to us, fear of God is not anxiety and panic but something of use where, according to Hebrews 2:15, there are "those who all their lives were held in slavery by the fear of death." It is thus service in freedom. And of this Luther spoke beautifully and in a captivating manner: "What is not service is robbery."[15]

15. This saying, attributed to Luther, appears to date back to a sermon he delivered on March 29, 1523. Martin Luther, *Dr. Martin Luther's vermischte Predigten*, ed. Ernst Ludwig Enders, Dr. Martin Luther's Sämmtliche Werke 2 (Frankfurt am Main: Heyder & Zimmer, 1878), 38.

The Decisive Aspect

From what was said we must draw the consequences for the *Kirchentag*. Naturally, that cannot be done over the entire breadth of that market of many possibilities which traditionally helped to determine the scene of the last *Kirchentag*. Every individual must experience the "Fear not" individually and by it be drawn into the sphere of the fear of God. This applies as well to the various groups of young and old, healthy and disabled, conservatives and rebels—across social, cultural, political, and racial differences. To draw a blueprint for all of this is impossible. But, in conclusion, what is needed is a comprehensive aspect into which each individual detail can be fitted and by which the particular situation is indicated, just as our position in general, as well as that of the 1981 *Kirchentag*. I will take up what just loomed up with the keyword *Barmherzigkeit*. Whoever was at the 1980 World Conference for Mission and Evangelization in Melbourne, or heard of it, knows of the hour and theme of Christianity today. Whatever may be most splendidly said or done at the *Kirchentag*, it remains unclear, does not aim at what is decisive, when "Fear not" is not understood as a beatitude for the poor, because what is at issue is not equilibrium (as is usual in the secular and church bureaucracy) but rather what is unambiguous in terms of 1 Corinthians 14:2ff. It must be formulated harshly and pointedly, but also very earnestly and convincingly, that we have not heard the "Fear not" in the concrete when before anything else it is not shouted to the Third World, then from the Third World back to us. Those who do not hear it today in a primarily ecumenical way hear it merely as edifying, as abstract; they are at best occupied with navel-gazing and confuse God's kingdom with their group and confessional interests. We all have our little aches and pains, our anxieties and conflicts, and must all die. Nonetheless, as the speaker from East Germany said at Melbourne, our environment in West Germany, perhaps even in East Germany, is determined by the affluent society. But this rests on the sweat, tears, torture, exploitation, and murder of people of color and the white proletariat.

Our society must see its image in the mirror of a world of poverty. Only provincialism will not want to allow this, in order to remain dumb, self-righteous, and hypocritical in the warmth of its own nest. Each of us here is implicated and jointly responsible. For our society continues to defend its positions of power and traditional privileges with brutal resolve and under misleading slogans. Still, all who profit from it or who worry about exports, workplaces, and pension increases make the present luxury the basis and norm of their behavior. We live in conditions in which the person becomes a wolf toward others near and far, for the most part without thought, but often in shameless frankness. Alms must cover over global injustice like crumbs thrown to the dogs from the set table.

This does not even reach those 3.3 billion German marks we spend each year on house pets. A synod of the German Evangelical Church reacts with indignation when the redistribution of the world's resources is held to be necessary, though the same remarks already appeared in the 1976 church document on *Social Justice* and were repeated in the *Brandt Report*[16] a short time ago. The synod fears revolution and the attack on sanctified property, while in Calcutta, Mother Teresa gathers the dying and corpses on the street. Here the function of the motto "Fear not" is altered, as if to say, "Be of good cheer, keep a robust conscience, capitulate helplessly, cowardly, or arrogantly to the status quo." The supposed pragmatism for which our children and grandchildren will pay cares cynically for the interests of those in power and their suppliers of raw material. Democracy reaches only as far as one gets back what is claimed to be sacrificed for freedom. The human rights so often conjured up are nowhere pursued and are, with us at least, bureaucratically administered and arbitrarily trimmed. The international solidarity of the work force no longer embraces the areas of misery in which a family must live on seven hundred German marks per year. Yet nothing hinders us from accusing others of materialism, atheism, the despising of human values. It is called realpolitik when in our time Cain asks, "Am I my brother's keeper?" [Gen. 4:9].

Into this apocalyptically polarized world of ours, which allows the rich to become richer and the poor poorer, goes the call of the Risen One according to Revelation 1:17f.: "Do not be afraid; I am the first and the last, and the living one. I was dead, and see, I am alive forever and ever; and I have the keys of Death and of Hades." It is only on the basis of the resurrection that our motto ultimately has meaning, whereas we on earth have to do with the global violation of human beings by human beings, demons, ideologies, and economic systems; whereas the Babylon of the White Man once more puts on all his might for display, and the ghosts of his victims rise from their graves to proclaim his imminent downfall. We should not hear "Fear not" as a general slogan, as if everyone who one way or another struggles through life and in the course of it encounters the unavoidable unpleasantnesses has a heavenly helper. To the poor, helpless, and humbled, the gospel is preached that God is on their side, does not abandon them to the grave and hell, but wills and creates their freedom. To the rich and self-secure, judgment is announced with the word of the curse from Matthew 25:45: "Truly I tell you, just as you did

16. The *Brandt Report* was a report from the Independent Commission on International Development in 1980. It was named after the first chair of the commission, Willy Brandt, a former German chancellor.

not do it to one of the least of these, you did not do it to me." It should be noted that this is spoken to pious people who want to serve God but separate the Creator from the creature and themselves from those in misery before their door. All who suffer and are alone are called here to remain in the discipleship of the Nazarene and to see themselves surrounded by the fellowship that shoulders its own cross, since in just this way their Lord makes his disciples like him and truly human. "Fear not" declares to all the churches that they do not have to bring alms to the Third World. The Third World points them to the place where the Beatitudes are more than edifying prattle. In the children of Israel's departure from the Egypt of the full fleshpots, that Word calls to the wilderness where the Father of Jesus Christ waits for them in his promises and with his tasks and where they may become witnesses to his glory and mercy. The decisive aspect of our motto to which we must pay attention today is its world-political dimension. Indeed, it applies to every individual, in personal distresses and apparent impasses, but never to the individual alone and never merely for Sunday and the contemplative hour in the chamber. It is called out to every member of the wandering people of God, in everyday life with its earthly ties, thus in responsibility for the conditions of society and a suffering world.

By themselves, orthodoxy and piety are not worth a measly penny for household use, because, together with bourgeois morality and the models of social well-being, they are offered at all kinds of markets. Where the Crucified and Risen One sends out his disciples, there is penetration of the kingdom of the principalities and powers that on earth teach us to fear. Then, "Fear not" means to go the way of the discipleship of our Lord to the end. Religiously foddered ideology spreads in heaps where one is protected from God's grasp and from that of the evil world, as well as from battle with the demons. But, according to 2 Peter 3:13, for the sake of the new heaven we also wait for a new earth in which justice dwells, and we must not tire of witnessing to such a promise in word and deed. Much can be said in criticism of the theology of liberation in the Third World. Nevertheless, no theology deserves the name "Christian" that does not dare to tear the masks from the faces of idols, that does not, with Daniel 2:32ff., uncover the clay feet of the world powers and attack the vested rights of the privileged, because among the privileged God's salvation is identified with one's own temporal and eternal well-being, and God's salvation is reduced to one's own. The 1981 *Kirchentag* will be measured by the breadth and energy with which it credibly sets forth this decisive aspect of the "Fear not" and dares to represent *Barmherzigkeit* [compassion], thus salvation for the poor in all the world, as the mark of our present state in the discipleship of Jesus.

╌╌ 16 ╌╌

The Eschatological Royal Rule of God (1980)

According to the New Testament, John the Baptist and Jesus begin their careers with the proclamation "Repent, for the kingdom of heaven has come near" [Matt. 3:2; 4:17]. The basic motif of their activity is their proclamation of that end time in which God appears out of God's hiddenness and makes known to everyone God's kingdom on earth. Authentic gospel must be measured by this message. Christians and church fellowships are credible only so long as the stormy cry is heard from them: "Thy kingdom come!" But if that is so, then we have to put the entire Bible, along with all of our traditions and expectations—in fact, the history of the world—under this one theme.

What Is the Meaning of the Eschatological Royal Rule of God?

The end of the world has often been longed for or feared. The New Testament proclamation of the imminence of the kingdom of God assumes that Judaism, whose fathers confessed in Exodus 15:18 that "the LORD will reign forever and ever," later saw the conviction of their faith threatened by earthly

A lecture given at the World Conference for Mission and Evangelization in Melbourne. First published in *Dein Reich komme: Bericht der Weltkonferenz für Mission und Evangelisation in Melbourne 1980*, ed. Martin Lehmann-Habeck and Walter Arnold (Frankfurt am Main: Lembeck Verlag, 1981), 114–23.

realities: "O LORD our God, other lords besides you have ruled over us, but we acknowledge your name alone" [Isa. 26:13]. We live in the conflict between the one true God and the wielders of power who compete with God in this world, and who actually appear to triumph over God. Now we must ask to whom the earth and its creatures really belong. In such a situation both the Baptist and Jesus answer: "Repent, for the kingdom of heaven has come near." In the New Testament, "repent" never means "change of mind," as in the Greek, but rather "return," as in the Hebrew. What appears to be a condition is actually a consequence of the promise of the kingdom drawn near, not a command but an invitation. In danger of being lost, one is called to return to the hope, to rely on the future of God, thus to move to the front line of those who wait. One need not doubt: God is coming to God's earth and to God's creatures whom God has not surrendered as God's creation. God will establish God's kingdom in the midst of God's enemies, unmask the idols, humble the proud into the dust, create power for the oppressed. When God's kingdom is spoken of from the Jewish perspective, it means first of all the revelation of the One who as king does not abdicate, but openly exercises God's rule everywhere. Naturally, this is not without an earthly echo, as angels, shepherds, and wise men give witness in the Christmas story. There is worldwide tumult and confrontation, just as at Easter and Pentecost. The community of believers is formed among rebels who deny their Creator obedience. This belongs to the end time. Where God comes near and breaks into the realm of the principalities and powers of this aeon, the earth becomes a battlefield, and everyone is drawn into the conflict over the true lord of their own life as well as of all others. God and the idols—this now becomes the decisive theme of world history, and no one can remain neutral here.

These statements, of course, exceed the message of John the Baptist. He spoke of the coming judge of Israel. His baptism was to be a sign of protection for those who renewed the covenant with God in the last hour. For Jesus, on the other hand, the inbreaking rule is constitutively a saving event opened with beatitudes; it brings forgiveness for sinners, help for the plagued, freedom for those in bondage; and, with deeds of power, it destroys the works of the devil. For Jesus, judgment is only the reverse side of grace, spurned by the self-righteous, and thus the end of the demonic violation of the creation. For this reason, Luke 10:18 reads, "I watched Satan fall from heaven like a flash of lightning," and Luke 11:20 bases the nearness of God's kingdom on the fact that Jesus drives out the devil "by the finger of God." The preaching of the Baptist is thus, as it were, reversed, without our being able to say how it happened. Here the appearance of the Nazarene is already determined by the secret of his mission. The difference between the Baptist and that which characterizes the bringer of the end-time gospel is twofold: First, God's kingdom is not merely at hand in the near future. It has already begun with Jesus's word and work. Second, salvation is where demonic power is broken, and thus it is no longer essentially limited to the boundaries of Israel. A world change has begun. Pentecost comes into view where heaven is opened, where the Holy Spirit obtains worldwide space in which to move, and where the *Pantocrator* is praised also by the gentiles.

The Kingdom of Christ

In a famous utterance, Origen called Jesus the *autobasileus* (the kingdom of God in person). Whatever the objection to it, in any event it exactly marks where the Christian view of the kingdom of God is separated from the Jewish. Judaism had already emphasized that the coming of the king determines the message of the kingdom, that this rule is not, for instance, just a new structure. Judaism too had connected (albeit not universally) the end-time kingdom with the appearance of a Messiah who, of course, was popularly conceived as a forerunner—that is, as a political liberator of Israel. What is Christian is the proclamation that the Savior not only of Israel or of his faithful but absolutely of all has become flesh in Jesus and, in all eternity, has become the Mediator and Revealer—as it were, the face of God turned to earth and its creatures. The Gospel of John calls him the way and the door, the shepherd, the bread, and water of life, the Word begotten of the Father and his sole exegete. The Pentecost confession of Peter in Acts 2:36 reads that God has made this Jesus Lord and Christ. In 1 Corinthians 15:24 Paul speaks of the One who will "[destroy] every ruler and every authority and power," then assigns world history this sense: "He must reign until he has put all his enemies under his feet" [v. 25]. The mighty hymn of praise in Ephesians 1:20–23 praises the Risen One who was seated "at [God's] right hand in the heavenly places, far above all rule and authority and power and dominion, and above every name that is named, not only in this age but also in the age to come." The Revelation of John, in 11:15, sums it up: "The kingdom of the world has become the kingdom of our Lord and of his Messiah, and he will reign forever and ever." Christianity knows of no end-time kingdom of God at whose center Jesus of Nazareth is not standing. If, according to Luke 4:43, his earthly task was to proclaim the gospel of the kingdom, then for his disciples he has become the presence of this kingdom with all its abundance of gifts and powers. This is what the disciples mean when they testify, "We have seen his glory" [John 1:14]. We will make clear what consequences this has for us.

We already indicated that right here, just as Christianity and Judaism part company, so also do gospel and mere ideology or religious utopia. For us, the kingdom of God is not primarily a theory but a praxis. However, to put it bluntly, it is not a praxis that mainly involves changed conditions, new possibilities, and goals. From the New Testament and Christian perspective, the kingdom of God denotes that action in which Jesus of Nazareth is our Lord and Lord of the world.

The first commandment was given concretion for us: "I am the LORD your God. . . . You shall have no other gods before me" [Exod. 20:2–3; Deut. 5:6–7]. This is now no longer uttered from the clouds as at Sinai. The Lord has now become Man, crucified, risen, Son of the heavenly Father, and at the same time the new Adam. Others may stylize him as a hero and model of their own choosing, a pioneer of humane, social, political ideas. This is not to be despised, but it no longer satisfies us. For he and he alone is our Lord, and there is salvation in no other, as Acts 4:12 laconically states. He and he alone separates us from all the idols to which we are otherwise delivered. What sounds like a command is a promise: you need no longer have other gods besides me, no longer need to reckon with them, fear them, pay them tribute. There is an open way as occurred with Israel in Egypt. His rule awakens free men and women and a fellowship of the free.

As the kingdom of Christ, God's kingdom begun on earth is the kingdom of the Crucified who sets his disciples together with him beneath the cross. Only those who (unlike the enthusiasts and ideologues) make no detour around Golgotha are truly freed by him and taken into his fellowship. My generation in West Germany learned that, like Israel, we were freed from Egypt and led through the wilderness in order finally as the church to dance around the golden calf. Even before Jesus has entered upon his career, the tempter offers him all the kingdoms of the world and their glory, and the Nazarene must defend himself against it, himself laying hold of the first commandment: "Worship the Lord your God, and serve only him" [Matt. 4:10; Luke 4:8]. This "only" leads to the cross, and on this "alone" the spirits, even in Christianity, always divide. Unmistakably opposed to all ideological temptation, Jesus describes himself in John 18:36–37 as a king whose kingdom is not of the world; it is, rather, the space of truth, of the sole rule of God spread abroad in this world. God's truth is hostile toward everything that appears in its own name, for its own honor, by its own reason or strength—in short, toward everything that trusts in itself and asserts its own will. All other conceivable paradoxes are transcended when, in Luke 12:37, the return of the Son of Man is described in analogy with the foot washing of John 13. Once again, just as once on earth, the One appearing in the glory of heaven will gird himself with the apron of a slave to serve his own. This is his law and his distinctive mark, because, according to Matthew 20:28, he did not come "to be served but to serve, and to give his life a ransom for many." The disciple is not above his Master, who, according to the psalm in Philippians 2:6ff., abandoned his equality with God and took on the form of a servant, as the prophecy of the despised and suffering Servant of God presaged it in Isaiah 53.

According to Philippians 3:10, "the power of his resurrection" is experienced in "the sharing of his sufferings," which make us "like him in his death." So, according to John 12:24, the wheat must die in order to bring forth much fruit. Grace does not make it cheaper for anyone: "Those who love their life lose it, and those who hate their life in this world will keep it for eternal life" [John 12:25]. The king of the heavenly kingdom continues his way on the streets of this world.

We have understood nothing about him when we seek him at the wrong place and proclaim him under false mottoes. He is always found only where redemption is needed, thus, according to Psalm 107:10, among those who "[sit] in darkness and in gloom, prisoners in misery and in irons." Here the Christian process of teaching and learning must begin, must be extended anew every day as the same Psalm says at its close: "Let those who are wise give heed to these things, and consider the steadfast love of the LORD." The one who serves has appeared among the possessors of power on earth, and he calls his servants in the midst of the reality of tyrants and idols ruining the creation. He does this to establish his benefits there—according to Romans 14:17, the kingdom of righteousness, peace, and joy in the Holy Spirit.

The Work of the Rule of Christ

The answer Jesus gives in Luke 13:32 to the warning about Herod's plans to murder him is very curious: "Listen, I am casting out demons and performing cures today and tomorrow, and on the third day I finish my work." Still, no one can ignore the fact that our Gospels continually narrate the healing of the possessed, that Acts continues this, and that the epistles of the New Testament, quite particularly the Revelation of John, celebrate the victory of the Risen One as deliverance from enslavement to the principalities and powers. By "principalities and powers" is meant all who torment, who seduce the world as well as every individual, who alienate humanity from itself, who plunge the proud as well as the desperate into disaster. Not by chance baptismal hymns, such as in Colossians 1:13, continually confess that "he has rescued us from the power of darkness and transferred us into the kingdom of his beloved Son."

We may criticize and demythologize the language and ideas of an ancient worldview as outdated. We actually must do so, since only then is the reality of our present life and our present earth perceived. But this reality does not cancel out the experiences of earliest Christianity. Rather, it sharpens them. The affluent society of the White Man may laugh about demons. But it can do so only because—blind, deaf, unfeeling, and stupid—it does not look beyond the shadows of its technical successes, its brutally defended privileges, and its traditional prejudices. Mountains of unrecognized guilt, and guilt unatoned for in one's own sphere as well as in the wide world, tower up ever higher. Churches become conformist with pious slogans that support the calculated optimism of politicians and economists. In a virtually blasphemous manner, unpleasant critics (to say nothing of rebels) are summoned to blind trust; to empty hope; to frivolous fearlessness; and, naturally, to discipline—so as not to endanger the prevailing power relationships.

We will not see and hear that our hour has long since struck, that we are in view, when 1 Corinthians 7:31 states, "The present form of this world is passing away." According to popular opinion, the kingdom of God and the reign of Christ are metaphysical constructions that, like islands of the blest, float above the clouds and, at best, are something to look for in places of worship and private edification. To most members of our congregations, it appears as heresy that, first of all, neither the kingdom of God nor the reign of Christ is for the purpose of urging the citizen to preserve traditional laws and orders or to be obedient to the higher powers. What is forgotten is that Christianity everywhere had to be a fermenting leaven; the voice of the oppressed; a critical conscience against possessiveness, the plundering of the earth, the violation of its creatures, and the enactment of the present status quo. Actually, 1 John 5:19 states, "we know . . . that the whole world lies under the power of the evil one." Yet, for the most part, we leave it to the dear God to deal with it, since (especially in the sphere of the White Man) things do not look so bad; prosperity and enjoyment of life are noticeably on the rise, while the sense for reality apart from money and success shockingly declines, and is perhaps actually smothered by political propaganda and demagoguery. We daily suppress the fact that, for the majority of its inhabitants, our earth is a hell; and we allow the truths that "the light shines in the darkness" [John 1:5] and that Jesus died in no-man's-land to be mere pious phrases. Only the one who denies these truths can deny that the gospel has a global political dimension.

Naturally, Jesus was no revolutionary. Nevertheless, his appearance had revolutionary consequences, and these were unavoidable. Universal conflict begins where the One who in 1 Timothy 6:15 is called "King of kings and Lord of lords" announces his claim to his creation, where truth and deception war over every individual, where the Crucified wrests his kingdom from tyrants and usurpers and destroys the work of the devil on earth. This is what is really involved when the demons appear in the New Testament as the real enemies of Christ, and for this reason all Christian service should always be seen as, in essence, a kind of exorcism—as the driving out of evil spirits. God's Spirit reigns on earth forever in the sphere of the demons, in challenging them and in victory over them. A Christianity that confesses that it believes in God's Spirit but does not draw the Spirit's power and victory into the depths, into the nooks and crannies, is a Christianity without credibility.

Everywhere our earth needs de-demonizing. For God's good creation arises and persists only where heaven is opened and sends down the Spirit. We have interiorized and privatized Christianity for too long, made of the Spirit of God only the power of sanctification in the community, consoled ourselves and others with a view of the blessedness of eternal life beyond temporal tribulation; and to the furious cry of hope and protest against all that exists we have, at best, dared to whisper in the lines from 2 Peter 3:13: "We wait for new heavens and a new earth, where righteousness is at home." The mission has applied mostly to souls; the diaconate was proof of love for the weak and suffering; alms were our homage to the fact that we were better off than many others near and far. All this embodied *caritas*, provisions for pilgrimage. But the new earth remained a dream; cooperation in the alteration of its structures was left to outsiders and, most of all, to enthusiasts. For this reason the proclamation of the resurrection of the dead was usually only the message of personal survival after death—a message written on gravestones but without any victory sign threatening bourgeois order. The Spirit who, according to Ezekiel 37, makes dry bones live and the beatitude of Matthew 5:6, that those who hunger and thirst after righteousness are already to be filled on earth, were held to be revolutionary fantasies, just like the triumph over fallen Babylon narrated in Revelation 14:8 and 18:2. We prayed the Magnificat in Luke 1:51–53 without taking seriously its words: "He has shown strength with his arm; he has scattered the proud in the thoughts of their hearts. He has brought down the powerful from their thrones, and lifted up the lowly; he has filled the hungry with good things, and sent the rich away empty."

This must be radically altered among us all if it is true, as Matthew 12:28 tells us, that Jesus was convinced he was driving out the demons by the Spirit of God. By express appeal to the kingdom of heaven drawn near, he commands his disciples in Matthew 10:8, "Cure the sick, raise the dead, cleanse the lepers, cast out demons." His work is to go on through us. Our time is to be a messianic time. We are not forgetting that he himself did not heal and set free all that came to him, that a paradise on earth absolutely did not begin with him, and that it was precisely his activity that led to his cross. The kingdom of God was carried by him into the demonic kingdom, but it was not finally and universally completed there. He gave the sign that it had come near, and the battle with the principalities and powers of this age had begun. We are called to nothing more, but also to nothing less. But this means that we do not leave the demonic kingdom undisturbed, but rather attack it at all its ends and corners, as witnesses of the resurrection from the dead and bearers of the Spirit of God, who does not share the kingdom with idols and wins back God's originally good creation, so that a new heaven may shine over a new earth.

God's Rule and Church

We cannot seriously doubt that, with his word and work, Jesus saw the in-breaking on earth of the eschatological kingdom of God and that, after Easter, his disciples daily reckoned with the end of the world. If at first only resto-ration of the old people of God lay within the vision of their mission, the host around Stephen set out on worldwide mission. The church was a host of disciples from among Jews and gentiles. Of course, we seldom realize, perhaps do not even want to see, how complicated this event was and how many problems it took on that continue to have an effect to this day. Outside Palestine, the first communities for the most part had no fixed—to say nothing of comprehensive—connection with one another. In doctrine, conduct, and form of organization they were largely dependent on their founders, and later on wandering prophets and their own teachers, so that differences and even contradictions could not fail to appear. Sacred Scriptures were available only for the second and third generations, and it is questionable whether all could manage to acquire an Old Testament, or at best a few books from it. Confes-sions and catechetical instructions were transmitted orally. For this reason, the eucharistic texts and the forms of the Lord's Prayer do not agree; the Easter narratives and the traditions of the four Gospels deviate from one another. This led to conflicts in which the early Christian community threatened to break apart. At least on two fronts there was no arrival at a final theological understanding. Despite the apostolic council and the dispute at Antioch, those loyal to the Torah and Christians who felt they were free of the Mosaic law never in fact overcame their controversies, but continually sharpened them.

In addition, the initially ardent expectation of the imminent end of the world was never completely extinguished. It led, rather, to intrachurch ten-sions. According to 2 Peter, whole congregations were misled in their faith because the awaited return of Jesus was delayed; according to 1 Thessalonians 4:13ff., Christians were worried about the fate of their dead; and, according to Hebrews, a wearied hope caused a crippling in the discipleship of Jesus. Yet there were two other tendencies. An enthusiasm attested to in 2 Timothy 2:18, and possibly already predicted in 1 Corinthians 15, saw the resurrection anticipated in baptism, and in death it allowed only the bodily hull to be stripped from the divine essence. And an ecclesiastical majority began to establish itself as a new religion on earth, with a specific morality [*Sittlichkeit*], under the supervision of authoritative offices until God would reveal God's heavenly kingdom. What is evident is the plurality of theological outlines in early Christianity, as is reflected in the New Testament. Coherent with them is the pluriformity of the Christian community already in the first century, which at times actually excluded dialogue and cannot idealistically be eased by the catchword *conciliarity*.

This state of affairs still has material significance for us. Properly understood, it allows for further theological insights for the present situation of Christianity. The confession of *Una sancta*[1] can only be established by that Lord who died for all; calls all to his forgiveness; and uses even the sick and dying in his service; who, by his Spirit, unites what differs; and who judges those who are still at odds with each other in their piety and yet stand under the commandment of repentance. There has never been an empirically demonstrable theological and organizational unity of the church. Still, repentance was always essential—not only for individual believers but also, and no less, for all confessions and Christian associations. Churches without repentance ignore their reality and deny the Lord who had to die also for them. They do not remain beneath the cross, under which all our guilt is uncovered and we are crucified together with our humanity. The Christian church—which on earth has existed only in theological and organizational pluriformity, often in individual churches opposed to one another—cannot, for this reason, simply be identified with the kingdom of God. Where we wait for a new heaven and earth, we will be permitted and obliged to reach out in longing and passion for a most profoundly renewed Christian church—each of us, naturally, in our own place and in contradiction to pious self-glorification or the idolizing of one's own fellowship. The coming God is never replaced by existing institutions, God's Holy Spirit never rendered superfluous by our religious tradition.

---

1. *Una sancta*, a term taken from the phrase of the Nicene Creed "*Una, sancta, catholica et apostolica ecclesia*" (One, holy, catholic and apostolic church) and referring to efforts at church unity since the sixteenth century, more recently to a high-church movement founded in 1938 by a group of evangelical pastors.

Given that our place on earth remains the station beneath the cross, and that in this period God's kingdom may not be separated from the crucified Christ, all churches and believers are at best signs and instruments for the end time broken in and for that consummation in which God alone will reign over the world, his competitors and enemies destroyed. They should certainly be signs and instruments of this end if God himself is not to be blasphemed as unbelievable. Viewed from such a task, the pluriformity, without which there never was a Christian *oecumene*, takes on a positive aspect. When God comes to us, no one goes away empty, no one may be excused from service. Everyone owes the Lord to whom all belong a witness that is personally characteristic, in one's own place, with one's own language, from one's own knowledge and tradition. No one is ever worthy or capable of deserving salvation on one's own; but one is always, in one's own way, in the position of handing God's salvation on to others as a fragile instrument and, by its power, resisting the demonic powers. In the New Testament what we call "laity" does not yet exist, only priestly members of the people of God. The Spirit of the present Christ needs the infinitely many and various functions of his earthly body in order to penetrate every part of our world, in order to create ecumenical solidarity. God does not make uniformity. God's kingdom works solidarity of the unequal because Christ died for all and can use each in his service.

God's Rule Today

Christianity does not live from canned goods that its ancestors left behind, and it does not yet live within the consummation of the blessed. It is set within the reality of the present day, the worldwide dimension of which we may not provincially, nationally, culturally, or racially restrict. Aside from the asserted abundance of possibilities and necessities, gifts and services, we ask in conclusion: What is ecumenically needful today? The New Testament urges three things on us as indispensable, which I will take up in slogan form. "Proclaim the good news to the whole creation," as is stated in Mark 16:15. There is no kingdom of God that is merely a theory or a mystery cult of pious souls. It exists only in the gospel's attack on the whole world for the sake of every individual creature. Love must be granted, guilt expressly forgiven, cares interceded for and shared, liberation proclaimed. I must learn that I too am really in view, that God will act on and through me personally. The earth must hear the voice of its true Lord as promise, claim, and judgment. Only to hearers of the Word are all the miracles of grace believable and visible. We must be called by his name to be something to the praise of his glory. Today the gospel defines Christianity as a resistance movement of Jesus Christ on earth against the power of the idols, against the possessiveness of the members of the affluent society, and against all who are destroying the creation. God's kingdom represents itself visibly where we are invited to the joyful meal at Jesus's table. This, of course, happens only when all whom the gospel calls to their Lord have a place here. The Crucified handed himself over to the godless, tolerated even Judas among his guests, promised in Matthew 8:11 that many from the east and the west would celebrate the meal of the perfected with the patriarchs. To all the needy he granted his fellowship, and in the midst of his enemies he gave the freedom of the reconciled. According to 1 Corinthians 11:27ff., only a fellowship in the body of Christ that is limited or denied renders one unworthy of the meal. At just this point, erecting walls of separation means preventing heaven from being open to sinners and all the disciples of Jesus; it means entering the ghetto of a closed society of only the pious or religious institutions and ideologies—whereas at the cross, salvation and ecumenical openness were established for the whole world. Does Jesus remain Lord at his meal? Or do we determine where its limit must be?

Ecumenical openness recognizes in the other the brother or sister of Jesus; thus ecumenical openness is also openness toward all. Christians cannot look neutrally or silently on the horrible inhumanity that is changing the earth into an inferno. The gospel is crippled where one separates soul and body, salvation and earthly help for the unholy, where one reserves freedom only for heaven and thus falsifies it on earth into an opiate for the exploited, martyred, and violated. The ideology of nonviolence is hypocritical if it is turned not against tyrants but against their victims. More, it is superstition when it demands more renunciation of violence than is possible from individuals or groups. There have never been spaces free of violence on our earth. Today we are witnessing a global class war in which affluent societies in wanton greed, and with all their scientific and technical capabilities, defend their privileges and allow whole continents to pay and bleed themselves out for it. For too long the old churches have struck a pact with the mighty and supported themselves on a bourgeois middle class while ignoring or actually despising the cries of the damned in this world of ours. Today God's kingdom proclaims with Psalm 12:5, "'Because the poor are despoiled, because the needy groan, I will now rise up,' says the LORD; 'I will place them in the safety for which they long.'" Will we go with this Lord on our way to his kingdom? We are invited to repent, each one alone and all in our community.

⊹ 17 ⊹

Where Eternal Life Begins
on Earth (1981)

A Sermon on Mark 10:17–27

This is a very moving, emotional, perhaps even most profoundly mysterious story. Beginning with a question, it hopefully leaves each of us questioning, having earlier led us step by step in a clear ascent to decision and separation. We can follow it as if we were the one who once in his life met Jesus on the way and, kneeling down, accosted the One passing by: "Good Teacher, what must I do to inherit eternal life?" For some of us, this theme of our text may have determined our own youth and become the theme of our life. If so, then we would have to speak of us too as rich and young. Taken as a whole, the theme states nothing less than that eternal life is the content and goal of an eager waiting for freedom and maturity, that much seems childish, worthless, and ruinous that to the world around is regarded as desirable.

My generation had a twofold reason for taking on the theme as a whole. Unlike it is today, for us the biblical call was well known early on, and almost self-evident. Its promise and command always aim at the whole, undivided person, at a life in shalom, at a world penetrated by God's love, held together by God's faithfulness, understanding itself in solidarity with the world by God's grace. But likewise in contrast to the present, we were situated in the

---

A sermon given at St. Egidien in Nuremberg on October 18, 1981.

mighty wake of German idealism, which, uncontested for a century, linked the bourgeoisie with the educational program of its classical poets and thinkers. Both were especially united in that philosopher who, during the wars for freedom, with his "Addresses to the German Nation," became the forerunner for the political ideals of his student hearers and their later heirs. Johann Gottlieb Fichte,[1] messenger of the truth he had experienced, wrote *The Way towards the Blessed Life*. In it he interpreted the Gospel of John, according to his understanding, as a witness to the glory of Christ; and as one seized by the message of the Gospel, he described the rebirth toward being a good person who, "if only consequent and resolute," is "stronger than a hundred evil ones."[2] He did this in contradiction to the world around him, in which "a well-educated man in a good society" does not eagerly speak of this truth of eternal life, is usually amused by it, regards it "brutally" as good for nothing, the knowledge of it as dubious and uninteresting, for which reason it meets with unbelief, absurdity, and lack of understanding when, despite everything, the one reborn sets out for it and follows in its track.[3] Those who are engaged here break out of the hustle and bustle of others because they treasure the truth as the highest good; they must allow it to cost them something, and more than something: their earthly life. If the rich young man of the Gospel becomes a disciple, he receives a share in the destiny of his Lord.

In a certain way, the great decision for my generation was that we had to learn to untie the knot that tied the biblical message with idealism. We cannot hear our story as participants mindful of their own youth, or as the aged still under the story's spell, without experiencing Jesus's reply to the question put to him as a shock. Should he not at least have understanding where others mock? From the outset, should he not love the questioner instead of taking him down a peg? "Why do you call me good? No one is good but God alone." This sentence deals the death blow to all idealism. The good is not in our reason and strength, whether conceived as the goal of devout instruction or as societal change or realized in the model of another person. Grasping for the whole, for a cure, for what is permanent, fetched from heaven to shape the earth after it, ends in failure. We experienced this too, we who once wanted all of it and dared it. If it all does not go bad, there are fragments, bits and

1. Johann Gottlieb Fichte (1762–1814), German philosopher, founding figure of German idealism, who developed his position from the writings of Immanuel Kant.

2. See Johann Gottlieb Fichte, *The Way towards the Blessed Life, or, The Doctrine of Religion*, in *Significant Contributions to the History of Psychology 1750–1920: Series A, Orientations*, ed. Daniel N. Robinson, vol. 2, *J. G. Fichte* (Washington, DC: University Publications of America, 1977), 496.

3. See Fichte, *The Way towards the Blessed Life*, 491.

pieces in our hands, clearest of all where once the gospel and politics were in wide agreement. We illustrate, to the extent we have survived, what happens when one has tried "consequently and resolutely" to force eternal life into one's own time and to get on against a world of resistances. It happened to us as in the fairy tale of the fisherman and his wife, who in the end demanded to become like God and, in the attempt (as the story harshly tells), landed in the piss pot.[4] The total healing we thought to create proved to be a total blinding. We plunged into the inferno and dragged the world into chaos with us. Now we know: "No one is good but God alone." We cannot seize the good like plunder. If we are to encounter what is perfect, God must appear in our lives as the Father of Jesus Christ and take it into God's own hands. But then we are removed from a dreamed-of heaven into what is preliminary, into everyday life with its possibilities and tasks, whole and blessed solely by the fact that we no longer belong to ourselves but have a Lord.

It is just this that our narrative describes in its continuation. Jesus rejects the sweeping question concerning the good in order concretely and soberly to name those commandments (haphazardly arranged like the many moments of an existence in a shared humanity) that every religious person knows: "You shall not murder; You shall not commit adultery; You shall not steal; You shall not bear false witness; You shall not defraud; Honor your father and mother." No one goes the way to heaven alone. Paradoxically, this way, rather than leading to the heights, leads to the depths and breadth of our world, into physical touch with our neighbors or, because the earth today has become so small, with the strangers in El Salvador, South Africa, and the Eastern Bloc. Faith must preserve itself in many different and changing conditions, pleased with it or not. And it must always recognize what is valid in other cultures, may not reduce East and West, North and South to a single denominator. In times of transition such as ours, it will share in political, economic, social, and intellectual change; and with a broadened or narrowed field of vision, helplessly or cleverly, calmly or passionately, it will enlist in or resist the condition that

---

4. Here Käsemann refers to a German fairy tale, "The Fisherman and His Wife," collected by the Brothers Grimm. The story is about a fisherman who one day catches a large fish who speaks to him and requests that the fisherman let him go because he is an enchanted prince. The fisherman lets the fish go, returns home, and reports the strange encounter with the fish to his wife, who responds by urging the fisherman to return to the sea to catch the fish again in order to ask the fish to grant them a wish. The fisherman catches the fish again, and the fish grants him a wish. At the urging of his wife, the fisherman returns to the sea again and again, each time with more wishes. Every time the fisherman returns to catch the fish, his wishes are granted, and the sea grows increasingly tumultuous. Finally, the fisherman and his wife wish to become like God. As a result, their home goes back to what it had been in the beginning—a "piss pot" (*Pisspott*), sometimes also translated as "filthy shack" or a "pigsty."

at any time may challenge it. It will be held in suspense by ever-new commitments and temptations. It must continually go out from itself into decisions for which it is no match—or into which it must actualize understanding, love, loyalty, patience, and self-denial. Each life has its particular mission, its own burden, an abundance of talents and responsibilities given it to share. But it also has its personal deficits and catastrophes. The beautiful word in James 1:25 calls us without exception to be blessed in our doing.

The rich young man is not yet at this point. Still, addressed respecting his standing under the law, he can answer, "Teacher, I have kept all these since my youth." In precisely this way, Paul, looking back on his Jewish past, called himself, "as to righteousness under the law, blameless" [Phil. 3:6]. The pious Pharisee speaks in this manner, and Jesus loves him because he believes him. We too continually meet persons whom we must love because a clarity proceeds from them, and in the midst of much entanglement and disunity they allow something to be detected of an unspoiled creation. They are people of decision. God is more gracious than we. God lavishly shares God's goodness even with the heathen and the godless. A faith that allows our hearts and heads to remain narrow, envious, or blind, or even to become so, is an egoistic and sectarian caricature of discipleship of the One who loved everything living, made room for beauty, and called even the radically pious to himself. That young man was a radical who wanted just one single thing: to keep the commandment revealed to him. It is hideous that Christians so often prefer middle-class mediocrity to the radicals because the radicals disturb their manners. If the Crucified is their Lord, they should belong to the "radicals" (the term literally means nothing else than to get to the root of things and to set this root, again and again, over and against the incessantly superficial). Jesus's Beatitudes do this very thing by expelling the stale air of custom, by bringing the kingdom of heaven to earth, where it disturbs the hypocrites and awakens the sleepers, where the cry of freedom gives hope to the prisoners and terrifies the mighty, the secure, and the idolater. At least in Christianity, the bureaucrats and the veterans of compromise—who do not want to antagonize anyone, who always count on the stronger battalions and balance on the trapeze of the flatly obvious or else peddle pious drugs—should not be allowed to increase. Who knows how many youth they drive away from worship because, in old age, they no longer understand the youth's needs and longings and no longer engage in adventure and experiment (though the God of the gospel descended to hell and opposed all the demons)? Perhaps we must still be young to understand the young man in our story, who, not content with the tradition of his fathers, for the sake of eternal life, longs to carry a heavier yoke and is old enough to be seized by it.

In any event, what he hoped for happened to him. Jesus enters into this radicality, just as he does elsewhere with the weak, lost, and possessed. He takes the young man at his word without checking whether or not his conversation partner has opened his mouth too wide and seen himself too idealistically. We may ask whether Jesus is referring to something greater than the commandments. In the early community, something like a monkish asceticism and the propertylessness of wandering prophets soon emerged, surpassing the usual discipleship in its denial of earthly goods. Actually, the new requirement would suggest a higher stage of Christian behavior. I will not deal with this difficult historical problem. In the context of our text, Jesus's requirement clearly concretizes and concentrates the sweeping reference to the Mosaic commandments. The disciples of the Nazarene are no longer to regard them as a guide through the confusion of everyday life, in which one can so easily be lured from a distance by the detail of so many possibilities. The religious person must continually consider what is to be done in the moment, what urgently deserves to be done, what is owed God and the neighbor, what has to be put right, what can be improved or omitted in the future. But in this way life loses its center, its direction, its profile. All commandments are correctly understood and helpful only when they point to the first commandment: "I am the LORD your God. . . . You shall have no other gods before me" [Exod. 20:2–3; Deut. 5:6–7]. Only under God is there an end to the worship that glorifies one's own self or something earthly, that violently or out of habit injures love. Otherwise, it is forgotten that faith has to live from the freedom of the children of God, preserve that freedom in contact with the creatures of the Father, and bring it to all the imprisoned and possessed.

There is no end to this highest commandment. To it we cannot say, "I have kept all these since my youth." Set within Christian freedom, we must daily withdraw from the lordship of the demons and must, for the sake of brothers and sisters, prepare for the exodus from Egypt. This is where the great adventure begins: "earthly still, yet heavenly,"[5] on the way to the promised but unknown future, trusting once again every morning the word that leads us. That word calls us to forsake altogether everything that hinders and weighs down—that is, our possessions, the force of the status quo, the fear of the wilderness to be wandered through, the seizure of the principalities and powers that, along with the body, claim our souls for their service. What I have described as the meaning of the first commandment receives its sharpest

5. This appears to be a reference to a line from the Lutheran hymn "Lasset uns mit Jesus ziehen" ("Let Us Ever Walk with Jesus"), the lyrics for which were written by the German poet Sigismund von Birken (1626–81).

expression in Jesus's word: "You lack one thing; go, sell what you own, and give the money to the poor, and you will have treasure in heaven; then come, follow me"—and carry your cross!

Dear congregation, when we were young we heard the first commandment in this form. It put us in an unavoidable position, directed us to our place on earth, and directed our path toward a blessed life. Few generations have been so blessed that with total clarity God's Word struck like lightning before their feet. Few have more radically come to know the severe glory of heavenly promise. We will not forget that, at that time, many of our good friends went away displeased or even sad. They not only had to fear for their possessions but also were ideologically possessed by what their fathers had left behind with them, which they themselves had appropriated by hard labor and no longer wanted to give up. The treasure in heaven can easily be spoken of in edifying fashion. To go with Abraham out from his father's house and from his friends into an unknown future, to leave the protection of the columns and the tradition, and to shoulder the cross, as if it were not a burden but only a support, is absolutely unedifying. Not by chance, most of those who then accepted the call to freedom beneath the cross have, in the present affluent society, become angry old men, rebels in church and politics. They must remain unedifying and nonconformist, as those who once resisted the assimilation required by church leaders. They can and will defend neither the basic values of bourgeois order nor the equilibrium sacrosanct to all bureaucrats (who always protect only the privileges of the mighty and well fed). They are troublemakers in every good and beneficial society, those who must say to society: "You lack one thing." Among Christians and churches, only the discipleship of the Crucified counts. Everything else is religious peddling of drugs.

The rich young man embodies the history of my generation, which once had to leave the past of its father's house and, for the sake of the one thing needful, had to leave the settled camps for the wilderness. Now there is dancing around us again, just as around the golden calf, and peace is construed as preserving what one possesses, making innumerable atomic weapons, guarantees of a freedom in which inhumanity triumphs. The class war has broken through regional and national boundaries and loosed damnation on two-thirds of the earth. Mammon is the god of our world. The One who goes to his cross truly speaks to our time: "How hard it will be for those who have wealth to enter the kingdom of God!" Church leaders who still propagate the national church [*Volkskirche*] seem to have forgotten that their Lord gives camels a greater chance of getting through the eye of a needle than those who can detach themselves from humanity but not from property have of entering the kingdom of God. The kingdom of God is not built on alms, however ready we are to give them. Hell cannot be exorcised with developmental aid, the capital of which flows back to us with interest. The White Man, even in religion and theology, is everywhere detested and hated by people of color because he wants eternal life already on earth at the cost of all other creatures. We have reason to be horrified together with the disciples: "Then who can be saved?" We have even more reason to consider Jesus's categorical answer, usually omitted by the pious soul-masseurs: "For mortals it is impossible." Most of all, we have reason to hear the conclusion of our narrative: "But not for God; for God all things are possible."

Our life has run its course between this "impossible" and this "possible," will be dragged back and forth until the last moment. Only those who have experienced, and who recognize every day anew, the "impossible" with respect to themselves and their world stand at the threshold of the Beatitudes and the kingdom of heaven and are suited for discipleship of the Crucified as messengers of the gospel. God rules among the broken, the dying, and the damned. God raises Lazarus from the grave and, unbelievably, has not only allowed us to survive but blessed us for service. Today God's revolution is still overthrowing whatever feels secure, still raising what is nothing out of the dust. We are its witnesses. Our earthly traces will be rapidly lost. But a new generation will appear in our place. Beneath Jesus's cross, those who already on earth experience daily the needed resurrection from the dead will find eternal life. There is no end to his call: "Follow me!" Nor is there an end to the host of witnesses of the gospel, of the fact that all things are possible with God, only with the One who sent his Son into our inferno in order there to erect his kingdom. He remains the Last One on the scene. It is salvation to remain with him and to be able to let everything else go. Amen.

⊹ 18 ⊹

What I, as a German Theologian, Unlearned in Fifty Years (1981)

W hen I was a child, I spoke like a child, I thought like a child, I reasoned like a child; when I became an adult, I put an end to childish ways." This word from 1 Corinthians 13:11 does not merely apply to an apostle. Wherever this cannot and must not be said in retrospect of all of our lives, this indicates that such a life may have reached a dead end, at some point having lost its courage for freedom. Whoever wanders in the open, whoever really lives, must, to the last breath—citing Paul once more—hear Philippians 3:12 as motto: "Not that I have already obtained this or have already reached the goal; but I press on to make it my own, because Christ Jesus has made me his own." In the New Testament the disciples of the Nazarene are, according to the original Greek text, called "learners." If this is correct, no one is ever free of learning, consequently also never free of unlearning.

When, for the first time in public, I tell of my life as a German theologian, the decisive question is, What have I learned from it? This applies to a professor even more than to others. If professors are not learners all their lives—thus not incessantly entangled in the adventure of new, better, comprehensive experiences—they are also of little worth as teachers. They have authority only as learners, and they give nothing important to their students if they do

A lecture given for the theological faculty at Marburg-Lahn on the occasion of the fifty-year celebration of Käsemann's doctorate, November 25, 1981.

not teach them to learn. But no one can learn who is not ready to unlearn. The only one who arrives in the open air is the one who breaks out of the given boundaries, who ventures out from fixed paths into the unknown, who does not allow heart and head to be crippled by stereotypes. Perhaps it may be said that only in what is unlearned does it become clear how and to what extent one is in a position to learn. In any event, Christian faith is not thinkable without that exodus in which Abraham turned his back on his father's house and his friends. It is doubtful whether life can be fruitful if it is not prepared to be in rebellion against old tradition and traditional privileges, if it is not prepared resolutely to throw off ballast where new horizons are to be won. My generation probably had more reason than many before it to leave well-worn tracks, thus to change views. We were forced to plow a new thing or—as we Marburgers heard it from Heidegger—to become radical, to penetrate more critically than usual to the roots and origins, to what is necessary.

How did this begin for me? Fifty years ago I would have said without hesitation that the conquest of the ideological theological liberalism by the so-called dialectical theology opened a way on which I had to distance myself from the inheritance of the previous century. (In part I actually had to give it up.) Today I maintain that the liberalism we as youth too hastily skipped over and took to be overcome has returned, and it has done so in terms of a dogmatism claiming to be confessional, as a fundamentalism once more on the move, not to be surrendered in church or in politics. Everywhere on earth human freedom is limited. From out of love, Jesus's disciples must give new space to freedom and resist the arbitrariness of the mighty. What appeared to us then as a departure for a new epoch (incidentally, not even in all Western Europe, and in general only from a scientific and church perspective) was in reality the forming of a buffer against the approaching fate of 1933. Dialectical theology made possible a sharp antithesis between evangelical faith and fascist ideology. I must expand a bit to make clear that, in addition, a breach was needed with the inheritance transmitted to us. In Germany, the Protestant bourgeoisie rooted in a romantic idealism was united with a reactionary nationalism. This fact has been too infrequently reflected upon in the church.

In addition, German history was decisively influenced by the French Revolution. Aside from a few years in the beginning, that revolution was able to inspire only minorities among us because its horrors appalled the citizens. The Napoleonic Wars completely obscured the fact that the era of democratic freedom had begun with them in the political and social sphere of Western Europe. The parochial state as reflected in the church—with its bureaucracy intent on preserving the spirit of servility and the renunciation of rebellious ideas—had, therefore, an antidemocratic effect. Of course, we could not avoid the nationalism of our neighbors, spreading among us with the wars of freedom. It became the decisive mark of the previous century, and finally our own fate. Since it was mainly linked to the rejection of revolution, in contrast to the scientific-technical development and the proletariat (both rising along with it), nationalism could only take on reactionary shape. Romanticism reveled in the past greatness of the Middle Ages and the dreams flying over earthly reality. Generally, with ordinary citizens, the world beyond their own church towers and mountains remained unknown, at least politically. The churches saw their temporal task as educating pious subjects. After 1848, their patriarchal pedagogy took expression in the Inner Mission,[1] in which the diaconate also served to preserve the social status. Until the end of the First World War, Christian citizens were not able to be in solidarity with rebels regarded as atheistic and without a fatherland; so today as well, even socialism appears suspect in many areas. In the main, we were still in the ghetto of mistrust toward everything that conservative tradition could have shaken when we had not arrived at unity and freedom but had become a nation, when economic expansion moved toward colonialism, and when economic and cultural liberalism forged links with Western foreign countries. Military might secured existence toward the outside. Intellectually, it produced an idealistic humanism resting on an ancient inheritance and neoclassicism. This humanism—to say nothing of world-political thinking—too seldom found its way to the outsiders of bourgeois society. Sworn to inwardness and self-discovery, it scarcely saw beyond the boundaries of its own nation. Its national yearning was directed toward a return of the old glory of the Reich.

This was the background of the normal theology of Protestantism. Family, school, university, military, state, and church took care that we grew up in this tradition, that we regarded our homeland as an arrangement of God to be defended with all our powers, and that all this would weigh on our consciences. For this reason, in any case for me and many of my generation, it was the profoundest shattering of our life when National Socialism ruthlessly let us experience firsthand the consequences of reactionary nationalism. It did not do so all at once. To our sorrow we learned that the demonic first camouflages itself as a heavenly messenger and promises to fulfill our desires for a better world. Until Stalingrad and even beyond, most Germans remained blinded. The deportation of Jews, the persecution of communists, socialists, and gypsies, and also of radical Christians, were naïvely or resignedly accepted as conditions accompanying the birth of a new epoch, though the inhumanity

---

1. The Inner Mission, founded by Johann Hinrich Wichern in 1848, was a lay movement that focused on charitable service to the poor in Germany.

of the system clearly came to light along with it. If we did not personally collide with the tyranny, we could close eyes and ears, hearts and heads, to the reality—which in our land is always fogged over by dreams and ideals.

Naturally, evangelical theologians at least had to know better, at the latest from the autumn of 1933 onward. If the demonizing of all liberal views and the shamelessly persistent and brazen hounding of Jews, as well as the aggressive political programs, did not already make it clear, now the theologians learned that, as it was said, the churches stepped into line and, to echo Goebbels, were organizationally stunted. It is a shame to have to admit that only a minority saw itself forced to resolute resistance. Apart from the psychological hindrances, the imminent threatening danger, the contradiction of many earlier friends, and the civil courage seldom practiced in the church and among citizens—with the majority, even the majority of Christians, nationalism remained so strong that one compromise after the other followed the initial enthusiasm. From time to time, the gulf between the so-called intact provincial churches and those already institutionally ruined (more precisely, between the leading theologians and administrators of each) and the gulf between the pastors and the members of the individual congregations were more painful than the pressure of the Nazis. To this day, we who suffered under it cannot forget the cowardice and diminished fellowship of that period. For our whole life, and in every area, we became the "partisans," as we are still denounced by church leaders, and more and more also within the area of scholarship. We had to remain so, because the time after the war was decisively determined by old men. Coming from the previous century, they did not take up the inheritance and organizational forms of the radical Confessing Church, but they carried on restoration and chased after the questionable ideal of a so-called national church. The rearmament of West Germany and the affluent society simultaneously growing along with it at times promoted shipwrecked national movements and the current deep political polarization between the two great parties that extends into the very Christian communities themselves. Clearly, in the Nazi period our resistance was only halfhearted. We defended the gospel and church orders but did not go directly to the political underground as a common humanity often demanded. Even during its greatest disgrace we have always given the nation more than we should, thus less to Christ and God's creatures than we owed. The discipleship of the Nazarene seldom allowed for penetration of the profanity of mundane life in the world, because we were entrenched behind sacred walls of pious tradition. The shape of German provincial churches, long since overtaken, was retained as if it were a more adequate expression of the "wandering people of God"—a phrase that, from a cell in 1938, I programmatically envisaged as the henceforth valid definition of Christianity. Only in the period following did my friends and I succeed in leaving the father's house marked by the slogans of bourgeois humanism, the idealism of which still appears today at the side of global capitalism, just as in the social wars of the previous century. If we had freed ourselves radically from the views and habits of Egypt, we would not have been drawn into the veritably atheistic dance around the golden calf, into the ideology of the market economy, which seeks to secure and increase possessions, success, and enjoyment of the White Man at the cost of the rest of the earth. The promise drives to the wilderness march.

I will be briefer in the next sections. They are to make concrete what for me almost as a matter of course resulted from the departure just described. If I wanted to report the changes in the area of theological research during the last fifty years, time would not suffice even if I limited myself to Germany and my speciality in the New Testament field. I was fortunate because in this area I likewise became a witness and participant of a drastic change and by it was forced to think more intensively, to enter upon new experiments and adventures, to break with old fronts, though at the cost of many friendships of my youth. In order to offer a comprehensive picture, I would have to tell of the emergence and almost fifty-year dominance of dialectical theology, of intense hermeneutical, confessional, historical, and religio-historical controversies, of coming to terms with Anglo-Saxon theology almost unknown earlier, of the relapse into apologetics and historicism.

Nevertheless, from all this I will choose a theme that most profoundly influenced my journey—that is, the debate with my teacher Rudolf Bultmann. I think that one may call him the last significant representative of that radical historical criticism founded about 150 years ago by Ferdinand Christian Baur of Tübingen.[2] Baur's great half-length portrait in my study daily reminds me of where I belong and where I do not. In Germany's universities, at least since the Enlightenment, schools gathering around one teacher have dominated the entire profession. Since Humboldt's[3] call to reform, the desire was to educate the elite—more precisely, to educate men who could think independently and in good idealistic fashion, thus who would make something of themselves everywhere. Just like Socrates, the teacher was the midwife. He took a position in the never-ending battle for the truth. In discussion with him, his opponents, his friends and pupils, one grew step by step toward one's

2. Ferdinand Christian Baur (1792–1860), German Protestant theologian, founder of the Tübingen School of criticism, described earliest Christianity as the opposition between Jewish (Petrine) and gentile (Pauline) Christianity.

3. Friedrich Wilhelm Christian Karl Ferdinand von Humboldt (1767–1835), Prussian philosopher, government functionary, diplomat, and founder of Berlin's Humboldt University.

own discovery and thus toward greater or lesser independence in the area of personal responsibility. Today such a pedagogy likely seems, far and wide, to be grotesque and totally out of date. Yet my generation surrendered to it passionately. We cannot deny its enormous value, though we were conscious of its problematic and ran the risk of being regarded as petrifacts of a bourgeois education. The life and death of a civilization actually depend on the individual's never surrendering critical thinking, and it is precisely community that gives the courage for it.

Historical and theological radicalism united Baur and Bultmann. We learned from them that there is no end to questioning as long as the question is reasonably put, that with everything and everyone there is a need to get at the root, that radicality is not merely a method of research but the presupposition of intellectual life. On the other hand, Baur and Bultmann differed in that the one looked for the course of world history, the other for an anthropology of the believer, both in that respect thematically obligated to their time and environs. For a long time I was not directly influenced by Baur but always preferred to study him. He appears to me now as the real ancestor. At the same time, I more and more strongly found Bultmann's central concern too narrow. I cannot contest the historicity of existence. But I learned that the question of the meaning of universal history was key to the problematic of existence and the center of the New Testament as well as of the Bible itself and of Christian proclamation. As our theory found it necessary, the conversation between grandfather and father and son took a very dialectical course. In that respect, it is probable that my own time and environment influenced me, though our study in the twenties really took place in an elephantine tower. In the main, decades of laborious exegesis returned me to Baur's neighborhood, though in that respect too he had greater influence on my thinking. Without considering the self-understanding of the first Christians, the expositor of Scripture would fall prey to a mythical-speculative interpretation of history. Conversely, there is no doubt that the Old Testament is concerned with the global validity of the first commandment, a validity made concrete in the New Testament by its witness to the kingdom of the crucified Christ in and over the whole earth. The self-understanding of the disciples of Jesus results from their discipleship, not from an idea.

For me the first doubts about Bultmann's exegesis arose over an interpretation of the Gospel of John. This interpretation made the evangelist the editor of a pagan speech-source [*Redequelle*]. By this means it was possible to allow all mythological statements to be attributable to the source. Now the incarnation of Christ and, derived from it, the believer's becoming human could appear at the center of the Johannine proclamation. The formal as well as material criteria of this hypothesis did not stand up to my penetrating reexamination. Still less was I able to accept a pagan speech-source. When Bultmann actually drew Ignatius of Antioch into his existential interpretation and, to put it pointedly, set Kierkegaard at the beginning of the second century, was the first time I had to separate myself from him. Karl Barth once described the relation of teacher and pupil impressively in his debate with Wilhelm Herrmann[4] and showed how the tears and fissures at the periphery gradually penetrate deeper and deeper, so that finally the dissent actually affects the center. I must describe this as representative of my development as well. Because I denied the existence of a speech-source and its pagan origin in the Fourth Gospel, statements of a mythological sort had to be interpreted as Christian, and after many attempts over forty years I could do it only when I stood Bultmann's interpretation on its head. The Gospel reflects and projects the Easter event into Jesus's earthly life. The Johannine Christ is already active on earth as the Exalted One. He is the Son of God, and thus his glory is the central theme, his becoming flesh only a means to its revelation.

Consequently, a second conclusion resulted. As a Protestant and dialectical theologian, Bultmann had always related the Christian faith to the hearing of the kerygma. We do not receive the new self-understanding from what is within us but solely though the Word of God coming to us from the outside, mediated through Scripture and church. This genuine Reformation inheritance was nonetheless so radicalized by Bultmann that the history of it could become almost irrelevant. In a certain way, his demythologizing, as the Norwegian Dahl[5] correctly emphasized, was a dehistoricizing and, as such, a witness to his idealistic inheritance. The collapse of the life-of-Jesus research in the previous century, the Reformation bequest, and the idealistic anthropology given key position were united in his theology, which, for this reason, despite its classically simple language, was left with a profound ambiguity, depending on whether one approached it from the Reformation or from the Enlightenment aspect. This appears most sharply in the problem of the earthly Jesus. For Bultmann, he is the occasion but not the content of faith; at best he may be regarded as its model. The gospel does not appear on the scene with him but with Easter. The word of Christian preaching—in fact, that of the

---

4. Johann Wilhelm Herrmann (1846–1922), Lutheran theologian, first a professor at the University of Halle, then a systematician at the University of Marburg, influenced by Kant, and thus in the idealist tradition.

5. The reference is to the Norwegian New Testament theologian Nils Alstrup Dahl (1911–2001), who wrote an influential review of Bultmann's *Theology of the New Testament*. See his "Rudolf Bultmann's *Theology of the New Testament*," in *The Crucified Messiah and Other Essays* (Minneapolis: Augsburg, 1974).

church—replaced him, just as does the Paraclete of the Johannine farewell discourses. Actually, the incarnation is the symbol of the Word taking on flesh ever new. But then, will we not have to ask whether ecclesiology overshadows Christology—modified, naturally, in Protestant fashion (that is, in that central emphasis on anthropology)? This would then also explain Bultmann's treatment of Pauline theology under the two headings "Man before the Revelation of Faith" and "Man under Faith." Even more, it would explain the astonishing sympathy that radical criticism found among Roman Catholic theologians.

By way of the example of the Fourth Gospel, I became aware that the New Testament contains different theological designs that cannot at all be united by a doctrine of the incarnation set at the center and by an anthropology connected with it. The Epistle to the Ephesians, the Revelation of John, and the book of Acts exemplify this in a range that actually embraces irreconcilable contrasts. Best of all, in its varying aspects, Christology is to be described as central. And content criticism of the canon is to be exercised on the basis of it. As important, indeed as irrevocable, as these aspects are in their relation to both believing and nonbelieving individuals, they still may never be solely or even chiefly related to individuals. Rather, what is proclaimed, and is to be taken most seriously, is the way of the Nazarene toward world rule become concrete and visible in the individual believer. The church as community of the disciples of this Lord is the breaking in of the eschatologically new creation. Preaching is legitimate insofar as it holds firm to the identity of Christ with the One come as Man into the inferno of the earth, with the one Crucified and exalted to be Lord of the world. That the Risen One can only be known by the sign of the cross distinguishes the gospel from ideology and myth. On this basis, the debate with Bultmann, begun over Johannine and Pauline texts, had to lead to conflict over the so-called historical Jesus. It too began at the periphery—that is, over the question concerning a minimum of reliable tradition—and ended in radical separation. For me, it is not the self-understanding of the believer as a call to the human becoming human but the worldwide lordship of the Crucified that became the focus of preaching and of discipleship. And it establishes a new self-understanding, makes possible a critical discerning of the spirits, and sets Christians off from classical idealism in all its ramifications. It may be that the teacher and the student disagreed merely in whether to give priority to the one aspect or to the other. Then the result would be that in all theology what is continually at issue is what should have priority and may not be exchanged. I am no longer prepared to give ecclesiology precedence over Christology, under whatever modifications that may occur.

In a third section, I will state what ecclesiastical consequences my theological decision had for me. I would like to begin with the conclusion. Today the ecumenical movement appears to me to be the most important event and the most genuine mark of our century's Christian history. It is also the answer to the ecclesiological problems brought home to me by Erik Peterson and that, in 1931, led to my dissertation, "Leib und Leib Christi." Here too occurred a reversal that decisively oriented my life. In my youth I was such a Lutheran that I would not have served as a pastor to a Reformed congregation. Now I came into conflict with most of my Marburg friends and again, of course, with the teacher, for whom the *oecumene* held no central interest. What for me is unforgettable is Bultmann's dictum in a seminar debate over the New Testament concept of *cosmos*. He said, "There is no such thing as humanity. That is an abstraction!" I had to learn that this was totally false, that the word "individual" denotes an even greater abstraction. The late convert, Peterson, who interpreted the New Testament from the history of early Christian dogma, had already reversed the switches, and a semester later Adolf Schlatter[6] threw a complicated host of questions at my feet with his theology of creation. In the church struggle, and afterward in the years of teaching at the universities, where I arduously had to fit in, there was little time for such a thematic. The wind was blowing in the opposite direction. Then came the 1963 World Congress for Faith and Order at Montreal, where for the first time I had before me in the flesh the *oecumene*, represented by five hundred delegates of every conceivable denomination. I was to report on the unity and diversity of the church in the New Testament. And to the intense frustration of most of the participants, especially of the Geneva leadership, I put forth the thesis that the biblical canon is obviously not the basis for a universal consensus but rather the basis for confessional variety. At any rate, in the same year it was seen that precisely my thesis allowed finding current ecumenical plurality already prefigured on the basis of early Christianity. The worldwide body of Christ, with its differing members in space and time, is held together solely by its Lord and makes this known in a given way in confession and discipleship.

This, of course, relativized confession and theological education, but it in no way dismissed them. I saw that, in the basically pietistic ecumenical movement, neither the Reformation nor critical theology had ever received the weight due them. Instead, the "apostolic tradition" set up by either side is nothing but a fiction lovingly tended by orthodoxy in all its visible forms—unless "apostolic tradition" is taken to mean simply that discipleship of the Nazarene never ended and that, according to our hope, it will not end. Of

6. Adolf Schlatter (1852–1938), professor of New Testament and systematic theology at the University of Greifswald, the University of Berlin, and the University of Tübingen.

course, "pure doctrine" is concretized in every sermon that allows Christ to be recognized as our Lord. But historical facts militate against understanding it as a dogmatic system. Doctrine is vital only when discovered and proclaimed anew. Confession and theological education must not, therefore, cordon Christianity off in a religious ghetto. The wandering people of God breaks through all enclosures and does not live from the canned goods it has taken along. Tradition will always be preserved anew, no longer possible when it cannot be made intelligible and attractive to others. In a period and in a world in which old and new religions are alive everywhere, we must begin to think ecumenically. God does not give up God's whole creation, but rather has the first and last word in it. Christ's body is that piece of the earth which has heard his promise and claim in such fashion that it no longer wants to resist its Lord. In a multiple mirroring of what is called God's image, and which impresses each of the body's members with Christ's image, Christian mission is carried on in worldwide service to the one who is to experience salvation. This does not occur without doctrine, but it must be independently developed in different places and times in order to gain entry everywhere. Here, however, doctrine is instruction in the praxis of discipleship, and theology a necessary function of the community, not a ruler over faith. Theology does not replace the Holy Spirit but aids toward discerning the spirits, and from out of love it weighs to what extent historical realities are and remain possibilities for moving into the present, or where and how they made dust of arable land, which needs plowing again in order to give bread to the world today.

Now I come to the last turning point on my theological journey. An ecumenical view freed me from the provincialism spreading in my land and from the schoolmastery of the confessionalists or pietists. But I had to learn that a theology related to the world has a political dimension whether that suits one or not. We once said at Barmen that no area of life is omitted by the gospel. Conversely, what was palpably made clear at the 1980 World Conference for Mission and Evangelization in Melbourne can no longer be ignored: Christianity is no longer determined by the White Man. Today, the majority of Christians, according to their number and in their passion for departure, are in the world of the people of color. This world would reject not only our intimate involvement with the bourgeoisie but also the tradition that rests on Greek civilization and that, from its own cultural assumptions, it no longer understands. In the next generation more of it will go overboard than is welcome even to the Christian rebels among us. We would have occasion to consider what emergency ration we need to retain under all circumstances and—this is an even more difficult problem!—how it will be received from us as indispensable. No theology and no church community should be secure against becoming a widely deforested territory on which will settle wild growth from another understanding of the Bible and another experience in discipleship. Finally, we may no longer close our eyes to the fact that the class war that began nationally in the previous century has now taken hold on all continents as a war to the death between the privileged and those who have been exploited for centuries. What is camouflaged as a harmless free-market economy and promises to benefit all is in reality the continuation of imperialism and colonialism by a capitalist system. It lives from the Third World's yielding its raw materials and accepting our finished products, to which, particularly heinously, all sorts of weapons belong. The result is that the slums, the reverse side of our affluence, continue to grow, and for three-fourths of humanity our earth becomes a hell in which hunger, murder, and prostitution rule, each person wrestling with the other for survival.

I would be grateful if no one detected propaganda in these restrained remarks, though an ideology that misuses actual conditions for its purposes has more of my sympathy than the usual suppression among us in the West. And I openly admit that my students have helped me considerably when they attempted resistance to their fathers in 1967–68. When, in the end time, according to Malachi 4:6, the conclusion of the Old Testament, God "will turn the hearts of parents to their children," it is surely no shame when professors learn from their students, at least occasionally, and in so doing allow themselves to be converted. To reduce it to a common denominator, I unlearned the spiritualization of the Beatitudes of the Sermon on the Mount. They promise that the kingdom of God—whose inbreaking on earth brings with it signs and wonders, healing and liberation from possession—will not only rescue earth from our egoism, sluggishness of heart, and hypocrisy but also from the tyranny of the powers enslaving it, taking each of us into its service and supplying the gifts needed for it.

I am no longer content with the Augsburg Confession, since the visible Christian community is made known just as much in the presence of the poor (with whose blessing in Matthew 11:5 the enumeration of Jesus's deeds ends) as in the preaching of the gospel and the administration of the sacraments. The context for it—from Israel's exodus from Egypt to the revelation of the new heaven and earth in the Apocalypse—is the message that the Father of the Crucified resists the proud, the rich, and the powerful. Since my dissertation, I have tried to define the nature of the church in ever new ways. In view of its worldwide task, and in view of the worldwide violation of creatures, I have arrived at the conclusion that in our time the church, also and precisely in its preaching and diaconate, must be the resistance of the exalted Christ in a world claimed by him and invited to his freedom. This is no doubt a political definition, as surely as I maintain that it is nothing less than pure doctrine. If the heart of the gospel (already contained in the first commandment) is concretized in the New Testament to signify that Christ is for us the true Lord of the world, then the gospel will not occur without political judgments in proclamation. Christ's lordship is over body and soul, heart and head, over disciples and demons—in this world and in the world to come—and is also a political fact. For the earth is always claimed by idols, whom only naïveté can call invisible. Who our lord is, and is to be everywhere, is the central question of existence. This earth of ours is, and remains to its end, the battlefield on which the decision is made either for Yahweh and against the Baalim or for the antichrists and against the Crucified. Resistance to the Nazis in our youth is an illustration of this. It would be senseless if we wanted to hide the fact that today the burden of this decision has become heavier, its dimension wider, its necessity clearer. For it continues, and whoever wants to can hear that all creation cries out and in yearning waits for the glorious freedom of the children of God. There can be no mere prattle about it; we must live it.

I will break off, though here is where my heart is beating, which meanwhile and for various reasons has turned away from scholarship. Everything has its time. An old man has to learn this lesson daily. All that we do turns to dust along with us, or becomes an artifact to be deciphered by those who are younger. I have always had enjoyment in life and in my work and, where possible, have tried to exceed limits; I have fought with many opponents and—unfortunately!—with all my friends, when a gauntlet was thrown at my feet. I have also paid the price for it and no longer tolerate healing wounds. Whether, in the academic sense, something decent has become of me, others may tell. It does not interest me. At least I have trained myself to change fronts, each time according to my understanding of Scripture and situation, not to store my seed but to cast it into the wind and to unlearn what others taught me. In this way one becomes lonely and, gradually, probably simpleminded too. Still, evangelical freedom demands its price—even, in the end, life itself. But evangelical freedom is the one thing that gives sense to all learning and unlearning.

Scripture Index

Subject Index

Abel, 123, 139

Abraham, xxxi, xxxii, 1, 15, 20, 64, 77, 85, 103, 121, 213, 216

abstraction (theological), xxvii–xxviii, xxxii, 13, 50, 63, 99, 100, 102, 147, 194, 223

Acts, book of, 24, 33, 35, 36, 96, 201, 222

Adam, xxxiii, 49, 51, 74, 81, 85, 137, 139, 175, 177, 200

affluent society, 28, 30, 90, 99, 110, 114, 121, 126, 176, 183, 188, 194, 202, 207, 213, 218

Africa, xvii, xx, xxvii, 78, 140, 182, 186

alms, xxxi, 91, 101, 102, 115, 123, 156, 183, 195, 196, 203, 213

American colleagues, 28

Ananias, 96

Anglo-Saxon literature, 28

anthropology, xxxii, 3, 4, 5, 59, 142, 147, 220, 221, 222

antichrist, xxvii, 3, 42, 44, 50, 178, 226

Antioch, 32–36, 148, 204, 221

Apocalypse, the, 35, 43, 44, 48, 62, 178, 225

apocalyptic, x, xv, xviii, xxvi–xxviii, xxix, 9, 15, 112, 195

apologetics, 142, 175, 219

apostolic tradition, 11, 223

apostolicity, 37–38, 41, 53

Argentina, vii, xxii–iii, xxv

armament, military, 25, 28, 189, 218

Arnoldshain Theses, 22, 22n20

Asia, xvii, xx, xxvii, 35, 38, 78, 132, 140, 182

atheism, 77, 157, 193

atomic weapons, 30, 43, 213

atonement, 70–71

Augsburg Confession, xxiv, 24, 33, 225

Augustine, 145

Auschwitz, 189

autobasileus, 199

Baal, 13, 73, 78, 226

Babylon, 79, 156, 195, 203

baptism, 7, 10, 15, 22, 27, 52, 86, 87, 106, 107, 123, 125, 165, 170, 198, 201, 205

baptismal hymns, 201

Barmen, Synod of, xi

Barmen Declaration, xxv, 19–21, 30, 138, 224

Barmherzigkeit, 193–96

Barnabas, 34–35

Barth, Karl, x, xxv, xxviii, xxix, 16, 19, 221

basic communities, 124

Baur, Ferdinand Christian, 219–20

Beatitudes, the, xxvi, 51, 62, 163, 180, 184, 188, 194, 196, 198, 203, 211, 214, 225

Berlin, xii, 83, 94, 105, 130, 131

biblical theology, 16, 109

Black theology, viii, xx, xxviii, 182

blasphemy, 61, 184

Bloch, Ernst, 136, 147

Blumhardt, Christoph, 110

body, 4, 5, 86, 93, 94, 96, 116, 156, 171, 182, 206, 207, 212, 226

body of Christ, x, xi, 2–10, 32, 37, 41, 47, 52, 62, 83, 84, 86, 87, 89, 91–93, 116, 125, 183, 207, 223

Bonn, x, 2, 3

bourgeoisie, xxv, xxvi, 20, 25, 29, 39, 50, 66, 99, 101, 122, 129, 132, 136, 137, 150, 156, 157, 182, 196, 203, 207, 209, 213, 216, 217, 219, 224

unity, 17, 23, 24, 38, 40–41, 43–46, 48–49,
  51–54, 57–58, 60–64, 92–93, 124, 137, 140,
  152, 205, 217, 223

victims, xix, xxiii, 99, 114, 153, 160, 175, 181,
  195, 207
Vietnam War, 130
Vilmar, August Friedrich Christian, 7, 7n6
Volkskirche (national church), xiii, 6, 12, 13,
  14, 188, 189, 213, 218
Voltaire, 190
von Soden, Hans Freiherr, 2, 2n2

walls, xxi, 21–22, 26, 43, 59, 64, 120, 126, 139,
  191, 207, 218
Weber, Max, 189, 189n9
Western democracy, 13
Western Europe, 216
West Germany, ix, xviii–xx, 131–32, 134, 136,
  187, 194, 200, 218
Westphalia, xii–xiii, xv, 22
white bourgeois, 78

White Man, the, xxv–xxviii, 13, 25, 29–30, 101,
  125, 145, 158, 174, 182–83, 191, 195, 202,
  214, 219, 224
white proletariat, 194
white supremacy, xvii, xxi, xxvi, 25, 30
Wichern, Johann Hinrich, 110, 110n1, 217n6
wilderness, the, 12, 15, 17, 30, 77, 103, 158,
  196, 200, 212–13, 219
Wolf, Ernst, 8
World Conference of Faith and Order in Montreal (1963), xxiv, 23, 223
worship, xii, 3, 8, 18, 22, 24, 34, 37, 50, 76,
  79–80, 82, 84–85, 88–89, 95, 99, 105–9, 112,
  116–17, 121–27, 136, 141, 143, 152, 161,
  163–64, 169–70, 179, 182, 200, 202, 211–12

Young Reformation movement, 19

zealots, 54, 155, 157, 160, 182
Zieverich, xi
Zionism, 16